Art Classics

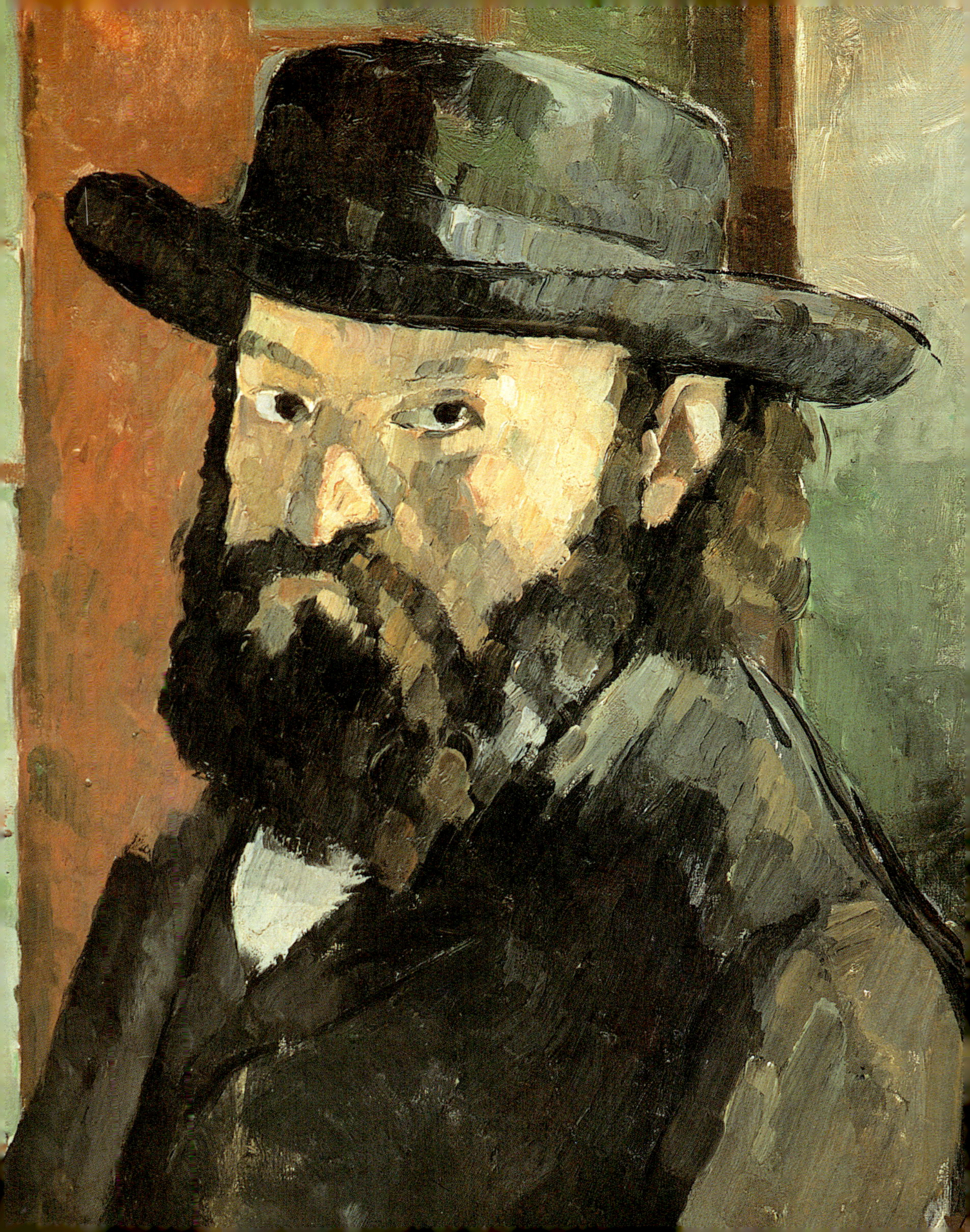

Art Classics

CÉZANNE

Preface by Alfonso Gatto

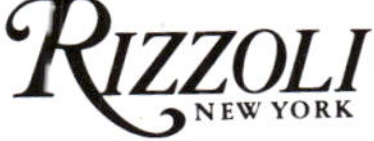
RIZZOLI
NEW YORK

ART CLASSICS

CÉZANNE

First published in the United States
of America in 2005 by
Rizzoli International Publications, Inc.
300 Park Avenue South
New York, NY 10010
www.rizzoliusa.com

Originally published in Italian by
Rizzoli Libri Illustrati

www.rcslibri.it
First edition 2003
Rizzoli \ Skira – Corriere della Sera

2005 2006 2007 2008 2009 /
10 9 8 7 6 5 4 3 2 1

Printed in China

ISBN 0-8478-2731-3

Library of Congress Control
Number: 2005922006

Director of the series
Eileen Romano

Design
Marcello Francone

Translation
David Stanton,
Timothy Stroud
(Buysschaert&Malerba)

Editing and layout
Buysschaert&Malerba, Milan

cover
Still Life with Apples and Oranges
(detail), 1899
Paris, Musée d'Orsay

frontispiece
Self-Portrait with Hat
(detail),
1879–1880
Bern, Kunstmuseum

The publication of works owned by the Soprintendenze has been made possible by the Ministry for Cultural Goods and Activities.

Contents

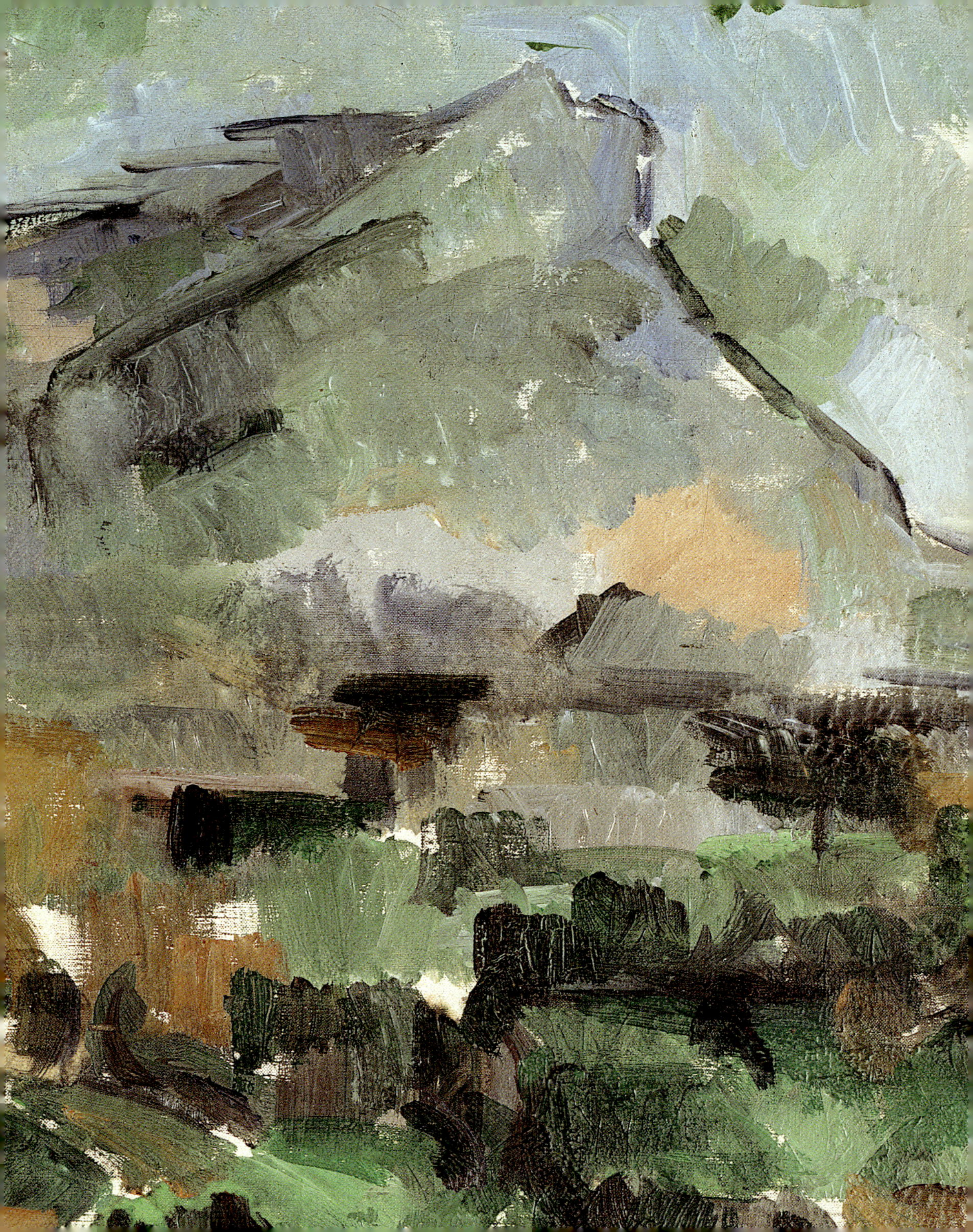

The Eye That Sees Its Own Vision
Alfonso Gatto

When imagining Cézanne—because they are certain and unpredictable, all difficult men have to be imagined—it is necessary to see him before a court, at the very moment the confused and awkward judges are pronouncing a sentence that has already been decided and that he has done everything to deserve without any blame, as a result of opening our eyes. Cézanne has told the truth, more truth than he was able to understand: a disturbing truth that will reach the institutions and churches, like all gospels. All the pictorial "churches" of the twentieth century, all the subversive or conciliatory institutions derive from him, celebrating the words with which until his death he sought to understand his "inability to go any deeper," as the Italian poet Giacomo Leopardi wrote, his obstinate "realizing" in order to give the color—the planes of color, the "colored sensations"—what it took away from the discretion and authority of the light.

In June 1904, two years before his death, Cézanne confessed, when writing to Émile Bernard, that he lived "under the impact of sensations" and, despite his age, "clinging to painting." A month previously, replying to Bernard, still fleeing from abstraction—characteristic of literature and of a light that, assisting the painter beforehand, ensured him from black to white of a support of "sign" and tone that stopped him just as he should have "taken firm control of himself"—he insisted on recognizing that "one is never overscrupulous, nor too sincere, nor excessively subject to nature" and that "it is necessary to penetrate what we have before us and continue to express oneself."

Mont Sainte-Victoire (detail), 1905
Zurich, Kunsthaus

The eye became the "centralizer by dint of observing and working." The stubborn artist, in his last letter to Bernard, just three months before his death, encouraged himself "to attempt whatever appears to present serious obstacles." He continued with his studies: "I study every day after nature and I feel I am making slow progress." He acknowledged that nature would give him the means necessary for correcting the errors of neoimpressionism, the "accentuating of forms with a black line," and all the "causes of abstraction that prevent the canvas from being composed and the outlines of the objects from being rendered where the points of contact are tenuous." Cézanne died at the age of nearly sixty-eight while painting. For him, he had recognized his age, but still let things take their course.

Portrait of Achille Emperaire (detail), 1867–1868 Paris, Musée d'Orsay

This is a style of painting that exists and leaves no room for the "appeals" that were asked of it or provoked, not even that of its own monotonous or obstinate words. Perhaps only Derain, until he lost his way, was able to understand the bitter truth that, as Cézanne put it, in "giving the image of what we see, forgetting what has appeared before us," we are part of a natural history of art that has become nature itself, as well as non-knowledge, a tough geology that cannot be described except to construct it and arrange it every time in the strata of its change, in the duration of its last legacy. This is all nature has done and all painting can do to understand its meaning when creating a "parallel harmony" for it. Light, as the successful idea of "colored sensation" that alone may extract it, "does not exist for the painter" (letter to Bernard, December 23, 1904). It must always be pursued and committed in its dense genesis, even if there is the risk of eliminating the planes and outlines that a more lasting, insatiable study allows us to contend with the impressionist tone. This extreme peace that comprises a poignant conviction of common sense for the ineffable—that is, for what cannot be said, but, in painting, must be said—is Cézanne's silent, rustic dignity: the task of creation, rather than of art, and stubborn faith in a positive dimension that is no longer dialectic, but is rather foolish and absolute.

In our imaginary court there will always be a Radomsky who will insinuate with sibilant delicacy: "The question is not here, but in this point: if your feeling were true, if it were right, if it responded to nature, or were not instead simply

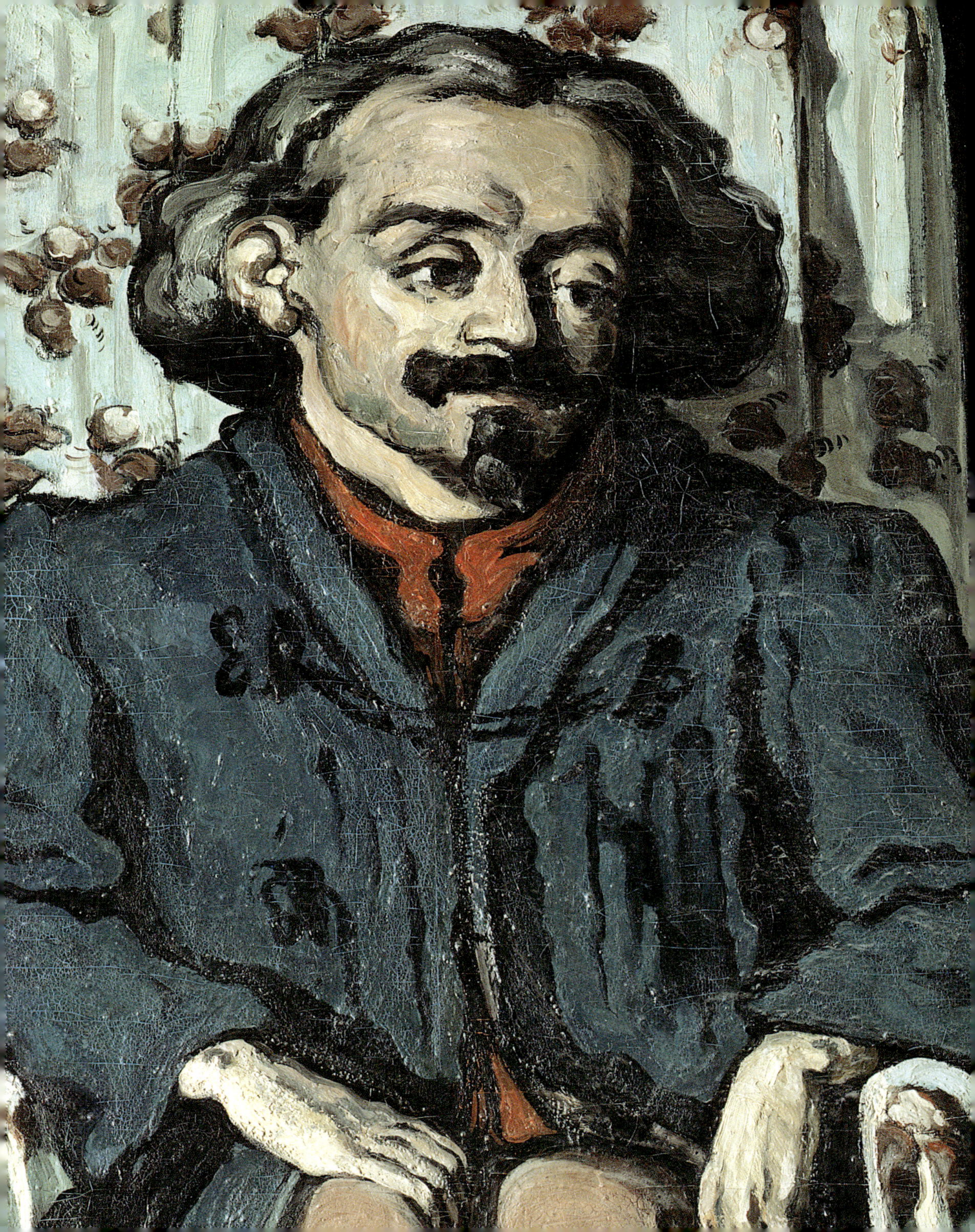

cerebral exaltation." Cézanne, too, as boy or as a young man in the scholastic poetry he sent to Zola—perhaps because he already recognized as difficult the natural state of grace in which he sought his positive goodness—attempted to redress the dangers of idealization with humor, doing his best in the romance of his own innocence. Now, with the last words preceding the reading of his sentence, which is already a foregone conclusion, he could say that, until the very last, his faith in painting was his identifying himself with the little that it takes to become a painter for all that he must realize (the obstinate, stubborn word that he never abandoned), that not even the good or bad experiences could ever have resolved for him, before the work, the grace and the malignancy that vied with him for the human contest of existence in action.

Before this court, the innocent man who receives the destiny and glory of the accusation must have the face that he gave himself in the *Self-portrait* of 1878 –1880 (Phillips Collection, Washington), the face of "a man who wants to master himself with submission to the outside world," as Jean Leymarie put it. Dostoyevsky would have made it his. The court knows that Cézanne is only a painter and that, nevertheless, he is not one, from the few clues of the natural grace that when he was a boy already occupied his gaze. Until the very last he penetrated with his eyes the impenetrable that was in him and almost preceded him in making external, compliant, and objective in visible nature the secret taking root of his mysterious frenzy, the existence in himself and in the difficulty of the obstinate patience, unencumbered with atmospheres for a demonstrative and emergent enchantment, where credulity itself is consumed.

This man who does not make mistakes, who does not deceive, can only be feared, if he fears himself and is only sure of what he touches, feeling himself sought-after and besieged in his own absence, which is all one with him to attack him. The mystery becomes accentuated, almost untenable; the calm manifestation of the power in the blast of the apparition is rapid on each occasion, and Cézanne keeps the steady pace of the violator who returns to "the motif," to the places that he has consecrated with his silence. As in the Gospels, Cézanne keeps his distance from any indulgent ending or from a vague memorial legacy: he is impervious and admonitory. "Sensations are the basis of my work; I believe I am impenetrable": these are the last words with which he defended himself from both himself and history (that of art, above all) that was never able to explain it. It is his insurmountable tautology, his certainty that he exists because of the coming into being always from the beginning in the beginning of being, in seeking the light of the shoots that from the burnt stump of the perpetual facture have difficulty with and then overcome their own force, the color woven by the grain of his myriad, never impassive, never inert. He is "impenetrable" because he is condemned to "penetrate what everyone has in front of himself." This is a virile condemnation: the "sensations," the more they are alert and adroit, prevent him from penetrating them further, realizing them, or holding them, beyond the impromptu that catches them, for a lasting period, typical of love as a *fait accompli*, without phenomena even of dismay, for a positive calling that is only the simplification of a duty. Every joy of reference, every gaiety of grasping is omitted in the work that recommences, in the damned "realization." Thus we have a man and his painting that have never taken infinity's name in vain, still less invoked the cause that allows it. Yet he declared: "Everything we see vanishes, doesn't it? Nature is always the same, but of what appears, nothing remains. Our art must give us the thrill of its duration; it must allow us to taste its eternity. What lies behind the natural phenomenon? Maybe nothing, maybe perhaps everything. So I clasp these wandering hands of mine. I take from the right, the left, here and there, everywhere, its colors, its nuances, I fix them, I juxtapose them, and they form lines, become objects, rocks, trees, without my thinking about it. They take on volume… My canvas clasps its hands, it doesn't waver… it's true, compact, full." Nature allows itself to be instructed, collected, and fashioned by the ever-renascent abundance of its dispersion as long as the painter works in the finite, in the sense, and also on the natural structure, the settling of the earth's strata. The ineffable of the creation, surviving from its vague promises, is thus to be obtained in the reality and word of the work, with its demonstrative, homogenous, and plenary habeas

following pages
A Modern Olympia (detail)
1873–1874,
Paris, Musée d'Orsay

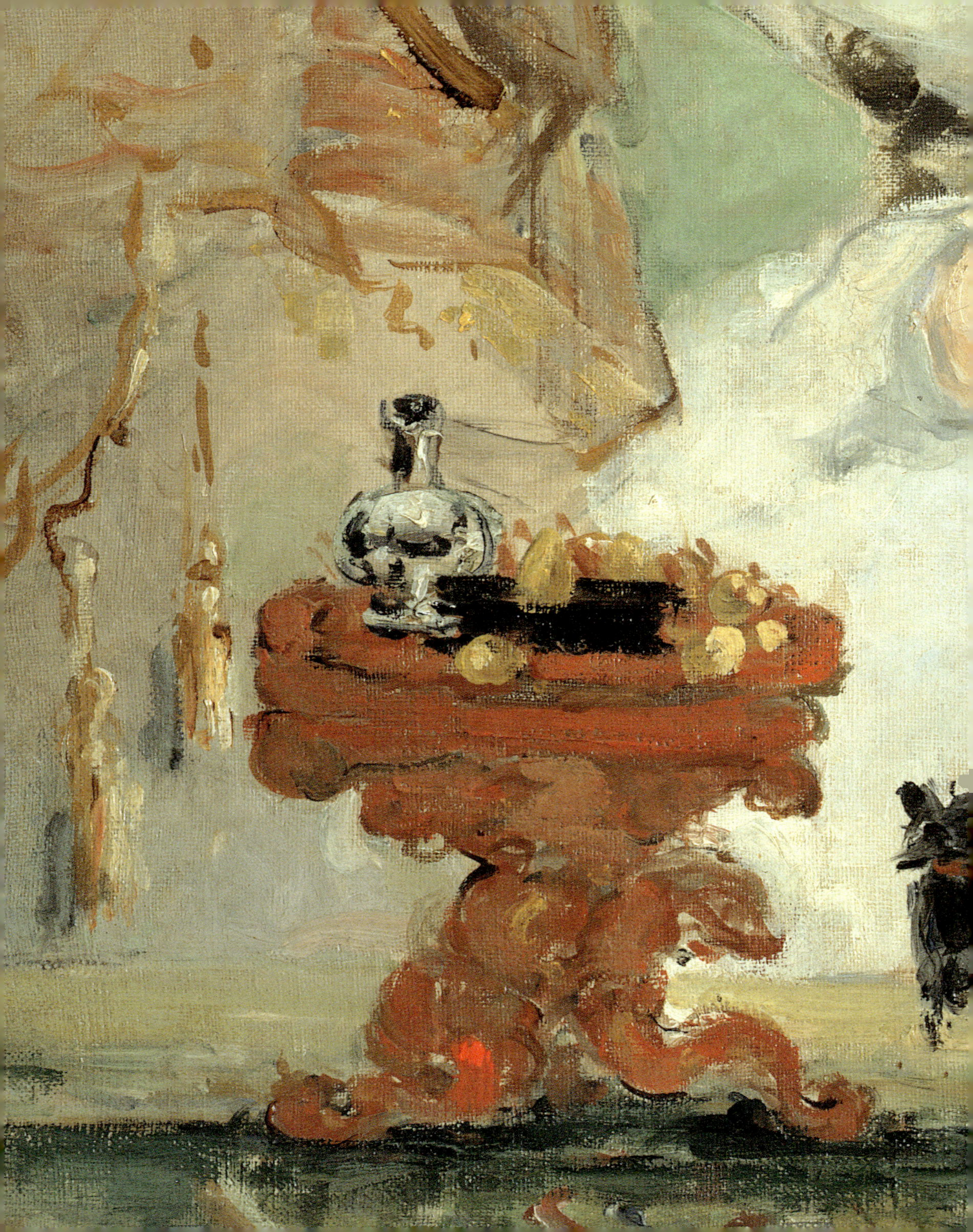

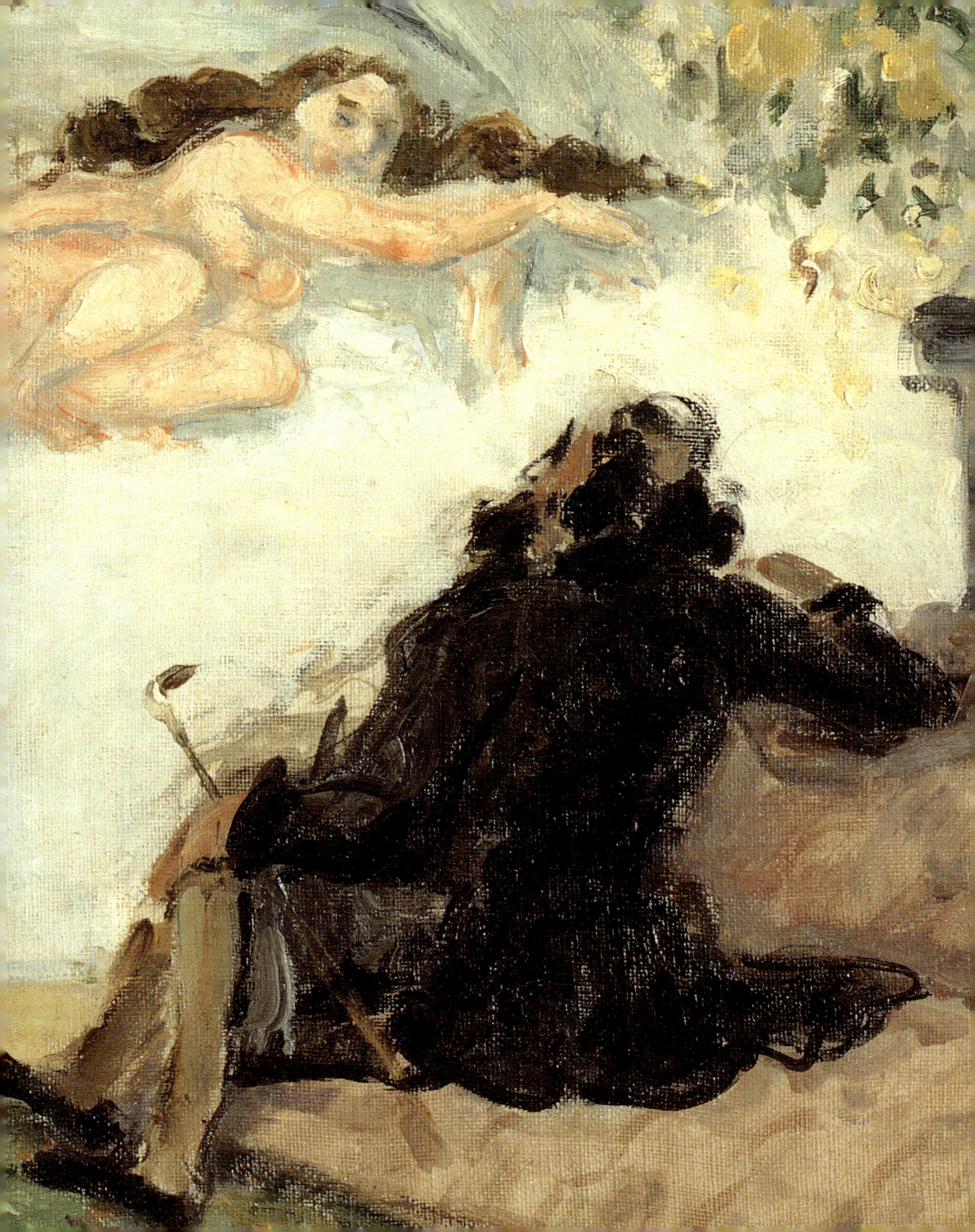

corpus: the paint is the only protagonist of the real image, of the concentrated gravitation that also attracts the solid—the volume—those hands carried away by their eagerness to take hold of, stop, and fix.

The Smoker (detail), *c.* 1891 St. Petersburg, The State Hermitage Museum

These "wandering hands" touch on the raw where, following them, the more the eyes scheme their staying power the more they seem to follow the unattainable—the inexpressible—and vie for it with the same ephemeral atmospheres that give rise to it. And one realizes how the impressionist temptation—the poetic aura that in its joy seems to touch the hazy horizon line before degenerating in the appointments of the hours and seasons—unleashes the amorous dialectic of the opponent who cannot do without having it in his eyes. It is all the more ephemeral when he is induced to restrain it and make it last, with his hatred for the "fantastic image," with his love for the real but heroic image.

Not by chance, Cézanne had recognized in his friend Pissarro "the painter who more than any other came close to nature," the "humble and colossal Pissarro." What Zola wrote about Pissarro in 1876—"Austere and sober painting, great attention paid to truth and precision. A tough and strong will..."—could equally well apply to Cézanne, aside from "precision," which could refer to Corot and to the greater glory of that love for truth, "tough and strong" truth, which is to be found in Courbet. For the impressionists, Pissarro had signified the land, the solid land that flees from tenderness when giving it deeper and more serious roots. In Pontoise, from 1872 to 1874, Pissarro seemed, with his own example, to be showing Cézanne, who joined him there, what his silent and contemplative neighbor could already call his own. These were the years of *The House of the Hanged Man*, *The House of Dr. Gachet*, and *View of Auvers*. "We were always together, it is certain, however, that each of us kept in mind the only thing that counted: his own sensation."

The artist had already gone beyond the impression inherent in appearances and objective in its scientism, in the mastery of the Cézannian word, in the annunciation of the "feeling" that is also "realization" through adversity—beyond the ephemeral that passes, the silence that remains, unexhausted and feverish of itself.

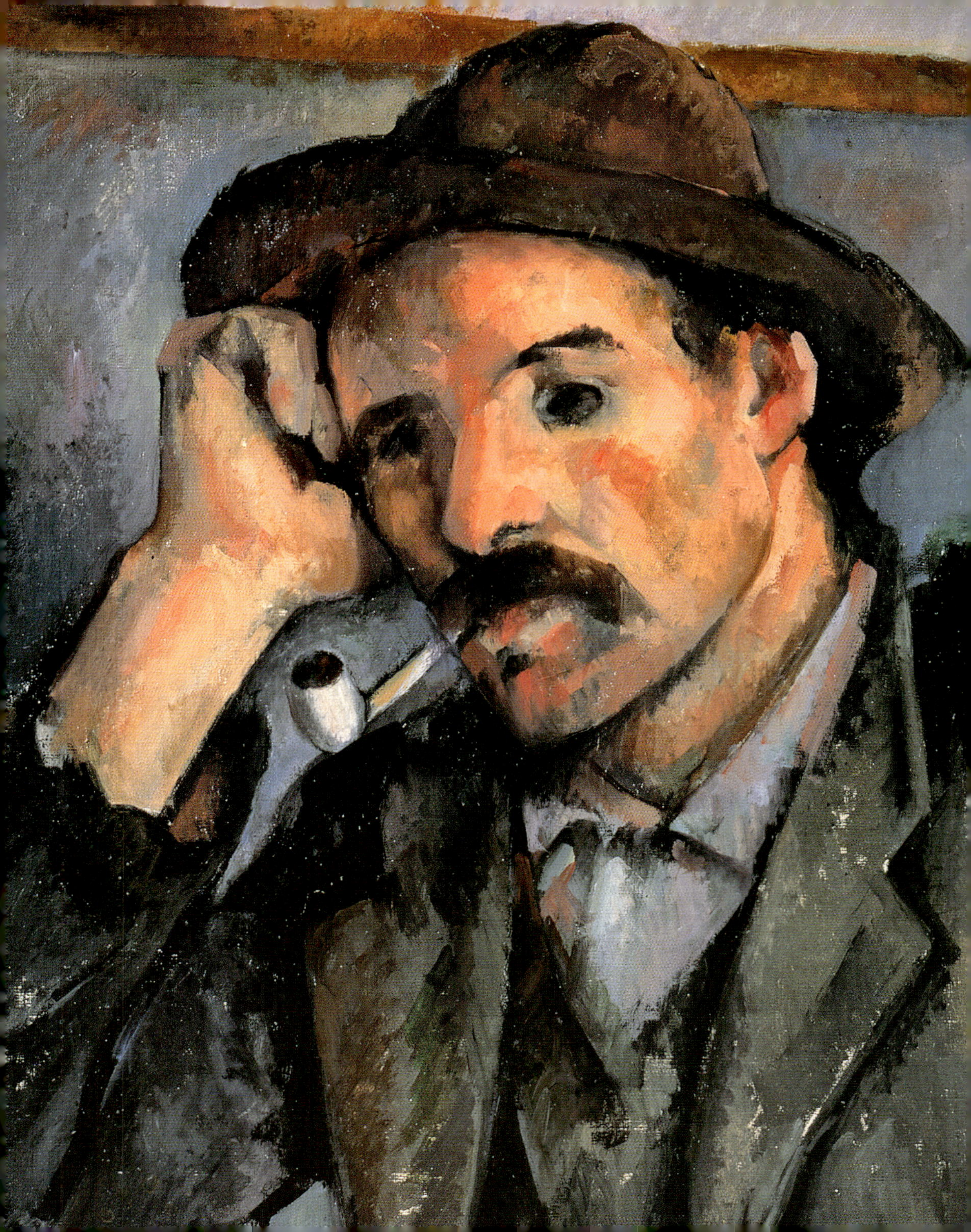

In September 1879 he wrote: "The countryside is truly surprising; it seems as if there's greater silence. Here are the sensations that I cannot express. It's better to feel them." Similarly, the poet Giacomo Leopardi wrote: "Sensations experienced at the sight of the countryside, as if one could not go deeper in and enjoy it more, as well as not knowing how to express it." Cézanne always painted this silence. Pathos is consumed in taking note of what is to be seen and making its secret visible: the surface, the appearance provokes the suspicion of being, of appearing: and the painter stops on each occasion, before bursting in, working, in his own harmony in order to devastate it, to construct it, to make it silent again in the now independent will of its meaning. It seems that Cézanne, when repairing the damage done on each occasion, and for each work until his death, kept increasingly solid this mysterious nature that he settled with the only scruple that he was permitted to have: that of patient and resolving matter that decides his absorbed spirit, the erethism of calm, indifferent to his calculation of the punishment.

Rimbaud's "Je est un autre" (I is another), before any other dreamlike, surrealist interpretation, is the recognition of clairvoyance that rather than "seeing" also the inexhaustible Goethean vision, is the discovery of the *inconnu.* The unknown: this integral reality of nature and man that is inside it to the point that it has it in itself. Cézanne appears to have taken into account—with guile or with even mischief—a passage from the letter that Rimbaud wrote in 1871 to Paul Démeny, the famous "lettre du voyant" (clairvoyant's letter): "So then, the poet is truly a thief of fire. Humanity is his responsibility, even the animals;... if what he brings back from beyond has form, he gives it form, if it is formless, he gives it formlessness. A language must be found..." The *là-bas* is so indicative of the vagueness that it must be certain of the consensual and conspiratorial impression to be taken back to the sign of its own contrast, and of the identity of "feeling" with "expression," to leave no doubt for Cézanne regarding its resolving power of conception inside the work. The eye that sees inside its vision is Cézanne's eye. This is solitude that has been transformed into a raptus or the nobility of cries, or else gravitating into its foundations of stone, like a planet that syllabifies all its clues of enduring life: the consanguinity of being "I" or "other" together. Cézanne suffered and fled from the "dérèglement des sens" (disturbance of the senses), like one of Georges Bernanos's heroes, his feet planted firmly on the boards of his watchtower, on the alert for himself, as if for an allurement, to the point that he denied himself a model for his *Female Bathers*, as Bernard recalls. This is extreme, desperate classicism which results from realization by gravitation, burnt by heretical calm, where no utterance is in vain and the conscience is impassive and ardent like fire: small, inexorable steps of victory reluctant in the immobility of perfection, until a state of sophism is reached. No hero's fast feet can beat this Cézanne-tortoise, which has the extreme form of its formlessness, the stubborn shell of a stone that breathes and knows it exists. Thus was born the sea of L'Estaque, purity that is intact yet bound to the suspicion of its rift, as to the eye of an inhabitant of the underworld that gazes so high that it is melted. Such a man is afraid of having always realized his own trap, the pride of putting himself aside in the things he isolates with his vision of painting, because the light, the cold incandescence of the color in the volume and in the curve of the form—the distance that comes closer and things close by that move away, to the bright point at the top that it is always suspended from it —comes as it was in the case of Rimbaud, or as it was, in another way, for Leopardi, from that unyielding and impetuous *là-bas* that may urge in a lonely heart, even if its opens the doors to the unknown and innovation.

The invitation to flee, the allegory of change, the thirst of the Baudelairean swan, the immured clairvoyance, and the Leopardian "one could not go deeper in" are resolved for Cézanne in the stubborn adherence to his roots, which were for him like the secret affluence of tacit communications that only he understood, the poignant modesty of physical vitality. "The colors are the expression of this profundity of the surfaces." "Each brushstroke that I apply is rather like my blood mixed with that of my model, in the sun, in the light, in the color. We must get on well together, my model, my colors and me." And even clearer: "Color is biolog-

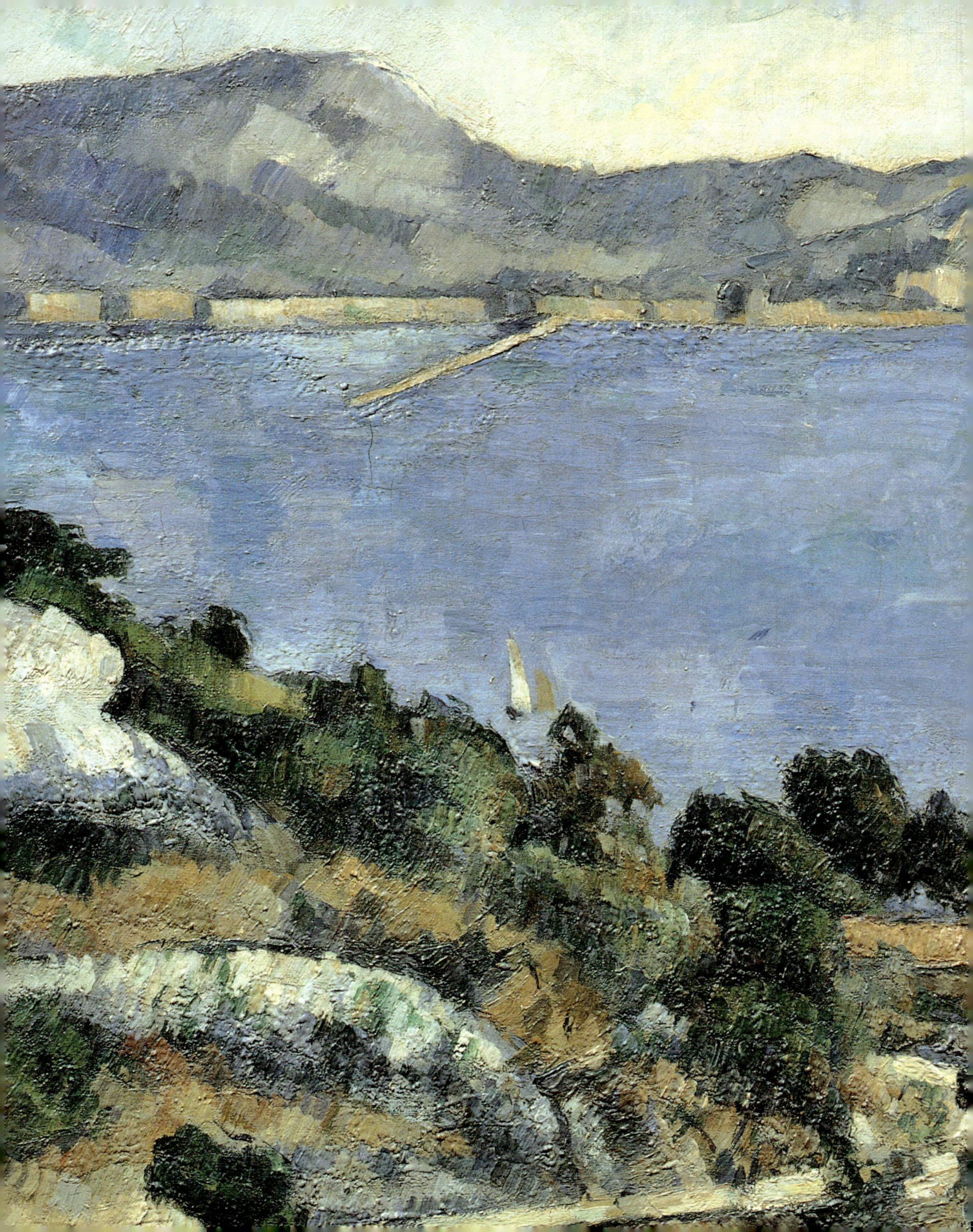

L'Estaque (detail), 1882–1885 Paris, Musée d'Orsay

ical, I mean it's living, it's the only thing that brings things to life." But life is not aware of its blood; the perfect organization of its circles silenced the sap that nurtured it. Those who, like Cézanne, needed to use its blood, had to wound themselves and heal, knitting themselves to the cut that once again would injure without hardening. It is not Cézanne who says this, but his painting and in it the stoic pride of a man targeted every day, in the streets of Aix, by the pranks of the innocents who put him to flight.

This is what the imaginary court accuses him of. Who is this weaver of life? An insect on the shuttle, the woodworm in its toughest knots, the worm that has climbed onto God's throne? Cézanne does not reply. He can only reply that he is the vector of hereditary characteristics, the only gene of the living cell of the new painting. He does not say, but he has painted; he has accused that the worm worthily climbs onto God's throne if it reaches it when attached, multiplied in the feet of its fatigue and not with the abstract wings of the hyperbole, if, in the humility worthy of "realizing," what he sees and his clairvoyance is recognized. But Cézanne would like to defend himself from his defenders, from those who, in order to show he was aware of his unitary spirit and his quest for truth, seem to guarantee him the overcoming of the Impressionist crisis, which also celebrated his paintings in the very period when he was working on his own way of making the impression last. It was, in fact, the Impressionists Monet and Renoir who confided to Durand-Ruel and Vollard, Monet regarding his dissatisfaction with his work, Renoir even more explicitly: "About 1883 [this was the year when they visited Cézanne in L'Estaque] something like a rupture appeared in my work. I had taken Impressionism to extremes and I realized that I didn't know how to how to paint and draw. To put it briefly, I was at a dead end." The year 1883 was when the twenty-four-year-old Georges Seurat, with his *Bathers, Asnières*—crystallizing his own version of divisionism, in which the Impressionist brushstroke was frozen and precisely defined—showed that he had learnt from Cézanne how to restore to objects and figures the light removed from the vapors and the ephemeral, the wandering of the Impressionist air. But he reconstituted, in narrated literary enchantment, the monumental stylism of a hierarchy that enclosed nature inside its idyllic expectations, exposed and overexposed to meditation on its meanings already beyond life—metaphysical, in other words. It was an open road after Paul Signac's grateful cry, who, however, could still reconstruct technically the "perfect harmony" of Seurat's canvas, almost planning its intentions. But where are Cézanne's life and his painting for life, entering the silence of nature attained that awaits him, still unreachable and suspended?

Farmyard in Auvers (detail), *c.* 1879
Paris, Musée d'Orsay

Before the imaginary court, Cézanne shakes his head. He would like to say it isn't true, not even for a Picassian paradox, that the Impressionists show us whether it has stopped raining, whether the sun is shining or whether the wind is blowing and never their painting; that it's not true either that he has taught only love for forms and volumes, concentration on rigorous drawing that is "not at all sentimental," as Léger attests for him; that his restlessness belongs to him just as his calm does; that Van Gogh, already divided, will give vent to his feelings on the schematic enchantment of Seurat, from the point to the stroke, to that fibrous color that, in its having as its tone the charge of passion, seeks to be both strong and "arbitrary," equal to the writing that instigates its symbol. Because Cézanne is, in Impressionism, the Impressionism that lasts and brings at the beginning what for his contemporaries, whether or not they be his companions, were the principles of their visual appearances. These "appearances," the more they are natural, give rise to his meditation, his will to "solidify": but he needs them as a point of arrival of the inexpressible that is never sufficiently realized and that once again awaits its organic structure and its bare synthesis as the very justification for practicing painting.

Certainly, what with appearances and surfaces made enamel-like with their own force and analyses of the planes of objects, and, aside from any neutral shadow and any linear perspective, the settling synthesis of volumes, in this geometry that is anything but abstract and illusory, Cézanne foreran everything, including Cubism—but he never was, with hindsight, a prophet of words, not even his own. Since treating "nature by means of the cylinder, the sphere, the

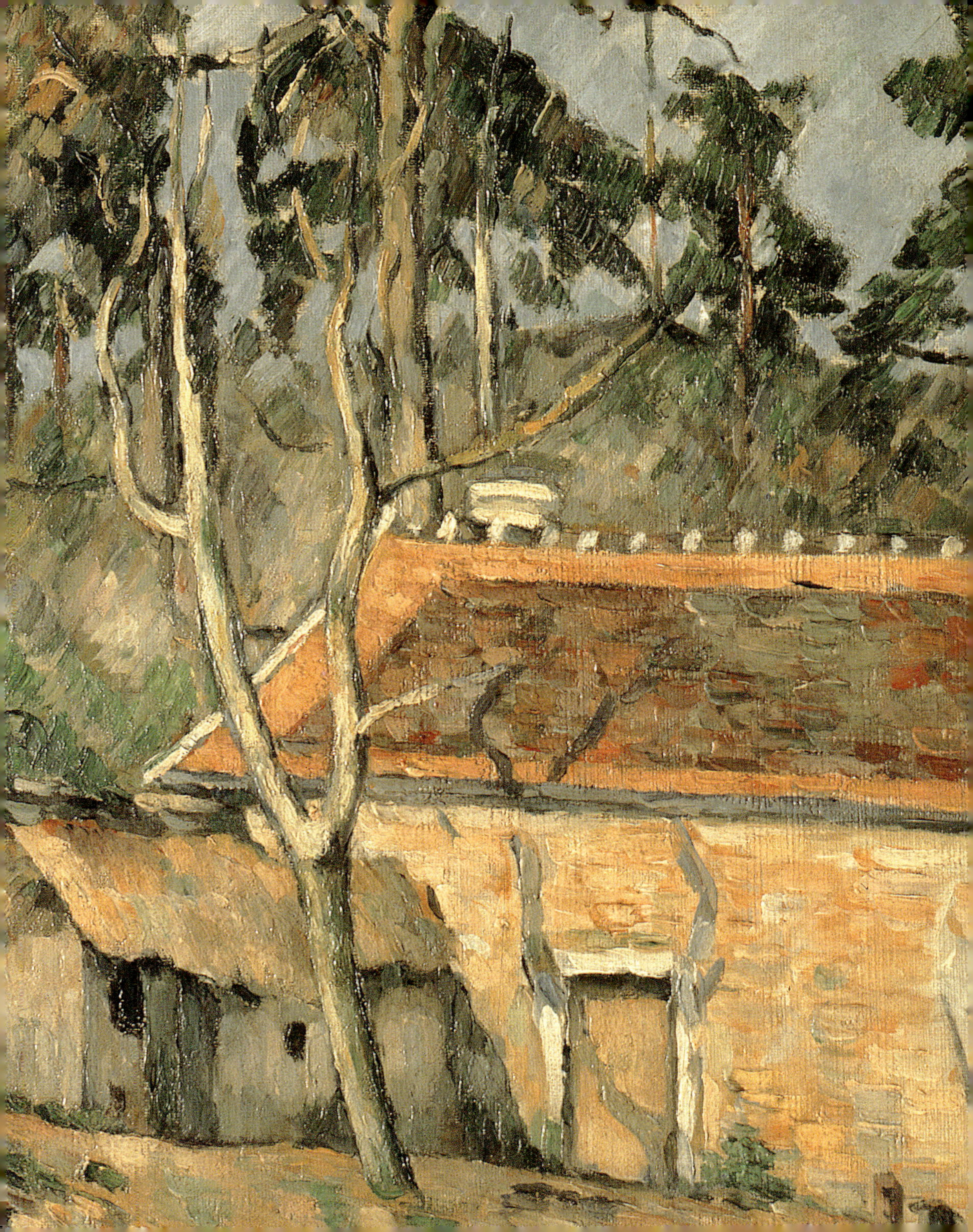

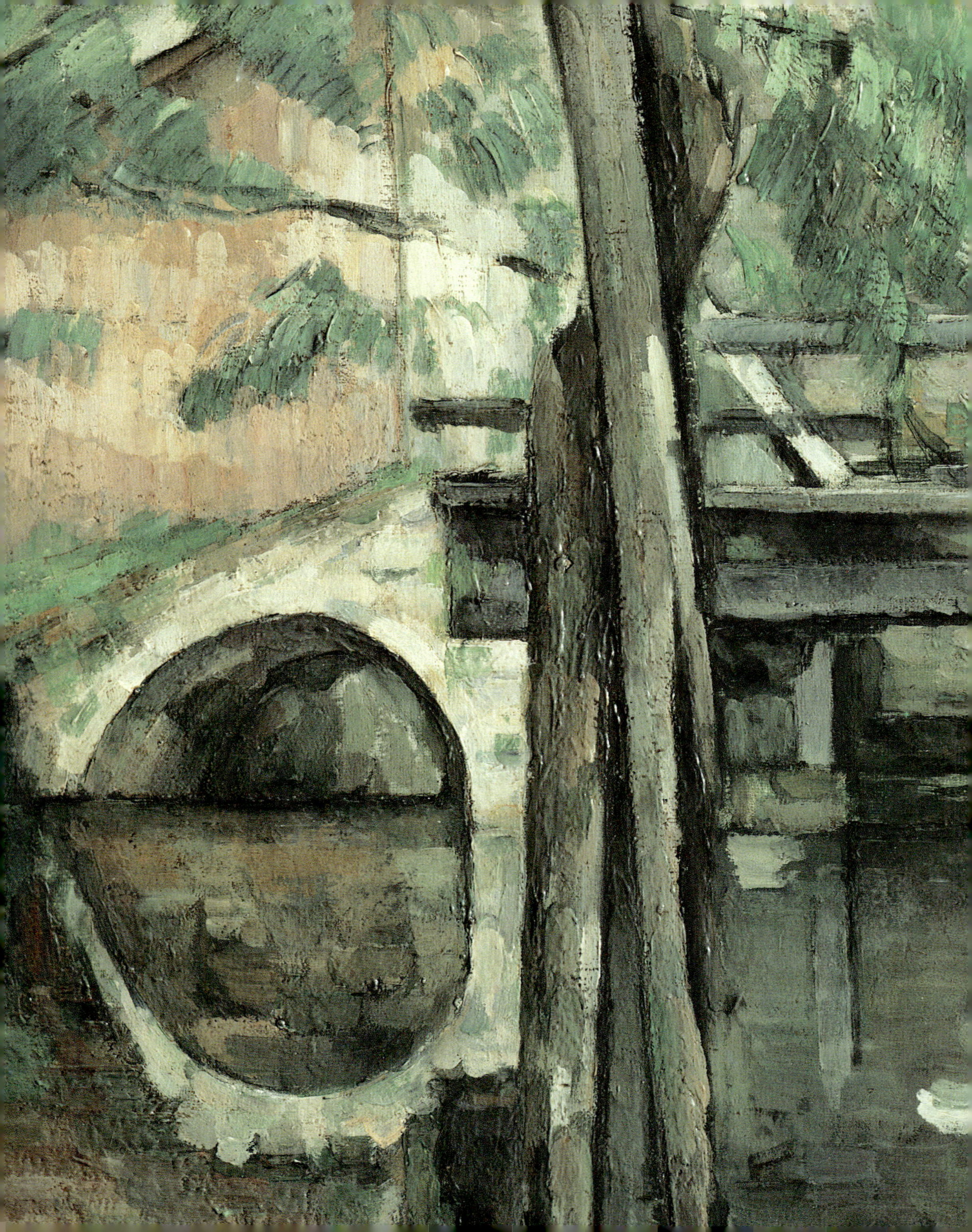

The Bridge at Maincy (detail), 1879–1880 Paris, Musée d'Orsay

cone, everything in proper perspective" meant for Cézanne bringing together at a peak of tension and penetrative secret his real suffering of the unfounded lightness of things and human nature, the decentered thoughtlessness that disperses life—perhaps in his most subtle analyses, but even more in the optical credulity.

Also in *Jourdan's Hut*, the last painting on which Cézanne's eye and hand dwelt before his death, the green over which Derain was to go mad burns with the arid dryness of the blue flame and it is the essence of the great oblivious remains that built the pyre of the first human transparencies. Already from Cézanne's first incredible watercolors—true miracles of life, the first words of existence for painting—this background transparency, more than infallible for virtuous fury, is an idea of space that is born at the moment of an utterance through its own voice. The accumulated moment of time revealed itself in the painting *The Railway Cutting*, in the Munich's Neue Pinakothek, dated to about 1870 (a masterpiece that seems to be subsequent to Fauvism, as has been said). It is, above all, the clear idea of what can (and must) be the extreme limit of bookish saturation or the weary human Petrachism, because it arouses to promptitude the spirit that burns and almost settles the reality of the earth in nature, starting the journey for which it will never be omitted, ambiguous in its belief and its opinion, but present, substantive, in the impact and secret of its identity. This is the secret of *The Village Street* of his late years (dated between 1899 and 1906), the three views of Mont Sainte-Victoire (dated between 1904 and 1906), belonging respectively to the Philadelphia Museum of Art, the Kunsthaus, Zurich, and the Kunstmuseum, Basel. Cézanne touched first of all—and it seems for the first time—what had always been inside him and his eyes: the coming into being of the earth from a bath of purity in color, cool humidity, transparent to an avid thirst; the impression, it seems of a huge shroud for its intense size where the most mortal frailty that a man has ever taken to win for himself is portrayed. The court does not pardon him, but it will pardon that "settling imperceptibly premature of the brushstroke that, before reaching its definitive equilibrium, allows itself the joy of groping its way," as Jacques Rivière saw so illuminatingly (his famous three pages devoted to Cézanne in 1910), in recognizing that "there was not a greater painter" than him. A painter who was "just a painter," the man without presence that hides, flees, to "serve" the things. Should we regret that he is just a painter? But the mountain from which he told (and will tell) the truth is still his and bears the name of victory.

Three Bathers (detail), 1874–1875 Paris, Musée d'Orsay

May this absent and incredible man who doesn't reply, this "servant of things," be convicted. He is capable of praying for his soul, as Émile Bernard saw him praying in the cathedral in Aix under Nicolas Froment's great triptych of the *Burning Bush*, in which the figure of Moses resembled him. Perhaps, before a real court, not even the Cubists would give him a hand—or else they would take part of it away. "He spoke badly about Gauguin," they would accuse and not even Van Gogh seemed convinced. He never detached himself from the Impressionists, continuing to tell them: "Pissarro came very close to nature, Renoir gave us the woman of Paris, and Monet a way of seeing: the rest doesn't count." And this "parallel harmony of nature," into which painting transforms itself, is an idea, a projection of nature or a challenge to the creation of the small meticulous worm that sees "profound and vertical"? He was obsessed by the verdant planes: the flat, inert, smooth surfaces almost burn him with shame; he had a horror of chinoiserie and literature. Literature, following the funeral of his mother? Cézanne, why did you refuse to do it? In order to run to the "motif" and cry on your own? And do you still identify with Balzac's Frenhofer, you who are also the author of an "unknown masterpiece," impotent like him, with the staring eyes, as in your *Self-portrait* (1885–1887), which Picasso copied in one of his drawings. Impotent or God, then? You have destroyed every idea of beauty in the name of the truth.

Cézanne doesn't reply: we'll never get rid of him, of his weight, of his absence, just as we'll never get rid of the earth or life, if it still remains for us to die (to keep silent) within their name.

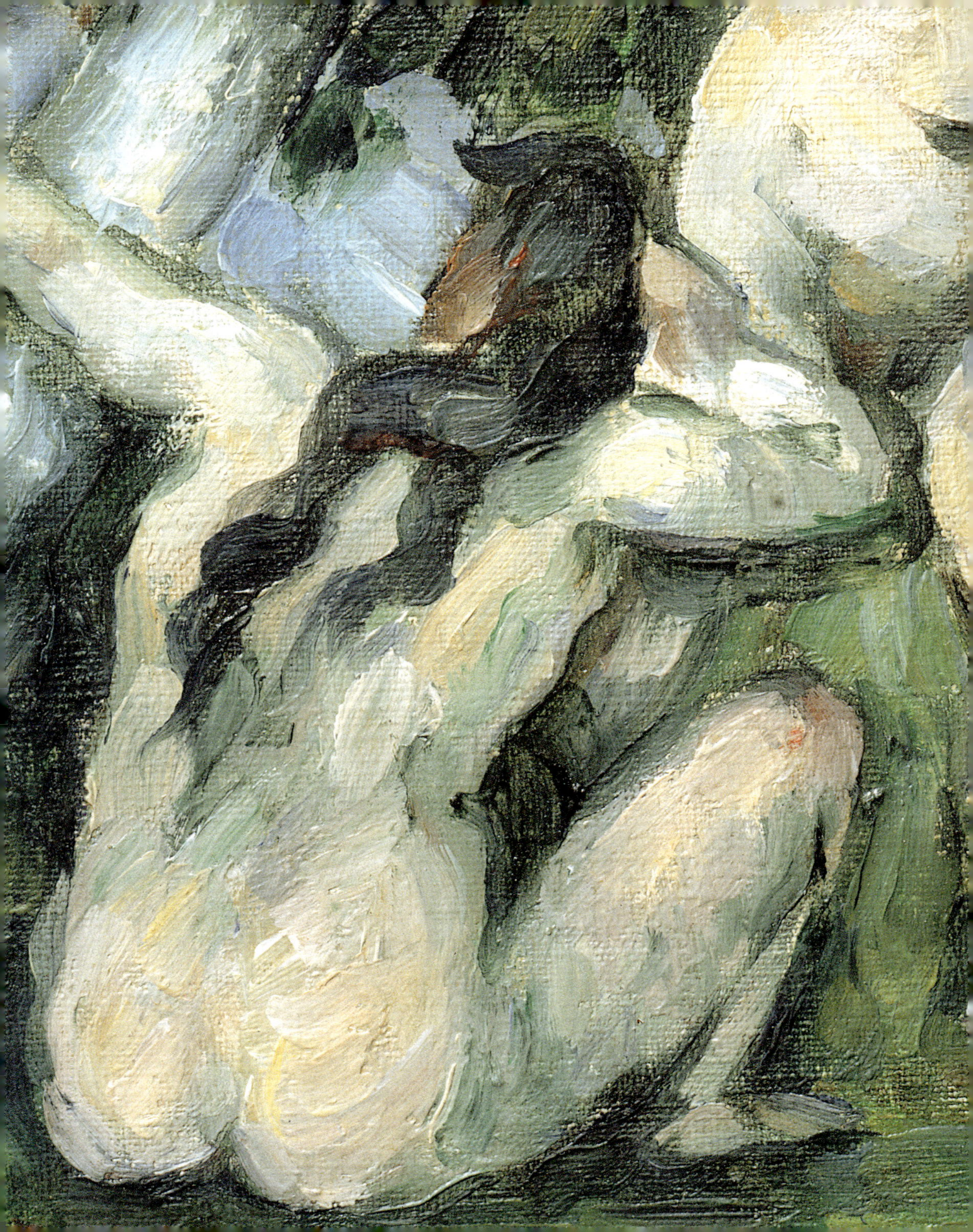

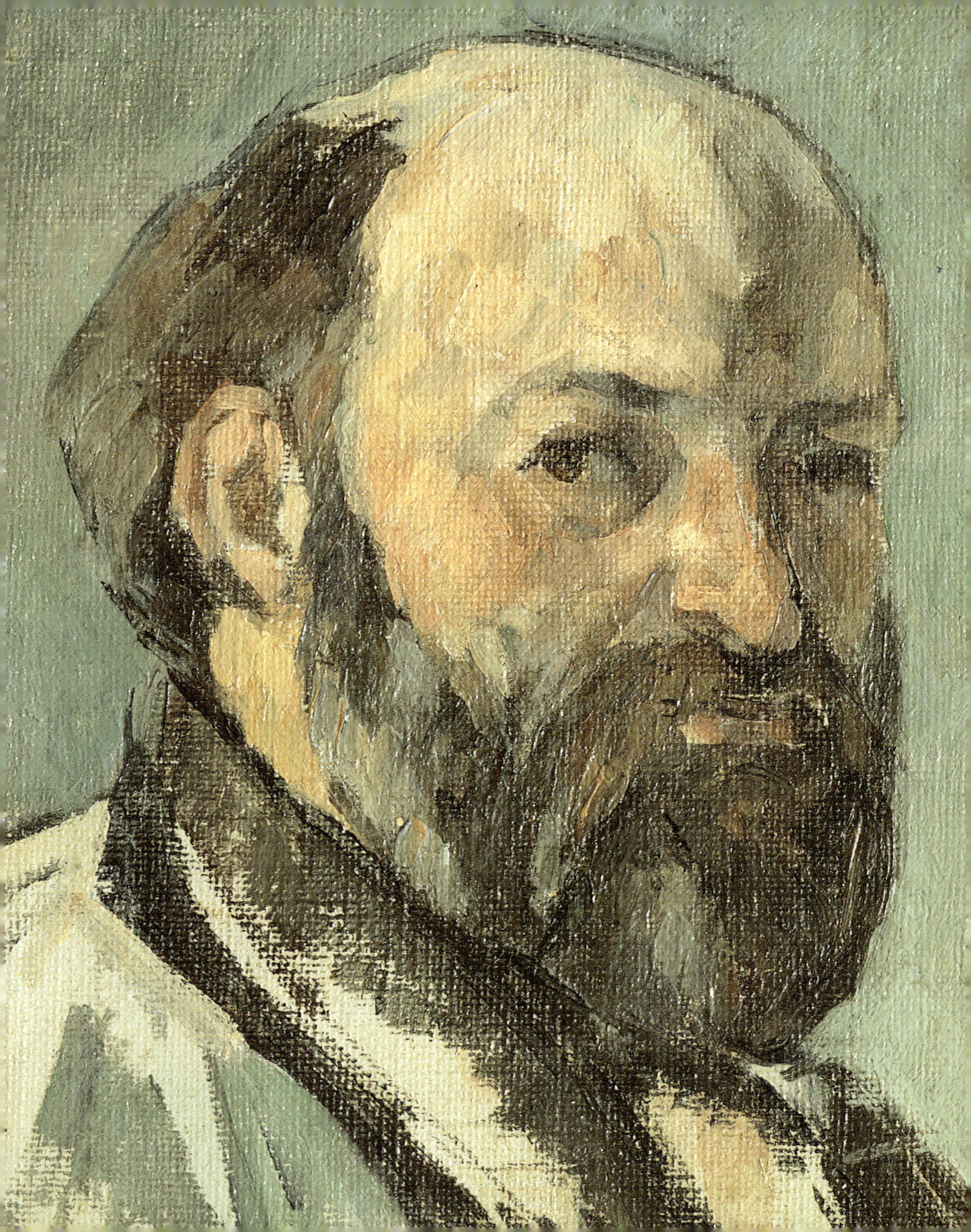

His Life and Art

"Today I'd like to tell you something about Cézanne. As far his work is concerned, he lived as a *bohemian* until he was forty, or so he said. Only later, when he met Pissarro, did he start to enjoy painting. And he spent the last thirty years of his life doing nothing but paint: without great joy, in fact, but with ceaseless anger, in conflict with each of his works, because none of them seemed to attain what he believed to be the most indispensable element. He called this *realisation* and he found it in the Venetians that he had seen at the Louvre and admired unconditionally. Convincing, becoming an object. Reality sublimated until it became indestructible through his experience of the object: it was this that seemed to be the most essential purpose of his work. Old, in poor health, worn out every evening completely by his normal daily work (in fact, he often went to bed at six o'clock, at dusk, after a supper gulped down absent-mindedly), angry, mistrustful, derided and disparaged whenever he went to his studio... he hoped, one day, to reach the objective that he regarded as the only essential one. In this way ... he had exacerbated the difficulties of his work in the most stubborn manner ... he moved back and forth in his studio, which had the wrong light, because the builder hadn't thought it necessary to listen to that old eccentric whom everyone in Aix agreed shouldn't be taken seriously. He moved back and forth in his studio, where the green apples were scattered around, or else he sat in despair in his garden and there he stayed. And before him spread the little city, oblivious, with its cathedral; a city for upright, discreet citizens, while he—as his father, who was a hatter, had foreseen—had become something else: a *bohemian* ... I wanted to tell you all this because in a hundred respects it's linked to many things around us and even to ourselves. Outside it's raining incredibly hard, like before. Farewell ... tomorrow I'll tell you more about myself. But you certainly know how much I've done it today too ..."

Thus wrote the poet Rainer Maria Rilke to his wife, the sculptor Clara Westhoff, on

page 26
Self-Portrait
(detail), 1880
Paris, Musée d'Orsay

October 9, 1907 from Paris, after another intense visit to the great retrospective the Salon d'Automne devoted to Paul Cézanne a year after his death.

Paul Cézanne was born in Aix-en-Provence on January 19, 1839, to Louis-Auguste Cézanne and Anne-Elisabeth Honorine Aubert. The artist's father, a successful hat dealer whose wares were much sought after by the provincial bourgeoisie, decided to take over the banking activity of Félix Alexis in 1848 and, together with a partner, founded a bank known as Cézanne et Cabassol, which henceforth ensured the family a comfortable life. The financial security allowed the young Paul to continue his studies without any problems. In 1852 he attended the Collège Bourbon, which gave him a solid background in religion and the classics and introduced him to the study of literature, including poetry. It was during this period that his passion for the Latin authors and for the work of Victor Hugo and Alfred de Musset developed, an enthusiasm that he shared with the young Émile Zola and Jean-Baptiste Baille, who was to become an engineer.

Linked by a bond of friendship, the young companions loved to spend sunny days in the open air walking, swimming, or reciting poetry. It was below the slopes of the Mont Sainte-Victoire, in the clearings in the woodland surrounding the Château Noir and on the banks of the Arc River, that Cézanne discovered the special charm of the Provençal landscape, with its wild, primitive beauty, and slowly the idea that he might have a vocation for painting took hold of him.

In 1857, a year before he received his baccalaureate, Cézanne decided to enroll —perhaps on the suggestion of Zola—in the École de Dessin in Aix in order to attend the courses held by Joseph Gibert, the principal of the school and curator of the city's Musée des Beaux-Arts. The young Cézanne drew from life with enthusiasm, but he also made studies of the plaster casts and marbles kept in the museum, following with commitment the traditional stages of academic training, divided between studies *en plein air* and drawings of antique sculptures. In 1858, Zola, his schoolmate and closest friend, decided to abandon the boredom of the provinces for Paris, the capital of art and literature, where he hoped to begin a career as a writer.

Despite the distance separating them, the two friends kept in touch with frequent letters. Paul's letters to Émile were intense and passionate and almost always contained poems reminding his distant friend—now swallowed up by the iron and stone jungle of Paris—of the gentle delights of the Provençal countryside. This is from a letter he wrote to Zola in April 1858: "With ardent force / an impetuous gust / blows over the city / rain that makes / the pleasant banks of the Arc fertile. / Like the mountain / our green countryside / feels the effects of spring: / the plane puts forth buds, / with its white tufts, the green hawthorn / is crowned with leaves."

His enthusiasm for drawing and the figurative arts—after his first experience in art school in Aix—became a passion and he decided to inform his family of his firm intention to devote himself to painting. His choice was strongly opposed by his father, a practical man for whom money was of primary importance and who had instead planned for his son a secure career as a lawyer that one day would allow him to take care of the family fortune. Constrained by his father, Paul unwillingly enrolled in law studies at Aix University. This is what he wrote to Zola on December 7, 1858: "Alas, I have chosen the tortuous path of law. 'Chosen' isn't quite the right word: they compelled me to choose it. Law, horrible law entangled with circumlocutions, will, for no less than three years, make my life horrible! O muses of Helicon, Pindus, and Parnassus come, I beg you, to soothe my despair. Have pity on me, a miserable mortal, dragged away against his will from your altars ..."

The urgent desire to paint, the need to express himself through forms and colors became increasingly strong and Cézanne began to alternate the tedious lessons of law with

Vase, Coffee Pot and Fruit
(Still Life in Black and White)
(detail), 1867–1869
Paris, Musée d'Orsay

drawing classes at the art school, where, in 1859 he was awarded second prize for a small head in oils.

In 1860 he decided to abandon the study of law and persuaded his father to let him decorate the grand salon of the Jas de Bouffan—the former summer residence of the governor of Provence on the outskirts of Aix, which the Cézanne family had bought a year before—with four panels representing the four seasons.

Meanwhile, Zola, who was convinced of his friend's artistic potential, insisted that Cézanne should join him in Paris. In fact, in 1860 he wrote to him as follows: "From six to eleven you could paint from life in a school, then you could have lunch and from midday to four you could copy a masterpiece that particularly attracts you in the Louvre or the Musée de Luxembourg. That would be nine hours of work. I think it would be enough; with a program like this you would be sure to make progress."

Cézanne stood firm against his father's opposition and, in 1861, managed to get his own way: with a modest monthly allowance, paid reluctantly by his family, he left for Paris hoping to enroll in the École des Beaux-Arts.

On his arrival, it was Zola who introduced him to the capital's artistic milieu, accompanying him to the museums and the official exhibitions of French art, the Salons. Thanks to his writer friend, Cézanne began to attend the Académie Suisse, a private establishment where, for a small sum, artists could make studies of models from life, without lessons or examinations, and landscape artists went to study anatomy.

Cézanne worked diligently for the entry examination to the École des Beaux-Arts: Claude Monet recalled his concentration, his brusque manners, and his unconventional method of working, which consisted in placing a black hat and white handkerchief near the model in order to establish the poles between which he could create his color values. Cézanne's retiring character, strong Provençal accent, and shabby clothes made him the butt of the other artists' sharp irony

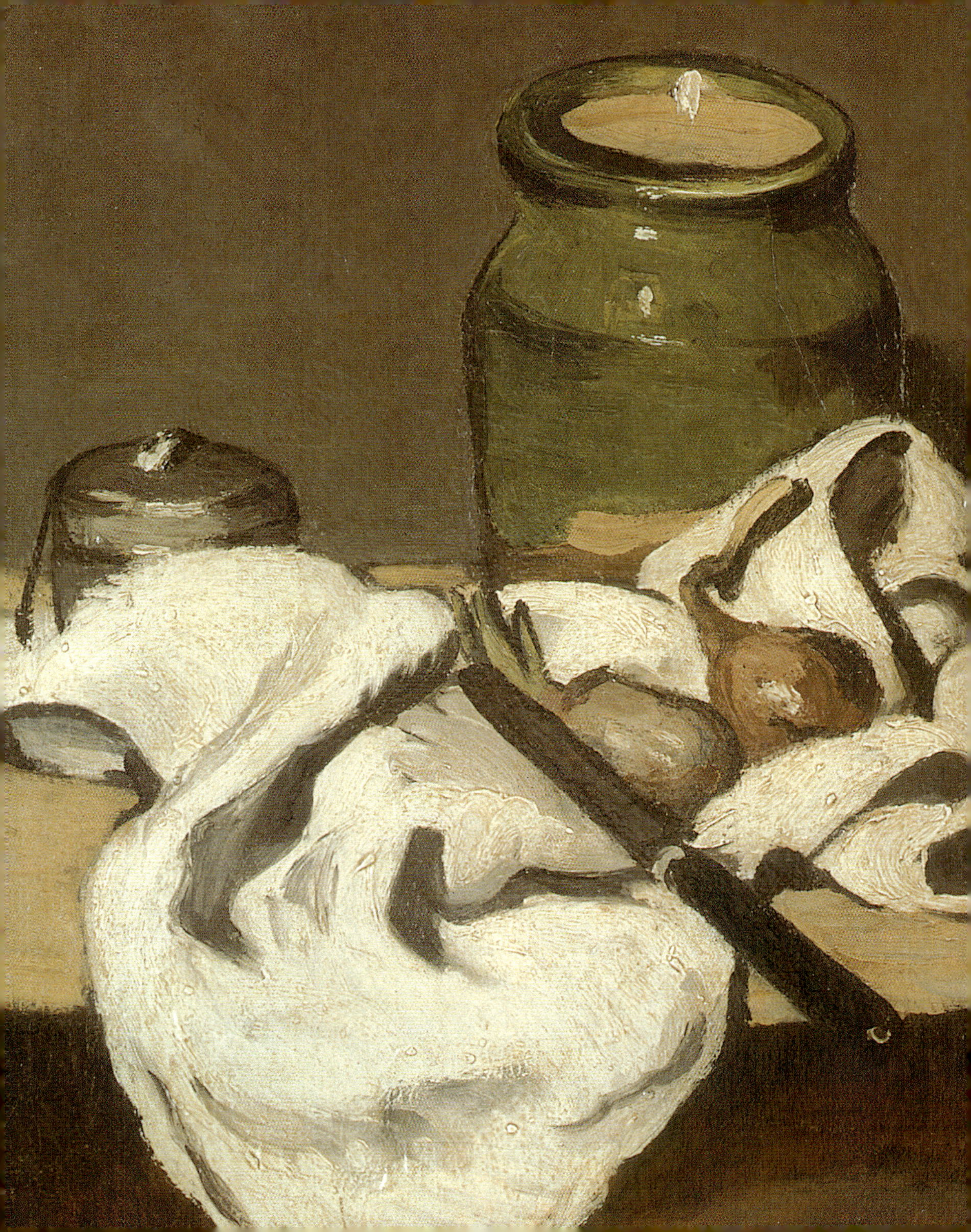

and he soon found he was isolated. Only Armand Guillaumin and Camille Pissarro, young painters attracted by the new realist style favored by Gustave Courbet, seemed to pay any attention to this talented young man with a bizarre, eccentric character, and proved to be friendly toward him.

In autumn, discouraged by the difficulties of life in Paris, the painter expressed his desire to return to Provence. He wrote to a friend in Aix: "I'm wasting my time. I can't see myself becoming a Parisian." In an attempt to persuade him to stay, Zola suggested he should paint his portrait. Cézanne began work on it, but soon, deeply dissatisfied with the result, he decided to destroy the painting. The rejection of his application for admission to the École des Beaux-Arts finally convinced him that there was no point in staying any longer in Paris and he decided to return home. His father immediately offered him a position in his bank, but Paul was not happy about this and persuaded the crusty Monsieur Cézanne to give him a small studio in the Jas de Bouffan, where he finished the *Four Seasons*, signing them ironically "Ingres."

The polemical reference to Ingres, the undisputed father of the new classical revival, is a clear indication of Cézanne's attitude to the official tendencies of French art during that period. Jean-Auguste-Dominique Ingres, the heir to the neoclassicism promoted by David at the beginning of the nineteenth century, was in fact the high priest of a cold mode of painting, based on formal perfection and the meticulous practice of drawing which frequently sacrificed color in favor of outline, which thus became the be-all and end-all of art. The insistence on exercise in the studio and the choice of mythological and historical themes remote from contemporary sensibility could not but arouse the strong reaction of a painter like Cézanne, who already felt an irrepressible attraction toward nature and the need for an authentic relationship with it in order to completely renew the practice of painting. This was now possible after the remarkable artistic contributions of Delacroix, the prophet of a new concept of art,

The Rape, 1867
Cambridge, Fitzwilliam Museum

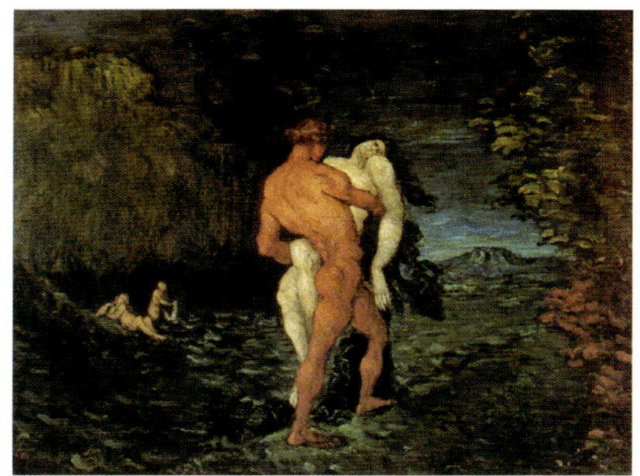

open to subjectivism and stylistically focused on the constructive and evocative power of color, and in the wake of the revolutionary and poetic approach of the Barbizon painters (Théodore Rousseau, Charles-François Daubigny, and Jean-François Millet), who began a new, vivifying relationship with nature and isolated themselves in the forest of Fontainebleau in order to paint *en plein air*. Meanwhile, a wind of change swept over Paris with the wholly innovative approach of Gustave Courbet, the exponent of a harsh style of painting without frills in which he explicitly chose to speak the language of modernity and reality. Cézanne was certainly able to see his works in Paris and no doubt he was deeply impressed by them. When, in 1862, he decided to return to the city, supported by a monthly allowance of 125 francs from his father, it was possible for the young painter to bring his artistic preferences into sharper focus. In the company of Zola, he visited the Salon des Refusés, the exhibition ordered by Napoleon III in response to the protests of the artists rejected by the jury of the official Salon. Here he encoun-

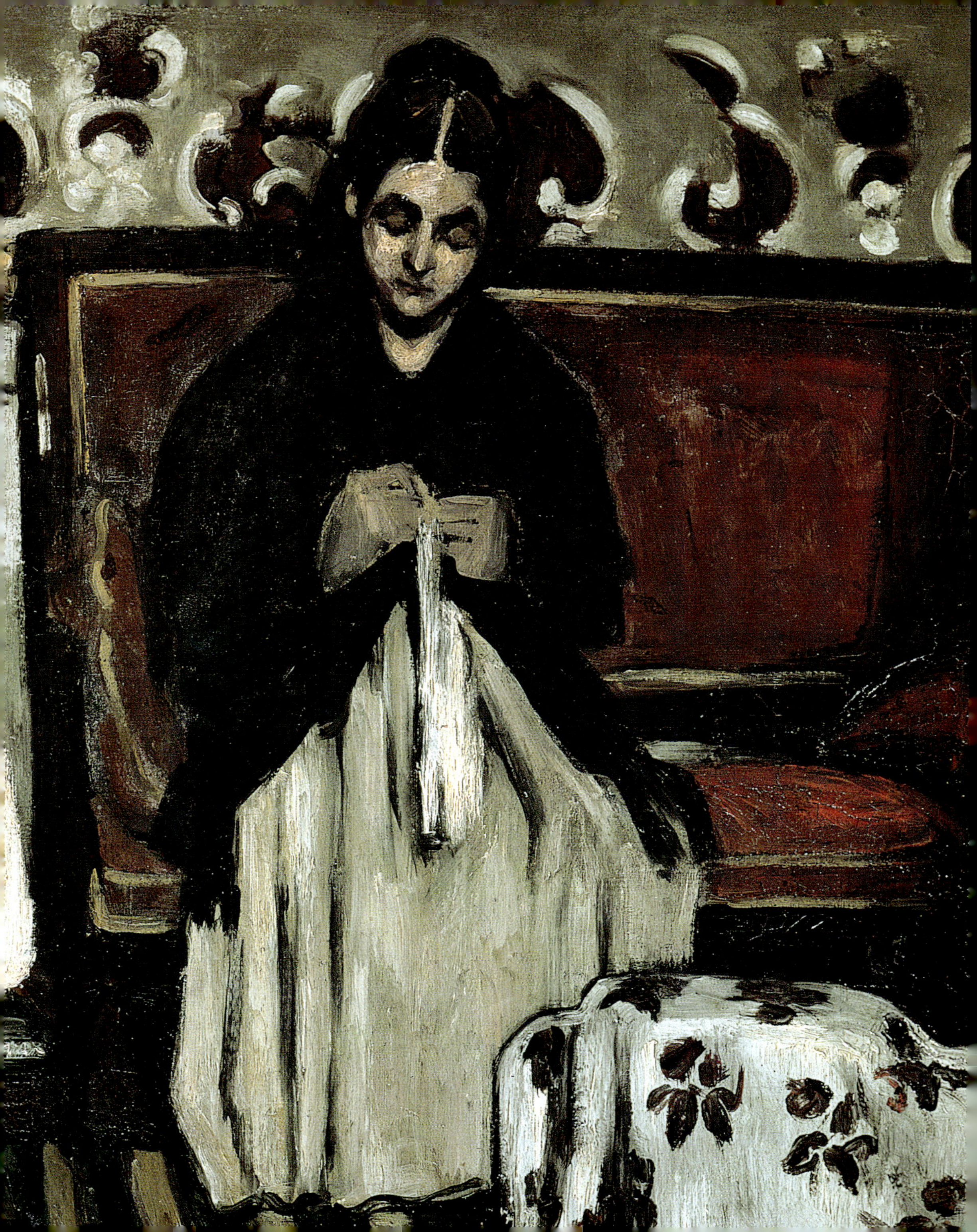

Young Girl at the Piano-Overture to Tannhäuser
(detail), *c.* 1869
St. Petersburg, The State
Hermitage Museum

tered the art of Courbet and Édouard Manet, the rising star of French painting who scandalized the Parisian public by exhibiting his *Déjeuner sur l'Herbe*, considered to be indecent because of the nonchalant representation of a female nude set in a realistic landscape together with fully clothed men and rendered in a rapid and simplified style. Courbet and Manet represented innovation, the revolutionary and liberating reaction to the dreary art of the academies, and they were supported by the young artists frequenting the Académie Suisse—such as Monet, Renoir, Bazille, and Degas—who met in the evenings at the Café Guerbois in Grand Rue des Batignolles to discuss art and culture. Cézanne rarely took part in these gatherings, despite the insistence of Pissarro, who was increasingly convinced of the exceptional talent of the young Provençal artist, who, however, tended to isolate himself and began to pay frequent visits to the Louvre in order to study the old masters. For him, the Venetian painters were a revelation: he sought inspiration in Titian's vibrant and luminous colors, studied Veronese's colored shadows, and developed his interest in Rubens and the Spanish painting of the seventeenth century, focusing particularly on the art of Zurbarán and Ribera. It was in 1864 that Cézanne first discovered the work of Delacroix, whom he was later to describe as "imaginative, sensitive to tonality" and to whom Paris devoted an exhibition a year after his death. The power of his color, the intensity of his line, the strong contrasts, and the force of the brush of this genius of the French romantic movement fascinated the young artist, now sure of the need to establish an authentic, if painfully subjective, relationship with nature and art.

Alternating brief, if tiring, stays in Paris with sudden trips back to Provence, Cézanne stubbornly continued to paint, despite his isolation and his deep lack of confidence in the value of his art. In 1865 the Salon rejected one of his works and the same occurred in 1867, when the Paris press attacked him bitterly, deeming his works ridiculous. On this occasion he was defended by his friend Zola, who, in an article

The Temptation of Saint Anthony
(detail), 1875–1877
Paris, Musée d'Orsay

in *Le Figaro*, offered a new, freer interpretation of his paintings. It was at this time, in fact, that Cézanne produced audacious works inspired by romantic literature and paintings; immersed in a dreamlike atmosphere and strongly symbolic—as in, for example, *The Rape* or *Pastoral*—which were executed with paint spread thickly over the surface of the canvas with the palette knife, in the manner of Daumier, one of the artists Cézanne admired most. The painter worked with great impetus, channeling the universe of his inner anxiety and the phantasms of a free and fervent adolescence into the limited space of the picture. The vigorous and ungainly figures are, in fact, constructed through the power of color, whether this be dense, dark, warm, or bright, and delimited by clearly visible evident black outlines seeking to restrain the forms and restore their stability and structural order.

Cézanne's dramatic painting—described by Manet as "dirty"—and his personal brand of romanticism clearly offended the sensibilities of the official critics, unleashing the disapproval of the Parisian artistic milieu, which did not seem to weaken Cézanne's faith in the validity of his own aesthetic convictions.

While Cézanne was staying in Aix he painted intensely, executing various portraits of members of his family, especially his Uncle Dominique. It was, in fact, in the period from 1866 to 1870 that he painted *Louis-Auguste Cézanne, Father of the Artist, Reading L'Événement* and the splendid *Portrait of Achille Emperaire*, a fellow student at the Académie Suisse who suffered from dwarfism and to whom Cézanne was particularly attached. In 1870 the artist decided to submit the painting to the jury of the Salon, who rejected it on the grounds that it ignored the rules of perspective and anatomy. Regarded as bordering on the grotesque, the portrait was targeted by the satirical journal *Album Stock*, which derided the artist's aspirations to realism.

When the Franco-Prussian War broke out in the summer of 1870, in order to avoid being drafted, Cézanne fled to L'Estaque, a small fishing village near Marseilles, in the company

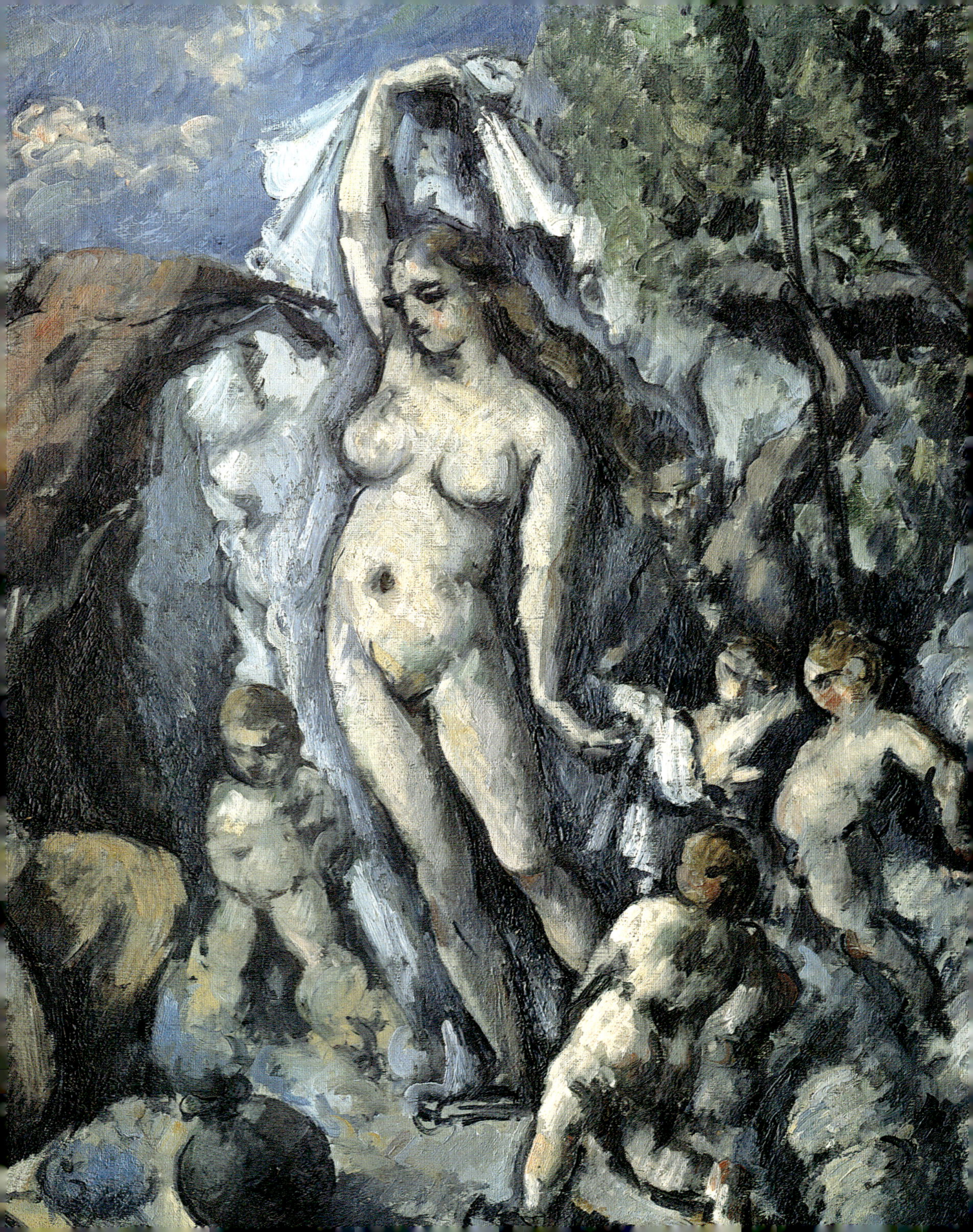

of Hortense Fiquet, whom he had met a year earlier in Paris and who earned a living as a model. The painter only paid occasional visits to his family and took great care to conceal his liaison from his father, fearing the latter's anger and that his funds would be cut off.

This was a period of ceaseless experimentation: the painter worked with total commitment, above all in the open air, seeking to come into close contact with the natural world, the ideal environment for the expression of his inner unrest. Dating from this period, in fact, is the intense painting *Melting Snow at L'Estaque*, a whirling interplay of curved lines and contrasting color effects, in which the painter seems to return to the dramatic expressiveness of his earliest works.

In 1872 Hortense bore him a son, Paul, for whom the painter always felt profound affection. Cézanne returned to Paris for a brief period, but soon became deeply depressed. Achille Emperaire recalled: "He was there [in his apartment in Rue Jussieu] abandoned by everyone. He didn't have a single close and intelligent friend. He didn't talk about Zola or his friend Philippe Solari any more. He was the strangest person you could imagine."

Closed to the world, now devoted only to his very personal aesthetic investigation, yet irritated by the ineffective results of his painting, Cézanne tended to isolate himself, avoiding contact with the other artists. The only relief from all this bitterness seemed to derive from his friendship with Camille Pissarro, who had studied with him at the Académie Suisse; an affable and generous man, Pissarro invited Cézanne to Pontoise in August 1872 to paint *en plein air* with him.

The two artists, one next to the other, immersed in the peaceful countryside of the Île-de-France, began to work together from nature. Pissarro, heir to the painters of the Barbizon school, who had promoted *en plein air* painting, taught Cézanne to lighten his palette, selecting only the primary colors (red, yellow, blue) and the complementary ones, and encouraged him to become a careful observer of reality. With him, Cézanne learned how to transform his broad, thick brushstrokes into very short dabs of color that sustained his confident, analytical rendering of the subject. By using Pissarro's technique, the artist discovered how to capture a general impression of the scene, with all the richness of its colors and forms.

Pissarro recalled, in fact, that "they always stayed together, but it cannot be denied that each of us remained faithful to the one thing that counts, the unique sensation."

The unique sensation, the close contact with the landscape: having abandoned the limited space of the studio, the painter, in Émile Bernard's words, "went in the morning and the evening to his *motif* ... observed the effects of the air on the local forms and colors; he analyzed, he sought, and he found." He trained his eye to contemplate things; he realized that the landscape required total attention and a notable effort to achieve objectivity.

Enthusiastic about the new method, in 1873 he decided to move, with his partner and son to Auvers-sur-Oise, a small village near Pontoise from where he could easily reach his friend Pissarro. During this time he executed one of his "impressionist" masterpieces, *The House of the Hanged Man*, which was strikingly different from the works the painters of Batignolles were producing. Cézanne countered the delicate, suffused light and weak, hazy outlines of Monet and Renoir with what the Italian critic Giulio Carlo Argan described as a "constipated" composition, constructed with masses of thick color "clotted like plaster." The deliberate, flat brushstrokes build up the forms in an orderly manner, seeking their structural truth and volumetric force, in order to entrust the power of color with the task of restoring the light. The "provisional" impressionist Cézanne reacted against the preoccupation with the fleeting moment with concrete, solid, well-defined painting intent on producing the clearest image in the world and focused on comprehending, fully and analytically, reality.

From this moment onwards the path that Cézanne's inquiry was to follow was that of making impressionism an enduring phenomenon, learning and developing the lesson on vision and on the direct contact with the subject formulated by the painters of Batignolles. Restoring to painting its role as the ideal method for investigating reality, this approach would lead, by dint of hard work and intense concentration, to totally innovative results. The painter knew that only the artist is entrusted with the task of renewing the way we look at things. The revealer of other worlds—or, rather, of the underlying structure of this world—he must teach others *to see*, to penetrate the profound sense of reality beyond the veil of appearance, beyond the provisional nature of the momentary vision. Observing, to the point at which he feels the model's blood mixing with his own—in Cézanne' words, "in the sun, in the light, in the color"—the painter receives from the world a "visual sensation" that his conscience is able to perceive distinctly, transforming it firstly into concrete thought, then into forms and colors on the two-dimensional surface of the canvas. The eye contemplates nature, therefore, while the brain engages in the "logic of the organized sensations" that gives the painter the possibility of expression. With the colors applied methodically, stroke after stroke, the artist reconstructs the outside world, offering it to the spectator purified, reduced to its essential forms or archetypes. "Everything in nature is modeled according to the sphere, the cone, and the cylinder. One must learn to paint on the basis of these simple figures; afterwards one can do what one wants," Cézanne told Émile Bernard in 1904, manifesting his noble ambition to comprehend what is unchangeable in the realm of the continuous, perpetual transformation.

At Auvers-sur-Oise, Cézanne painted meticulously, with extraordinary concentration. Paul Gachet, an eccentric doctor who was particularly fond of art and an early admirer of the young artist's work, recalled that he worked diligently for hours on end. The artist usually had second thoughts about his work twice a day, "once in the morning, once in the afternoon; one for gray weather and one for the sun; it happened on more than one occasion that he battled with a canvas, working on it from one season to the next, so

An Afternoon in Naples, *c.* 1875
Canberra, National Gallery
of Australia

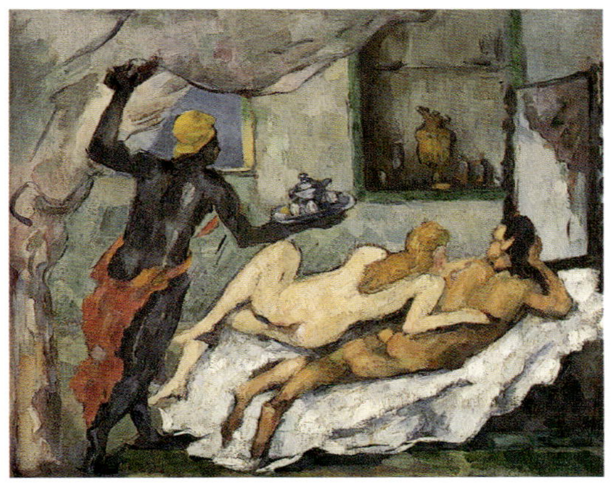

that a spring landscape painted in 1873 ended up by becoming a snow scene in 1874."

In this period, thanks to Pissarro, Cézanne also met Père Tanguy, a paint merchant who accepted his works in exchange for materials because the artist could not afford to pay for them. They immediately took a liking to each other and he became one of Cézanne's first dealers: it was in Tanguy's Paris shop, in fact, that the collector Victor Chocquet, already an enthusiastic buyer of Renoir's works, acquired one of Cézanne's paintings in 1875.

In Paris, meanwhile, the hostility of the official artistic circles had persuaded the young artists who frequented the Café Guerbois to seek alternative exhibition spaces to the Salon, and the project already entertained by Manet in 1867 took concrete form on April 15, 1874, when the Société anonyme des artistes, peintres, sculpteurs, graveurs etc., comprising Monet, Renoir, Sisley, Degas, Berthe Morisot, Pissarro, Edmond Béliard, and Guillaumin, and three of Degas's friends,

Boy in a Red Vest
(detail), 1888–1890
Zurich, Bührle Foundation

organized an independent group exhibition in the studio of the photographer Nadar on the Boulevard des Capucines.

Encouraged by Monet, Pissarro managed to persuade Cézanne to join the group; he participated with two landscapes (*Landscape at Auvers* and *The House of the Hanged Man*) and the "scandalous" *A Modern Olympia*, painted the previous year at Auvers-sur-Oise and purchased by Dr. Gachet. From its very title, this painting revealed the artist's intention to engage in a subtle polemic with Manet, whose *Olympia* (1863) had created such a scandal at the Salon of 1865 because its unidealized nakedness had shocked the Parisian public. Eight years later, therefore, Cézanne decided to go back to the same theme in order to offer a new version, alternative to Manet's, in the hope, perhaps, of focusing attention on his works on show at the Salon with a view to selling them. This was, in fact, a period of great hardship for the painter, who was often obliged to ask his friend Zola for financial help.

Cézanne's arrogance hurt the feelings of Manet, who, perhaps due to his presence, decided not to take part in the first exhibition of the group. The artists were subjected to a rain of ferocious criticism, derisive comments and indignation. This is what the critic Louis Leroy wrote in *Le Charivari* of April 25, 1874: "Oh, it was a hard day when I ventured to visit the first exhibition on the Boulevard des Capucines in the company of Joseph Vincent, a landscape artist who was a pupil of Bertin and has received medals and decorations from various governments! This reckless person came in good faith: he thought he would see painting like one sees everywhere, good and bad, more bad than good, but that were not contrary to artistic propriety, dedication to form and respect for the masters. Oh, form! Oh, the masters! There's no longer any need, my dear fellow, we've changed everything!"

The new, very free approach to nature initiated by the young artist had, in fact, profoundly revolutionized the concept and practice of painting: technique and palette were adapted to the urgent need to perceive the reality of the

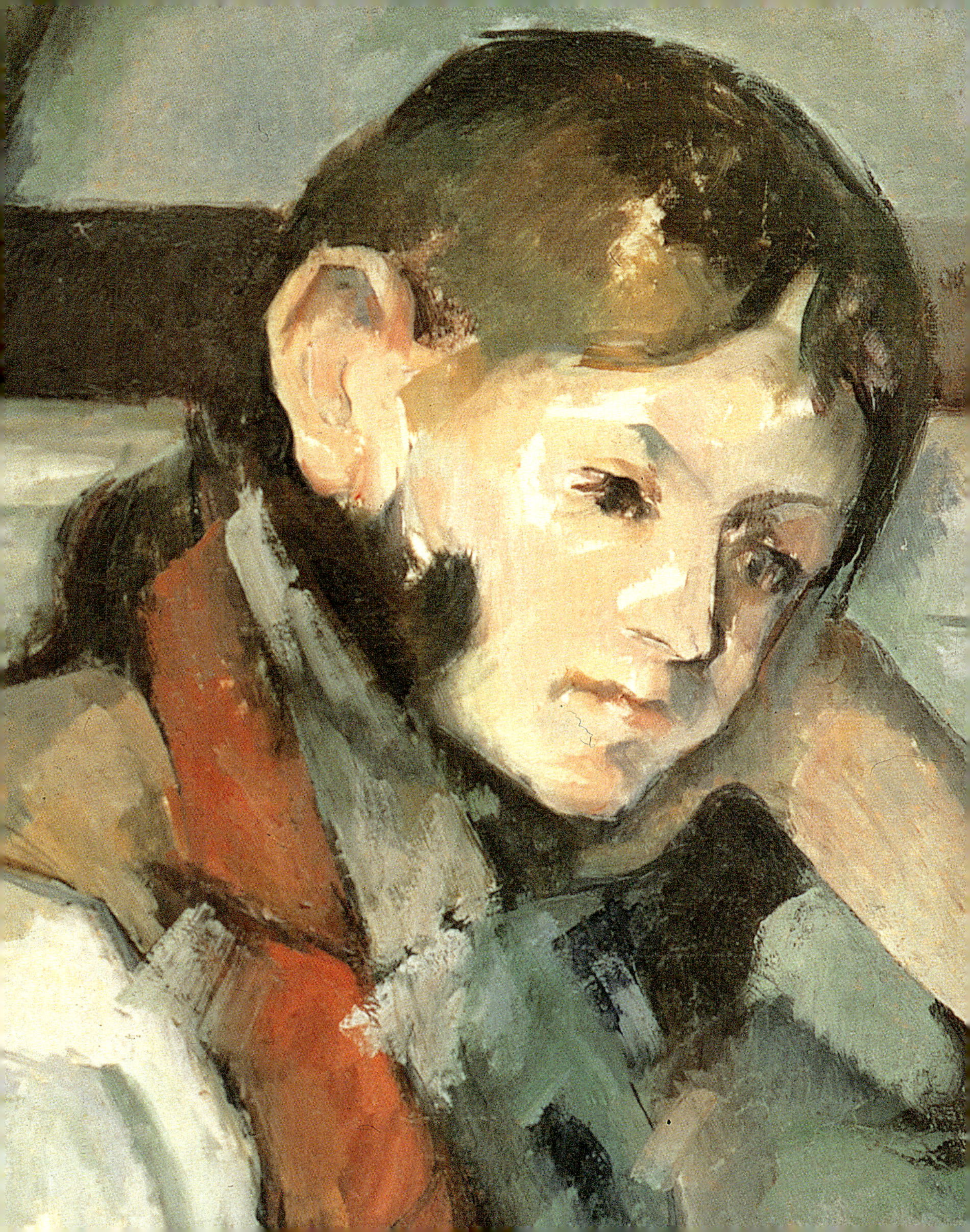

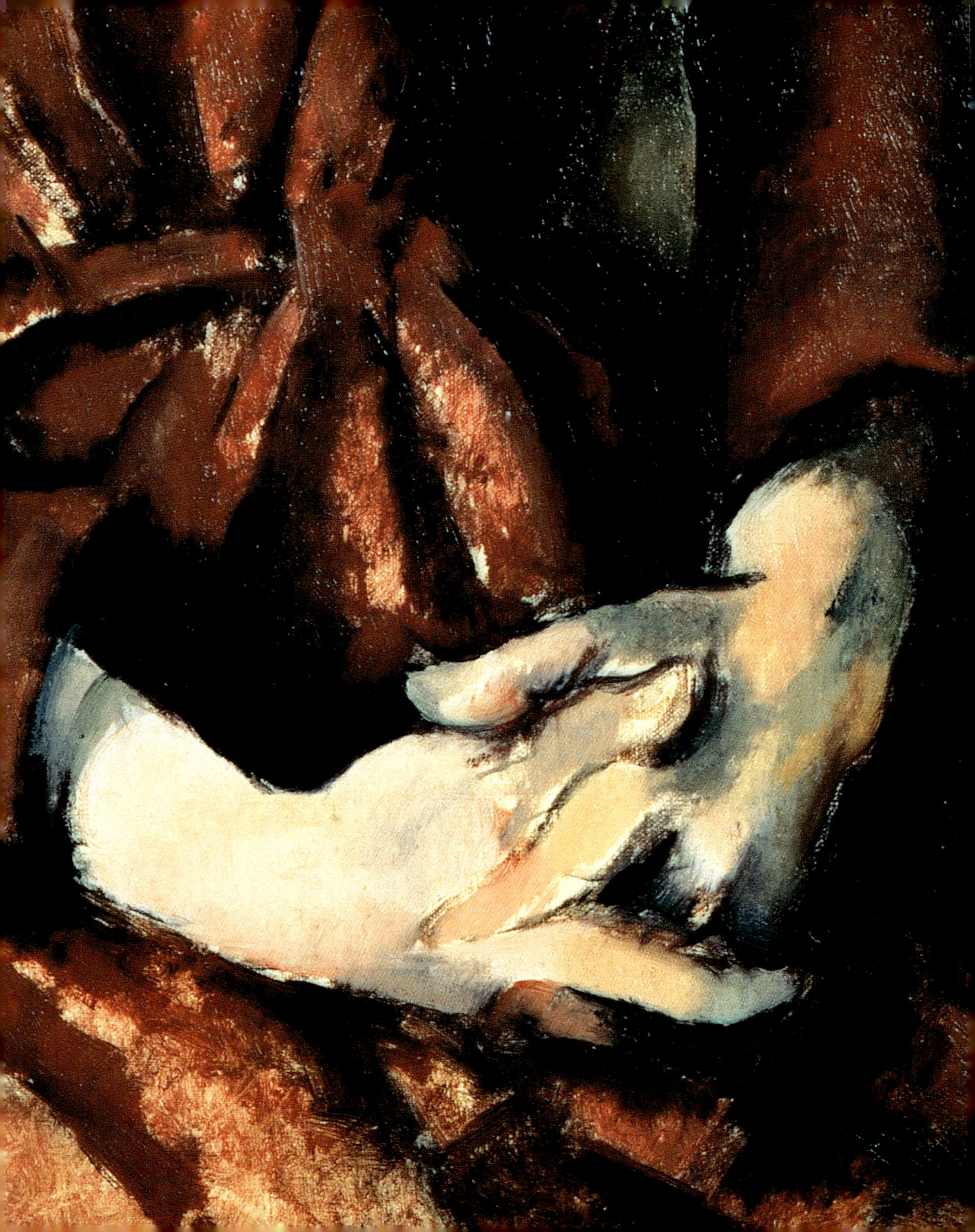

Madame Cézanne in a Yellow Chair (detail), 1888–1890
Chicago, The Art Institute

outside world directly, from life, without mediation. The harrowing experience of modern society had made a deep impression on them and they courageously decided to react against the conventional idea of "beauty" and what Émile Zola described as "bourgeois obtuseness" by proposing a type of art that was able to effectively interpret the spirit of the age. Sarcastic and malicious remarks were made about Cézanne's paintings, but the artist managed to sell *The House of the Hanged Man* to Count Armand Doria for three hundred francs.

Deciding not to take part in the auction of impressionist paintings held at the Hôtel Drouot in Paris, Cézanne then returned to Aix. He also did not participate in the second impressionist exhibition organized in 1876, preferring to present his paintings once again to the Salon, which, as before, rejected them. At the 1876 Salon Cézanne had, in fact, decided to present a difficult and bold painting, *An Afternoon in Naples*, which provoked the scandalized reaction of the jury of the Salon, who were disturbed by its explicitly erotic subject and the vigorous technique adopted by the artist, consisting of short, swift brushstrokes in the impressionist manner, which they judged to be totally unsuitable and offensive.

Tired of the criticism and of Paris, Cézanne decided to spend the summer of 1876 in L'Estaque. Here, he painted two views of the Gulf of Marseilles for the customs official Victor Chocquet, a refined collector of modern works of art and, like himself, a great admirer of Delacroix. The rugged, sun-drenched landscape of L'Estaque fascinated the painter, who, writing to Pissarro, described the "olives and pines that never lose their leaves," and the "fearsome sun" that transforms things into delicate "*silhouettes*, not only in black and white, but also in blue, red, brown and violet" that his brush reproduces meticulously. This is a synthetic landscape, flat "like a playing-card" that lends itself both to the compositional rigor the painter tried so hard to find and to his analytical approach to reality. The splendid view entitled *The Sea at L'Estaque* (Rau Foundation, Zurich),

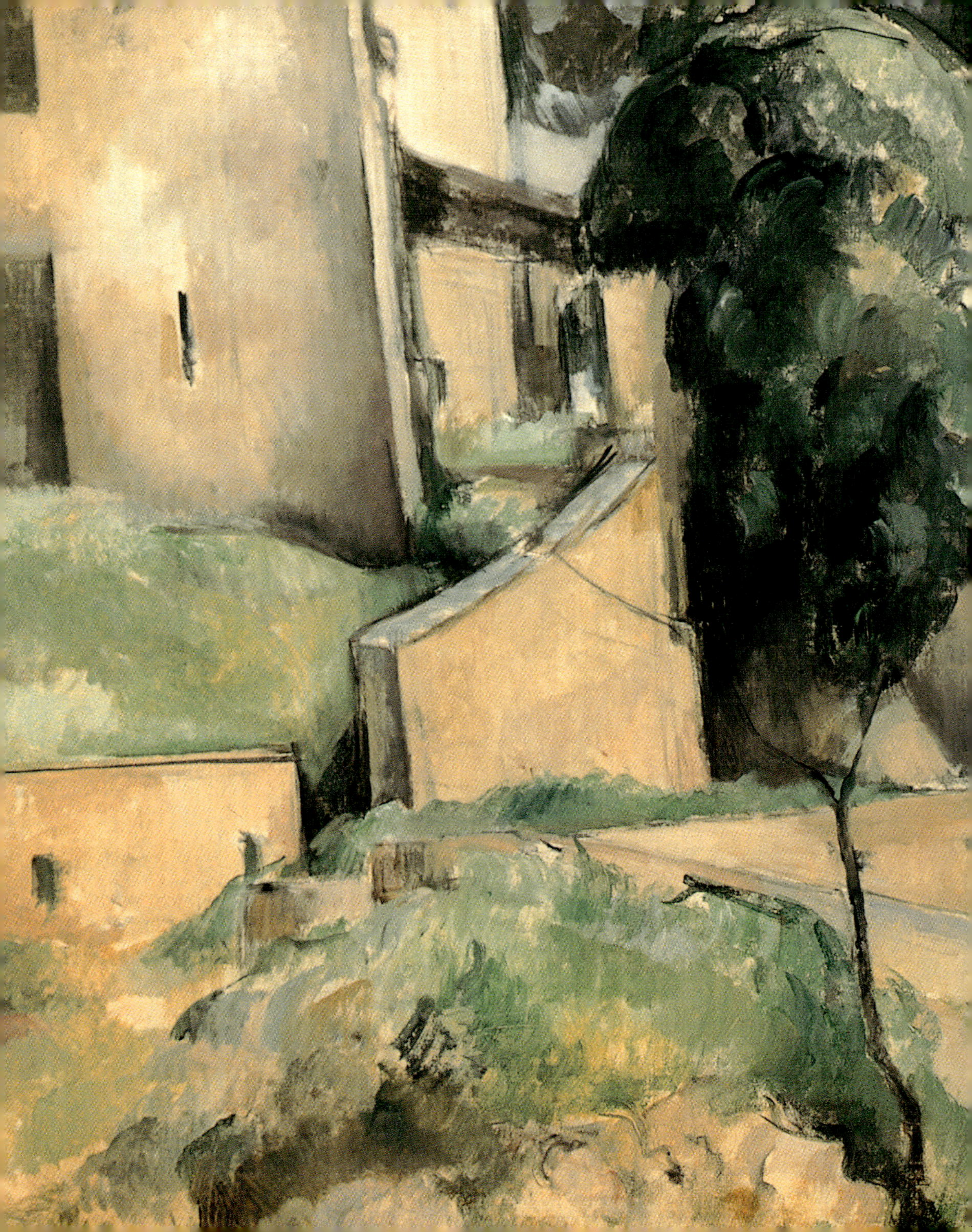

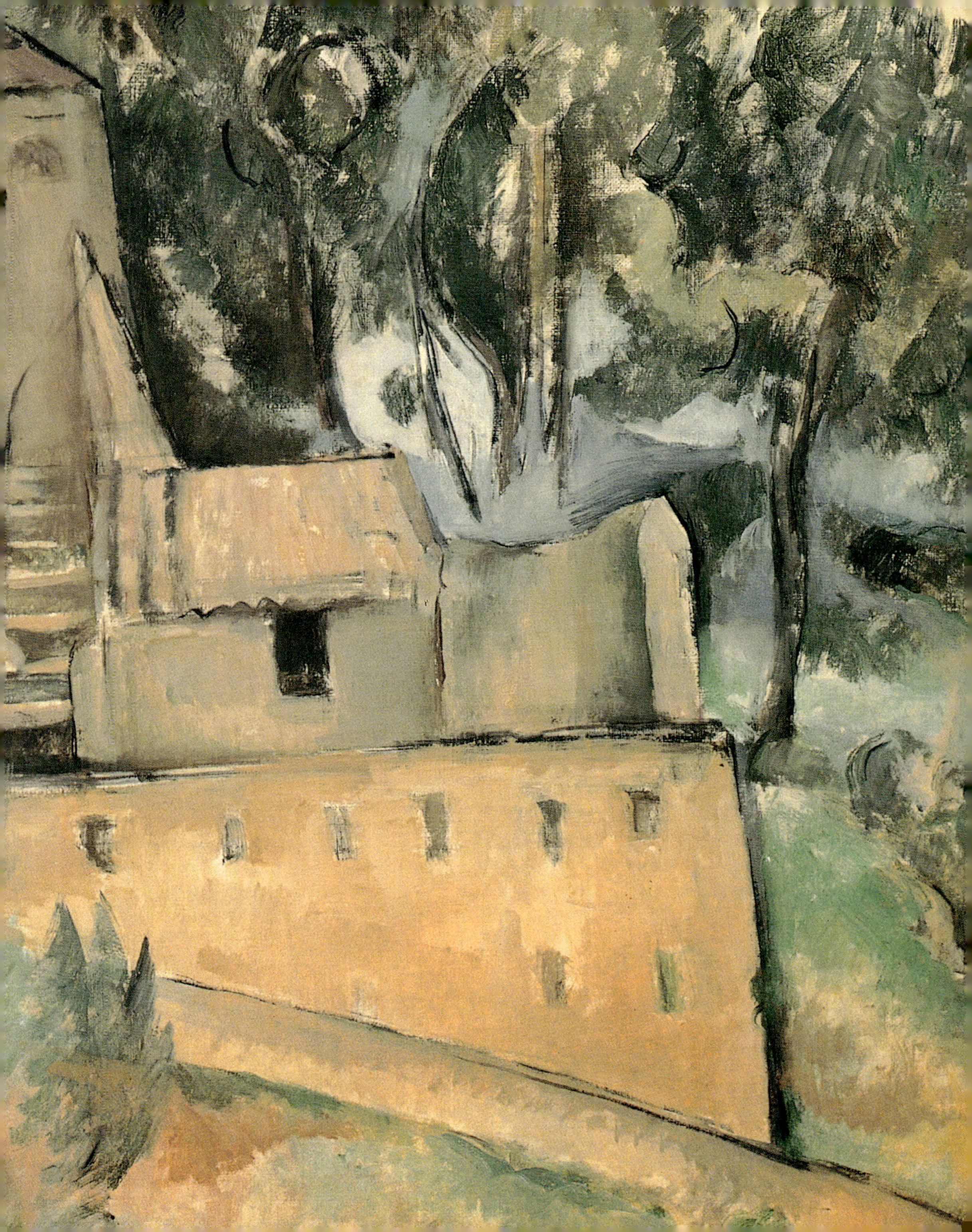

prevoius pages
The House at Bellevue
(detail), 1890
Geneva, Musée d'Art et d'Histoire

constructed fragment by fragment with small bright strokes of color, following a gradual and meticulous procedure moving from the foreground diagonally toward the distant sea, is one of the most limpid and innovative results of the artist's experimentation in this period.

When the third impressionist exhibition was held in 1877, Cézanne decided to show three watercolors and a group of twelve paintings (still lifes and landscapes), described by the artist as "studies of nature," a painting of bathers and a portrait of Chocquet.

The public flocked to see the exhibition, ready to laugh and make derisory comments that provoked the indignant reaction of Chocquet, who did his best to defend, above all, Cézanne, "whom he placed among the greatest" and was the victim of the most ferocious criticism. The group was also supported by the critic Georges Rivière and Émile Zola, the latter describing Cézanne as "the leading colorist of the group." Exalting "his Provençal landscapes with their splendid tones," the writer stated: "The canvases of this painter, so powerful and deeply felt, may cause the bourgeois to smile, but they show he has the makings of a great artist."

The need for isolation so he could undertake his artistic investigation independently caused Cézanne to associate with the group of impressionists less frequently: 1877 was the last time the painter took part in the exhibitions organized by Monet and his companions.

His visits to the Café de la Nouvelle Athènes, the new haunt of avant-garde artists and writers in Place Pigalle (regular visitors included Manet, Mallarmé, Verlaine, and Edmond de Goncourt) became sporadic, but did not pass unobserved. Thus Edmond Duranty wrote to Zola: "If it may interest you, Cézanne appeared recently at the small café in Place Pigalle. He was dressed as in old times: blue overalls, white linen jacket covered with spots of paint, etc., an old shapeless hat."

Cézanne's contempt for conventions was frequently the target of malicious comments, and people increasingly tended to gossip about him. The young Irish painter George Moore,

View through the Trees, 1882–1885
Private collection

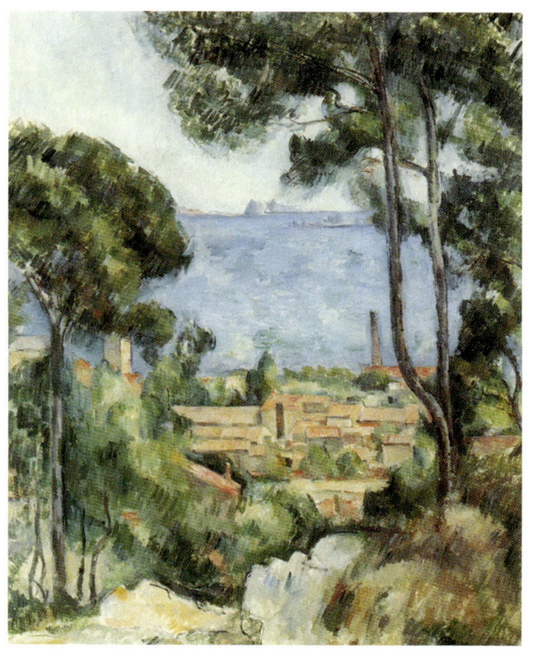

who had come to Paris to study art, although he did not know the artist, recounted (in his *Reminiscences of the Impressionist Painters*, 1906): "We used to hear about him—he used to be met on the outskirts of Paris wandering about the hillsides in jackboots. As no one took the least interest in his pictures, he left them in the fields. [...] It would not be right to say he did not have talent, but while the intention of Manet, Monet and Degas was to paint, Cézanne's intention was never, I fear, very clear even to himself. His painting may be described as anarchy of painting, the art of delirium."

Disturbed by Paris, by the noise and the distractions, Cézanne felt the need to return to the south and work in solitude: Aix was the ideal place to work in peace and, after 1878, the painter only rarely left Provence. That was the year when, by chance, his father discovered his secret relationship with Hortense and, although he threatened to cut off his allowance, in the end he decided to increase it. And this was the time when, like a "mystic" or "contemplative"—as Émile Bernard put it—wholly

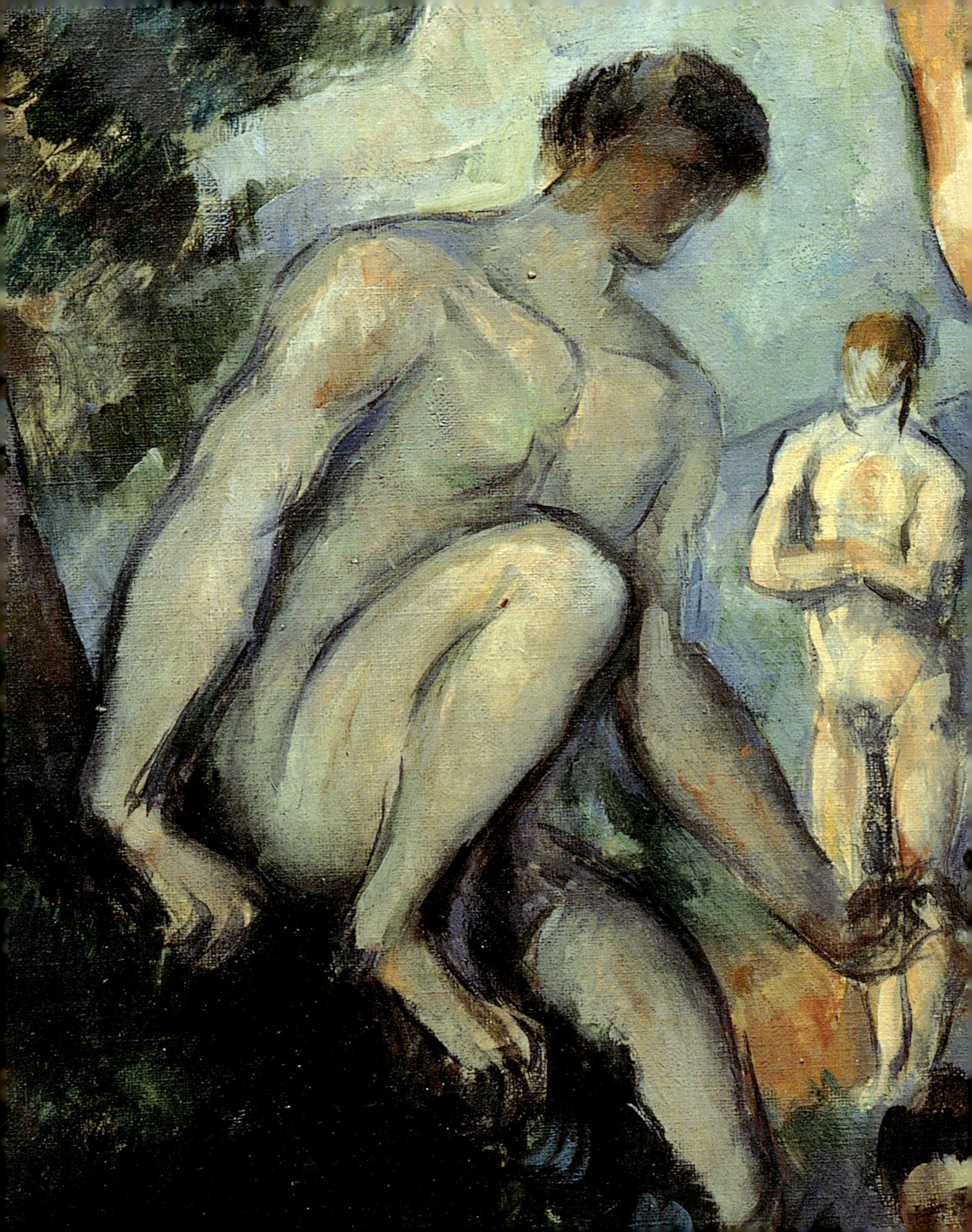

Bathers
(detail), *c.* 1890
Paris, Musée d'Orsay

devoted to painting, Cézanne began a period of intense research.

The painter selected his themes—those felt were most congenial and that he had tended to focus on since the beginning of his career—and it was on those and possible variants of them that he worked, patiently and indefatigably: the landscape, the still life, the portrait (and the self-portrait), the nude in the landscape (bathers, male and female). The painter worked on a number of subjects at the same time and applied the same method to them all; and, whether they were animate or inanimate beings, he posed the same aesthetic questions with regard to them all: "At the beginning, complete submission to the model; carefully, establish the position, develop the investigation of the lines, link up the proportions; then, in sessions of profound meditation, exalt the sensations of color, elevate form to a decorative concept; starting from color towards a harmonious whole."

Cézanne required his models to keep absolutely still—this was indispensable for him to observe them correctly ("You must be like an apple. Does an apple move?")—and then he went on to seek to understand the spatial relationships. His investigation, in fact, regarded essentially the form of the things and their relationship with the surrounding space. The painter was interested in generating an *authentic*, non-illusionistic vision of reality and, for this reason, he began to observe objects from various points of view, representing them in the painting in different perspectives that distort them and present them to the spectator in a wholly new version. Thus the objects show more than one side of themselves simultaneously, forming a new disposition on the canvas that allowed the painter to create relationships and proportions alternative to the academic and traditional ones, based on the perspective and single vanishing point typical of the art of the Renaissance. Color was also useful to this end: Cézanne used blue, for example, expressly for perspective purposes by exploiting its capacity to break through the space by thrusting things into the depth, thus suggesting distance to the eye. The painter told Bernard: "For us

Woman with a Coffee Pot (detail), *c.* 1895
Paris, Musée d'Orsay

human beings nature is more in depth than on the surface, which is why it is necessary to introduce, in our vibrations of light, represented by the reds and the yellows, a quantity of blue sufficient to give the impression of air." The painter knew, in fact, that nature reveals itself through color, that it "is biological… is living, it alone gives life to things" and, therefore, color—the medium of painting par excellence—is given the task of constructing the forms and generating the light. Cézanne does not, in fact, illuminate his objects from the outside—using a source of artificial light created ad hoc—but it is the objects themselves that irradiate light thanks to the color with which they are impregnated.

In a painting like *Kitchen Still Life*, datable to about 1888 – 1890, the results of this complex inquiry are already clear: every object in this crowded composition fluctuates in a wholly mental space and is revealed to the spectator in its own perspective that ensures it has the greatest possible representativeness. The sugar-bowl, pitcher, tablecloth, basket, and fruit are depicted by the artist independently, from different viewpoints, each of which then contributes to the overall harmony of the painting. Thus the equilibrium sought by Cézanne is not based on the submission of all the elements to hard and fast yet abstract rules of perspective, but rather on the multiplicity of the visual trajectories. In the same way, each element transmits light thanks to the power of the color and the effect of the chromatic contrasts. As Cézanne told Bernard: "To understand nature is to see it through the veil of interpretation as blots of color following each other according to a law of harmony. Neither the line nor modeling exists, but only contrasts. These contrasts are certainly not rendered by black and white, but by the *sensation of color*."

In 1879 Cézanne decided to abandon his Provençal exile temporarily for Melun, a small town southeast of Paris. Here he spent part of the winter in order to paint the landscape cloaked in snow, but then, suffering from the cold and without enough money to

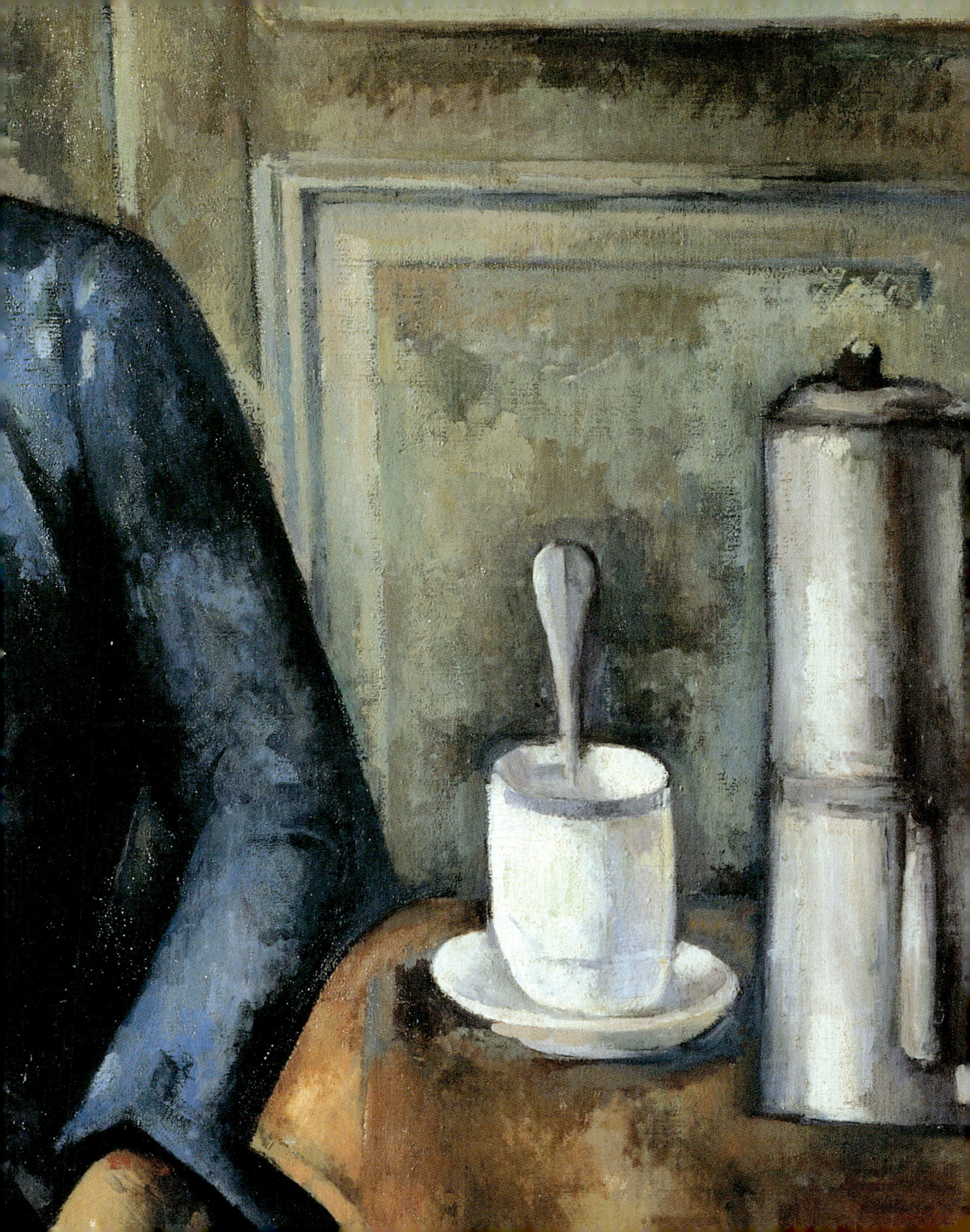

buy coal, he went back to Paris in the hope of being accepted by the Salon. Once again the jury refused him admission and it was only in 1882 that he managed to show the *Portrait of Monsieur L.A.*, receiving only a lukewarm critical response. He also spent part of the following year in Melun and it was here that the artist painted one of his masterpieces, *The Bridge at Maincy*, constructed with short, very bright green and ochre brushstrokes that, although disposed separately next to each other, endow the painting with notable structural solidity.

In August 1880 Cézanne again chose the Île-de-France for his painting: he visited his friend Zola at his luxurious residence in Médan on the banks of the Seine, where he spent a great deal of time painting *en plein air*, and also the following summer, when from May he followed Pissarro to Pontoise, not far from Médan.

In October 1881 Cézanne returned to Aix, where his father provided him with a studio at the Jas de Bouffan, where he lived essentially in isolation, receiving only rare visits from his old friends living in Paris.

In 1882 Renoir visited the artist in L'Estaque and was deeply impressed by the rugged beauty of the Provençal landscape. This is what he wrote to Madame Charpentier: "I'm learning a lot. The sun always shines and I can rub out what I'm doing and start again when I want. This is the best way to learn...." The painter started work with enthusiasm, but he was soon laid up in bed with a severe attack of pneumonia. Cézanne and his mother nursed him lovingly and Renoir later recalled their generosity in a letter he wrote to Chocquet.

In 1883 Cézanne was deeply grieved by the news of Manet's death. In December Monet and Renoir came to stay with him in L'Estaque.

Meanwhile, in Paris, the critics, even those with avant-garde pretensions, continued to ignore Cézanne's output. In his book *L'Art Moderne*, the novelist Joris-Karl Huysmans decided not to include an analysis of Cézanne's work, confessing to Pissarro that, for him, the artist embodied "the kind of Impressionist who hasn't made it," and that, aside from "certain still lifes," he would soon be forgotten. Thus

Cézanne was left in isolation, with no choice but to continue obstinately along the road he had already taken, despite the general lack of understanding he encountered.

Once again he took refuge at the Jas de Bouffan, where he began a period of intense work. The painter Émile Bernard recalled: "Immersed in the absolute of his art, he was not interested in what was going on outside this; he continued, in solitude, to develop his analysis. Slowly, with reflection and with strength, he worked away with the spade that one day would reveal the wonderful vein from which all splendors would emerge."

During this period he produced marvelous works with absolute formal purity, such as the series devoted to chestnuts at the Jas de Bouffan, where the structural tension reached remarkable heights: trees and buildings are distributed over the canvas with absolute rigor, while the whole painting has a rarefied and crystalline atmosphere that amplifies the sensation of silence and absorbed concentration.

In 1886 Cézanne finally decided to legalize his relationship with Hortense Fiquet, who lived most of the time in Paris with their son Paul, and they finally got married. In October his father died and he inherited a substantial sum of money: the very person who had done his best to thwart his ambitions now gave him the opportunity to be free from financial problems for the rest of his days. It appears that the artist stated on this occasion: "My father was a man of genius: he left me an income of 25,000 francs."

At the same time, Émile Zola's novel *L'Œuvre* was published in Paris; this was the account of a failed painter, Claude Lantier, driven to suicide by the irresolvable conflict between his ambitions and the inadequacy of his creative powers. Although the Parisian readers understand this to be an allusion to Monet and the impressionist movement, Cézanne sensed that there was an explicit reference to his early years and his hard struggles to affirm his artistic choices and he felt offended. On a number of occasions, in fact, Zola had expressed his disappointment with the continuous insecurity and

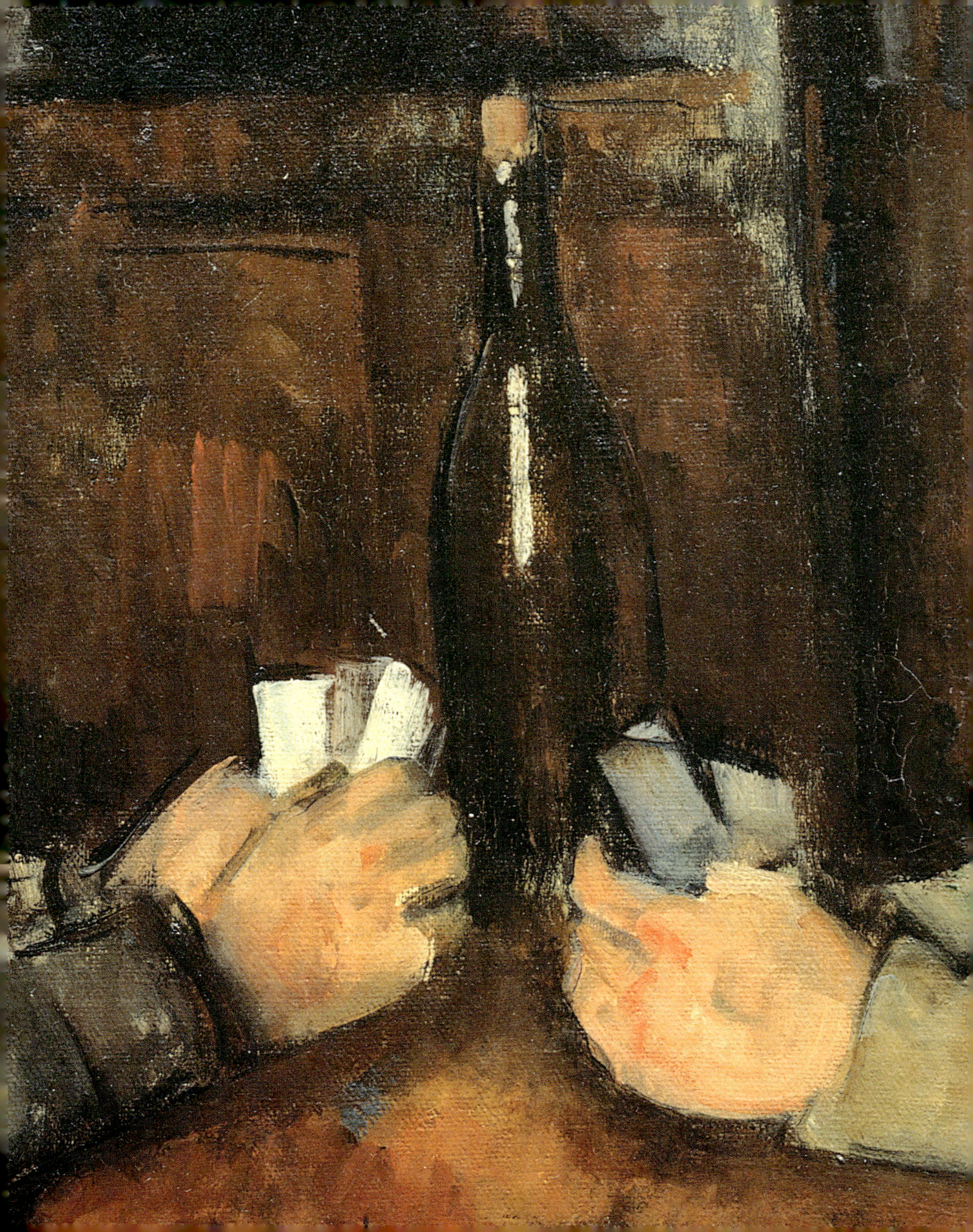

Card Players
(detail), 1893–1896
Paris, Musée d'Orsay

indecision of the painter, who was always dissatisfied with his work, and he became convinced of the absolute uselessness of his friend's efforts and of his substantial lack of talent. Cézanne interpreted the book as a distressing betrayal and in a letter he briefly thanked his writer friend for the copy of *L'Œuvre* that he had sent him. The two friends were never to meet again. In 1894 the Dreyfus affair exploded in Paris: this involved the intricate legal case of Alfred Dreyfus, a Jewish officer in the French army who was unjustly sentenced to life imprisonment on a charge of spying for Germany and was strenuously defended by Zola in the famous open letter (*J'accuse*) he sent to the president of the French republic in the name of truth and against the dangerous extremism of French nationalism. Cézanne reacted with indifference, revealing evident conservative tendencies that, as he approached fifty, replaced the libertarian and republican beliefs of his youth.

Nonetheless, the considerable fortune inherited from his father had not produced any change in the painter's austere existence. Cézanne continued to live in the usual way, totally concentrated on his painting. He only saw a few friends and those only rarely. Pissarro, Renoir, Chocquet, and Père Tanguy sometimes came to visit him in Aix, but the painter preferred his state of isolation so he could devote himself completely to his work, which was for him, as he once told Zola, "beyond all expectations, the only refuge where one finds real satisfaction with oneself."

He studied color assiduously and it was in this period that he started to use watercolor, which together with oils, became his favorite technique. From 1888 to 1890 he developed his interest in the human figure, which dated back to his early years, devoting four canvases to subjects drawn from the Commedia dell'Arte (*Mardi Gras, Harlequin*), while in 1890 he started to work on the series of card players, probably stimulated by the presence in the Musée des Beaux-Arts in Aix of a painting with this subject by a seventeenth-century artist, Louis Le Nain. For the first time the painter decided to focus on "social reality." It was only here that the outside world, with its complex problems, was able to invade his isolated existence consisting of art and silence. Although he treats the card players of Aix as volumes and although he is totally absorbed by the problem of their spatial relationships, Cézanne seems to want to endow the figures with a precise moral value, insisting on their dignified seriousness and their backs bent by the burden of hard work.

In 1890 Les XX of Brussels, a very active group of painters who had displayed works by Gauguin and Toulouse-Lautrec in Belgium, invited the artist, together with Sisley and Van Gogh, to exhibit a small group of paintings for them. In his reply, Cézanne wrote: "I had decided to work in silence until the day when I should feel able to defend the results of my work on a theoretical level, but in view of the pleasure that finding myself in such excellent company has given me, I shall not hesitate to change my mind." Slowly recognition arrived and Cézanne's painting began to attract the attention of younger painters. They stepped up their visits to Père Tanguy's shop on the Rue Clauzel, in Montmartre, which was the only place in Paris where at that time it was possible to admire the work of the mysterious painter of Aix. Émile Bernard, Maurice Denis, Pierre Bonnard, and Édouard Vuillard—future members of the Nabis group and exponents of Gauguin's dream of pure art—were among the most regular visitors to Tanguy's shop. Denis recalled that what most impressed them in Cézanne's paintings was the balance, the essentiality, the austerity, the sense of grandeur, the conscious abandonment of the impressionist premises, and the conquest of form, obtained through the quest for the eternal principles underlying the variety of nature. Cézanne had demonstrated to the young artists that it was possible to combine sensation and reflection, and that the eye, the heart, and the mind all contributed to the complete understanding of reality. Thus the artist had, in Denis's words, been able to "restore its fundamental role to sensibility," but he had also managed to "replace empiricism with reflection." For them, he represented "the conclusion of the classical tradition

Madame Cézanne in the Conservatory,
1891
New York, The Metropolitan Museum of Art

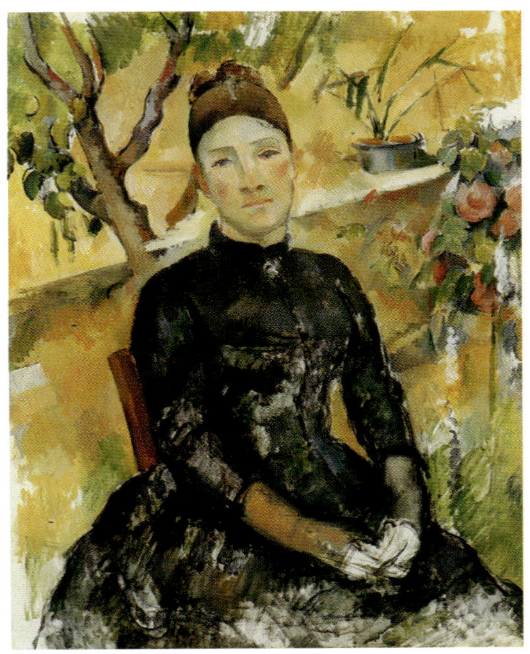

and the outcome of the great crisis of liberty and light that had rejuvenated modern art." Cézanne was now acknowledged by the new generations as the "Poussin of impressionism," the prophet of innovation.

In 1894 Père Tanguy died and the six paintings by Cézanne kept in his shop were auctioned off for sums ranging between 45 and 215 francs.

Thanks to Pissarro's sagacious advice, the young dealer Ambroise Vollard began to take an interest in Cézanne's painting and decided to exhibit his works. The artist accepted and sent fifty works for what was to be his first one-man show. The exhibition was held at Vollard's gallery in the Rue Lafitte and, although the Parisian public claimed to be offended by so much ugliness and the critics confirmed the underlying coarseness of their opinions, the impression of many visitors was of great power. Commenting on the exhibition, Pissarro wrote to his son: "My enthusiasm is very mild compared to that of Renoir and even Degas was fascinated by this refined savage, Monet, all of us… are we mistaken? I think not. The

Still-life with Apples and Oranges
(detail), 1899
Paris, Musée d'Orsay

only people who don't feel this fascination are the artists and collectors who, with their errors, have shown their lack of sensibility. As Renoir rightly said, these paintings bear a resemblance to the frescoes from Pompeii, so worn and so marvelous!... Degas and Monet bought some splendid Cézannes. I exchanged a poor sketch of Louvenciennes for a superb little picture of bathers and a self-portrait."

Gustave Geffroy also devoted an enthusiastic article to the exhibition: "Passers-by who enter the Galerie Vollard in the Rue Lafitte will find themselves face to face with around fifty paintings: portraits, landscapes, fruit, and flowers, on the basis of which they can finally give their verdict on one of the greatest and most refined figures of our times. When this happens, and it's high time it did, everything that is obscure and legendary concerning Cézanne will disappear and what remains will be the work of a lifetime, rigorous yet fascinating, masterly yet simple.... Cézanne is a great lover of the truth, passionate and naïve, austere and simple. He'll end up in the Louvre."

Thanks to Vollard's ability, Cézanne started to find keen buyers in Paris. The prices of his works rose, but his health was failing. He suffered from diabetes and became irritable and morose. He decided to retire to Aix, where he was comforted by the affection of Henri Gasquet, an old school friend, and the latter's son, Joachim.

Despite his precarious physical condition, he continued to work tirelessly. In 1897 he stayed in Le Tholonet, a village on the slopes of Mont Sainte-Victoire, where he painted a number of landscapes featuring the Bibémus quarry, which the artist studied carefully thanks to the precious information he received from Professor Marion, a childhood friend, who, during long Sunday walks, explained to him how the earth was composed.

After the painful death of his mother, which occurred in the same year, the Jas de Bouffan was sold and Cézanne moved to Aix, in Rue Boulegon, where he set up his studio in the loft of a small apartment. Émile Bernard remembered it as "a vast, high but drab room

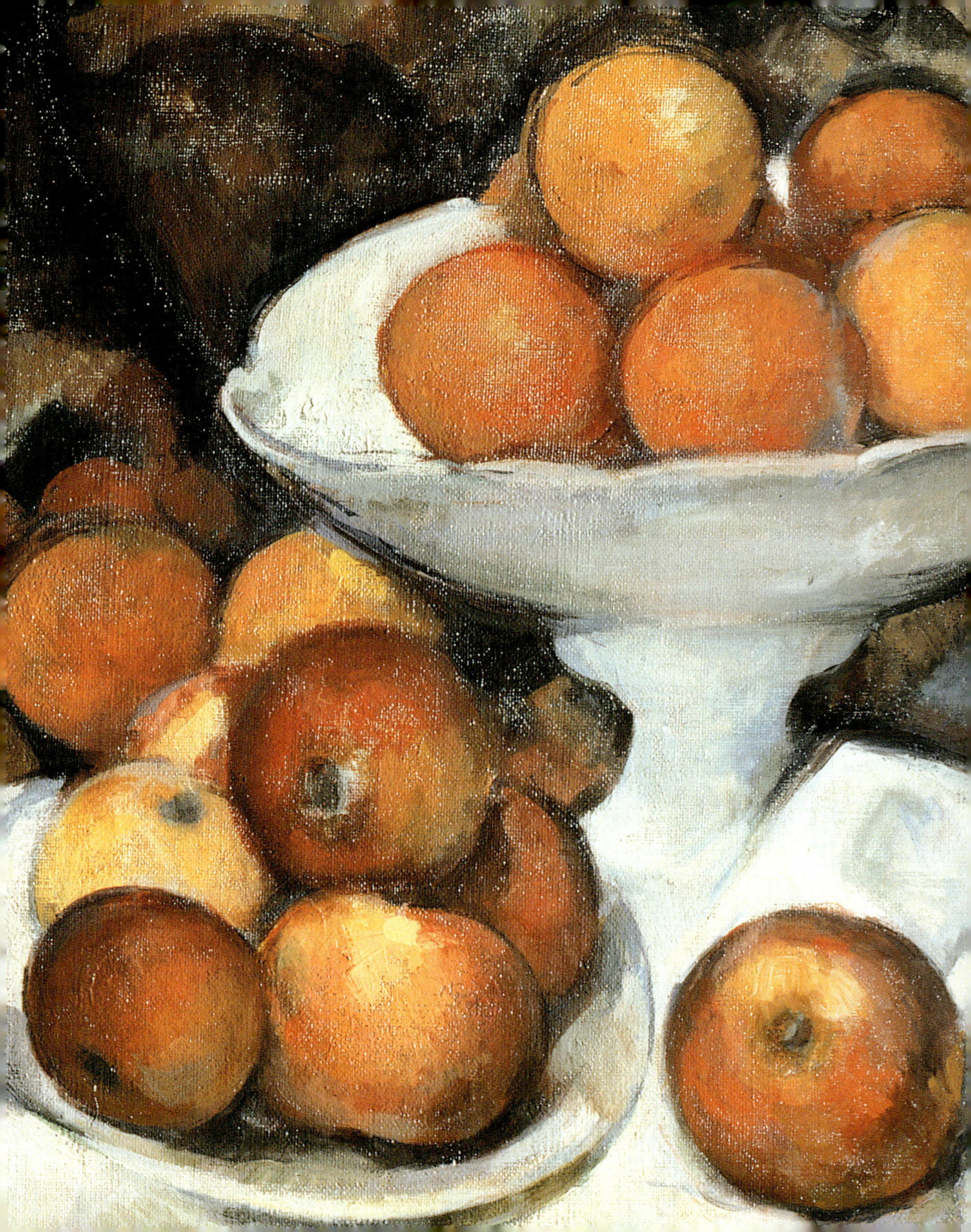

with bare walls, overlooking an olive grove," which evidently did not satisfy the painter's thirst for isolation, so he decided to rent a room at the Château Noir, an old neo-Gothic building not far from Aix belonging to a coal-merchant who had made a fortune, and here he established another small studio.

Meanwhile, in Paris, Vollard organized new and increasingly fruitful exhibitions. In 1900 Cézanne participated successfully in the Paris Exposition Universelle with three canvases, while he sent thirteen to a group show at the Galerie Cassirer in Berlin, where the poet Rainer Maria Rilke had his first opportunity to see the artist's work.

Cézanne's investigation of color continued without interruption: in fact, he progressively thinned down his impastos, preferring to paint with transparent glazes that he used in his now well-advanced process of decomposing forms. He paid careful attention, as Giulio Carlo Argan put it, to "the width and frequency of the brushstrokes so that every touch of color corresponds to a precise formal definition. With great clarity he defines the structural reason behind each *petite sensation* and its specific function in a context of spatial relationships." In the portraits and the long series of paintings devoted to Mont Sainte-Victoire he obtained results with a new structural solidity that never diminished the freshness and immediacy of his vision of reality. Proceeding rhythmically, Cézanne's brush gave life to myriads of colored strokes imbued with a transparent light endowing his subjects with an incredible intensity of movement.

Although Victor Chocquet had died in 1891, it was only in 1899, when his widow died, that his splendid collection was put up for sale. Encouraged by Monet, the dealer Paul Durand-Ruel bought a large number of paintings by Cézanne, while Ambroise Vollard purchased a splendid watercolor by Delacroix that the painter particularly liked and gave it to him. Cézanne, who had shared Chocquet's admiration for Delacroix, kept the painting carefully and even made a copy of it, now in the Pushkin Museum in Moscow.

Meanwhile, the prices of Cézanne's works

rose incredibly. The paintings of the "hermit of Aix", as Cézanne was called, were finally given the value they deserved, but the painter did not allow himself to be enticed by the prospect of easy financial success and continued to work in solitude.

Artists and critics, however, began to be curious about him, even seeking him out in Provence. Cézanne welcomed the visitors cordially; in particular, he appreciated the visits of the young artists in Gauguin's circle, who regarded him as the precursor of a new way of conceiving and producing art. "I believe that the young painters are more intelligent than the others," he wrote to his son Paul in Paris. "The old ones only see a dangerous rival in me." Those who visited him in Aix found a tall man, almost exaggeratedly courteous, who sometimes became somber and aloof. Cézanne only talked about painting and was irritated by those who questioned him about the theoretical premises of his art or asked him for ready-to-use abstract formulae. "One can say more—and perhaps better—when one is confronted by the subject than when one pronounces purely speculative theories in which one often loses oneself," the artist stated peremptorily when accompanying his visitors to the hills surrounding Aix.

Mild, humble, and very polite to those who showed they appreciated him, the artist agreed to exhibit at the Salon des Indépendants in 1901 and his fame began to spread beyond the borders of France. At the Salon de la Société Nationale des Beaux-Arts in the same year, Maurice Denis displayed his *Homage to Cézanne*, which portrayed a group of artists, including Redon, Vuillard, Bonnard, and Denis himself, gathered around a still life by Cézanne that formerly belonged to Gauguin, an early admirer of his work.

In 1902 the painter decided to leave his studio in Aix and build a new one on a piece of land located on the Les Lauves hill behind the city, from where he had an excellent view of Mont Saint-Victoire. He continued to work indefatigably, accepting the ever-increasing number of invitations to exhibit in the leading

Médan Castle,
1879–1881
Zurich, Kunsthaus

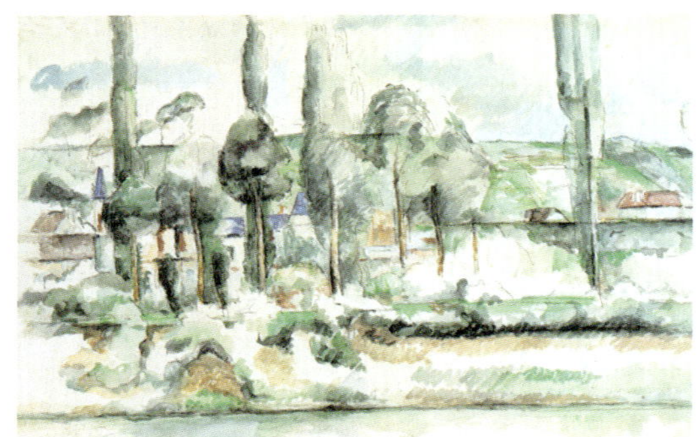

art centers of Europe. He alternated major events, such as the impressionist exhibitions of the Vienna and Berlin Secessions in 1903 and the Salon d'Automne, with small group shows like the one organized by a number of artists in Aix, where the painter asked to display his works with his name followed by the appellation "pupil of Pissarro," once again confirming the deep affection and esteem he felt for the artist, who died in 1903. In 1904 he agreed to meet the painter Émile Bernard, who had published an enthusiastic article about him. The young artist stayed in Aix for a month and was deeply impressed by Cézanne. In February 1904 he wrote to his mother from Marseilles: "He is an elderly man, simple, a little suspicious and eccentric—but a good man. He is a sort of lord of painting who handles dense impastos as if they were rich earth."

The two discussed painting at length and Bernard gradually learned more about Cézanne's technique. With his help he began to acquire useful information regarding his palette ("a real painter's palette"), composed of eighteen colors: five shades of yellow, six of red, three of green, and four of blue; and then he described his way of painting "in the manner of Ingres, starting from the details and completing some parts before proceeding with the rest." The artist confided his opinions about painting to Bernard and, in their long conversations in the Provençal countryside, Cézanne confirmed that he had no time for theorizing or the speculative exercises in art to which critics and artists were accustomed. He strongly advised Bernard, in fact, "to devote himself completely to the study of nature" and "to try to create paintings containing a lesson," without losing himself in abstruse speculations that have very little to do with the painter's craft. This encounter is recorded by a number of photographs of the artist and the book *A Conversation with Cézanne*, which contains a number of enlightening observations by the artist on his work.

Cézanne's state of health became increasingly precarious and, in a letter thanking Roger Marx for a number of articles he had devoted to him, the artist wrote: "My age and health will never allow me to realize the dream of art that I have pursued for the whole of my life. But I shall always be grateful to the public of intelligent connoisseurs who have had ... the intuition of what I have wanted to attempt in order to renew my art."

Although he was still working intensely on his female bathers—what Émile Bernard described as "naked young women, white bodies against diaphanous blues"—the artist continued to paint *en plein air*. He lived alone, and Vallier, his gardener, the favorite "motif" of his last portraits, looked after him.

On October 15, Cézanne left his studio as usual and went off into the countryside in search of a subject. Caught in a rainstorm while he was painting *Jourdan's Hut*, he collapsed and remained exposed to the inclement weather until he was taken back home on a laundry cart. The next day he got up and went into the garden to work; thoroughly exhausted, he had to go back indoors. He died in his bed at his studio at Les Lauves on October 22, 1906.

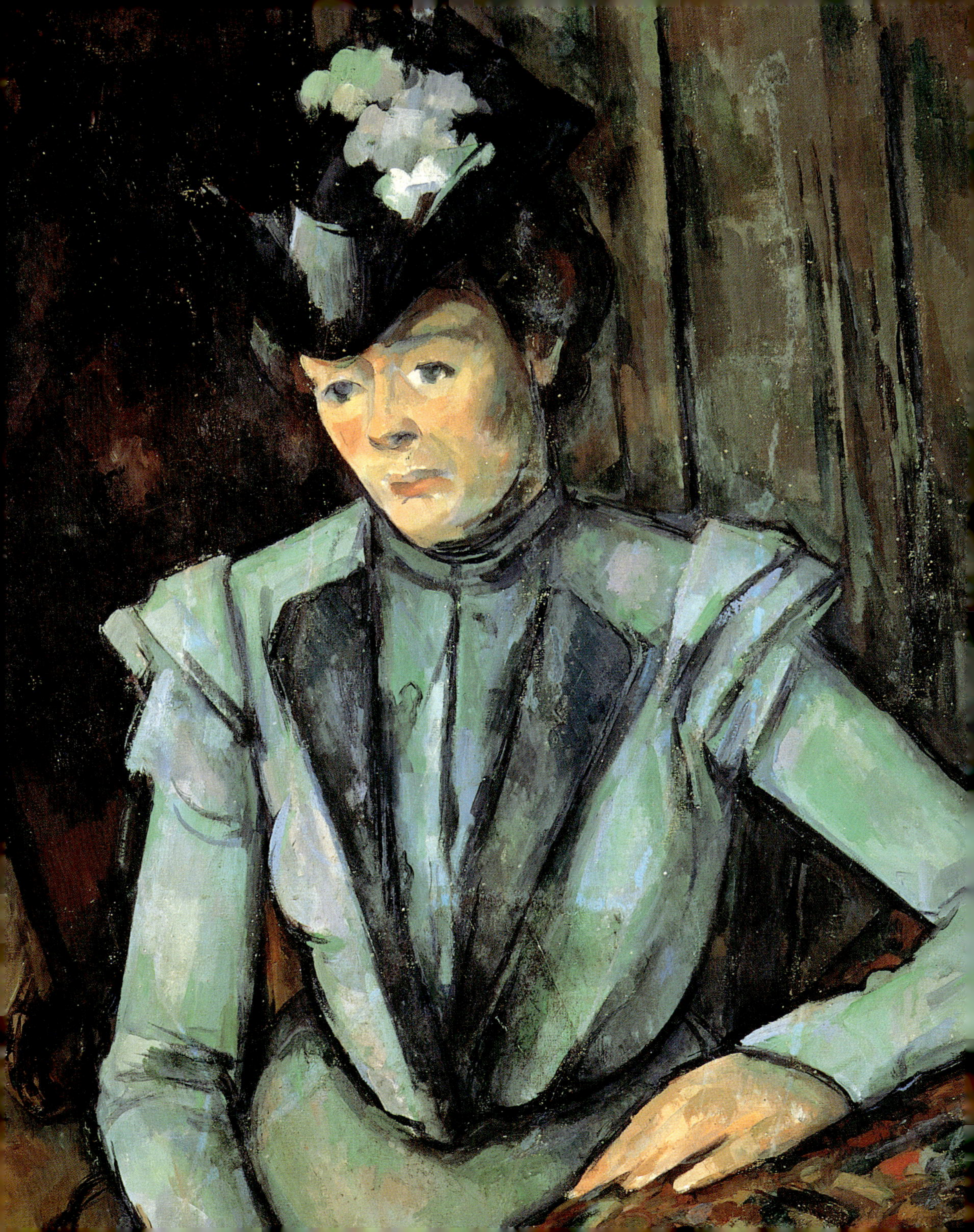

Woman in Blue
(detail), *c.* 1904
St. Petersburg, The State Hermitage Museum

With the vast retrospective that the Salon d'Automne devoted to the artist in 1907, Cézanne's audacious experimental painting met with the success that it had been denied for so long. Artists and writers wandered through the rooms of the Grand Palais, surprised and dazzled by so much monumentality and expressive power. The poet Rainer Maria Rilke visited the exhibition every day and, in a series of letters to his wife, Clara Westhoff, described his very profound impressions of this encounter. For Rilke, Cézanne was the high priest of a new concept of art that involved the complete elimination of his individuality in order to pursue the grand design to transform the invisible into the visible. In the great sacrifice of his solitude, the complete devotion to his painting, Cézanne managed to give substance to what is ephemeral, making it possible for the new generations to have a new ethical and aesthetic relationship with art: this is the "anonymous work from which things also spring forth," that of the complete renunciation of one's own subjectivity to become a diaphragm or sounding board through which the world is represented as it really is.

In the Grand Palais, in addition to Rilke, Gertrude Stein, and Guillaume Apollinaire, there were the young painters Georges Braque and Pablo Picasso who were well aware of Cézanne's remarkable contribution to the problem of *vision* and his final rejection of impressionism. Fernand Léger, who, with Braque and Picasso, theorized the principles of cubism, stated peremptorily: "Without Cézanne, I wonder what contemporary painting would be like. I studied his work for a long time. I was not able to tear myself away from it; I never ceased to explore and discover it. Cézanne taught me to love forms and volumes and made me concentrate on drawing." His investigation of the immutable structure underpinning nature and the consequent deformation of the volumes accompanied by the modulation of color are, in fact, the ineluctable premises of both the process of radical geometrization of the forms practiced by the cubists and of the principle of *simultaneous vision*. With Cézanne a new dimension of the pictorial space came into being; no longer constructed according to traditional principles, it was open to the creative impulse of the artist who could move, expand, and superimpose the objects in order to reconstruct the world in accordance with the laws of his particular intellectual universe. This was a coherent response to the demand for a break from the nineteenth-century forms that were one of the priorities of the avant-garde movements, which found in Cézanne a very clear answer to the wholly modern problem of the independence of art.

Also the crude appearance of certain works and the exaggerations Cézanne imposed on the forms, which the critics of the day regarded as negative aspects of his painting, were interpreted by the new generations as the revolutionary premises for the long-awaited process of liberation of art from the constraints of the painting of surfaces in accordance with the canons of beauty of a bourgeois stamp.

Inspired by his perspective aberrations and his daring treatment of the human figure (especially in the case of the female bathers), the avant-garde artists were able to definitively abandon the time-honored figurative tradition. Henri Matisse stated that "Cézanne is the father to us all," the prophet of compositional freedom and of the sumptuous, anti-naturalistic use of color. Thanks to Cézanne, painting became a universe in its own right, with its own laws. Toward the end of his life Cézanne stated: "I am the subjective conscience and my canvas is the objective conscience. Both the canvas and the landscape are outside me, but the latter is chaotic, casual, and confused, without a logical existence, without any rationality, while the former is enduring, categorized, participating in the modalities of the ideas."

His legacy impregnated the artistic movements of the early twentieth century. In 1912 Wassily Kandinsky declared that "Cézanne created a new law of the form … he was able to transform a teacup into an animate being, or rather he was able to identify the existence of life in that cup. Cézanne took still life to a level at which the things that are outwardly dead become inwardly alive. He painted them as he painted human beings because he was able to see their inner lives. He gave them chromatic expression, that is, a completely pictorial dimension, and enclosed them in a form that could be expressed in abstract, often mathematical forms that radiated harmony. He did not represent a man, an apple, or a tree, but used them to create something thoroughly pictorial that we call image."

The silent and absorbed sitters in Cézanne's portraits were later remembered by Amedeo Modigliani, who first saw the artist's work in the Galerie Bernheim-Jeune—associated with the Salon d'Automne of 1907—where seventy-nine of his watercolors were on exhibition. Modigliani, who had only been in Paris for a year, immediately recognized Cézanne's greatness and sought to render the ethereal sitters of his own portraits with the simplification and monumental power of the French artist's figures.

On the other hand, Cézanne's still lifes, "so marvelously occupied with themselves" as Rainer Maria Rilke put it, influenced another Italian painter, Giorgio Morandi, who appreciated his untiring devotion to his work, his preference for pure forms, his repeated studies of the same theme in order to obtain all the possible variations of light on the objects, his constant quest for an art form of his own and —again in Rilke's words—"the tangible immaterial means of expressing everything."

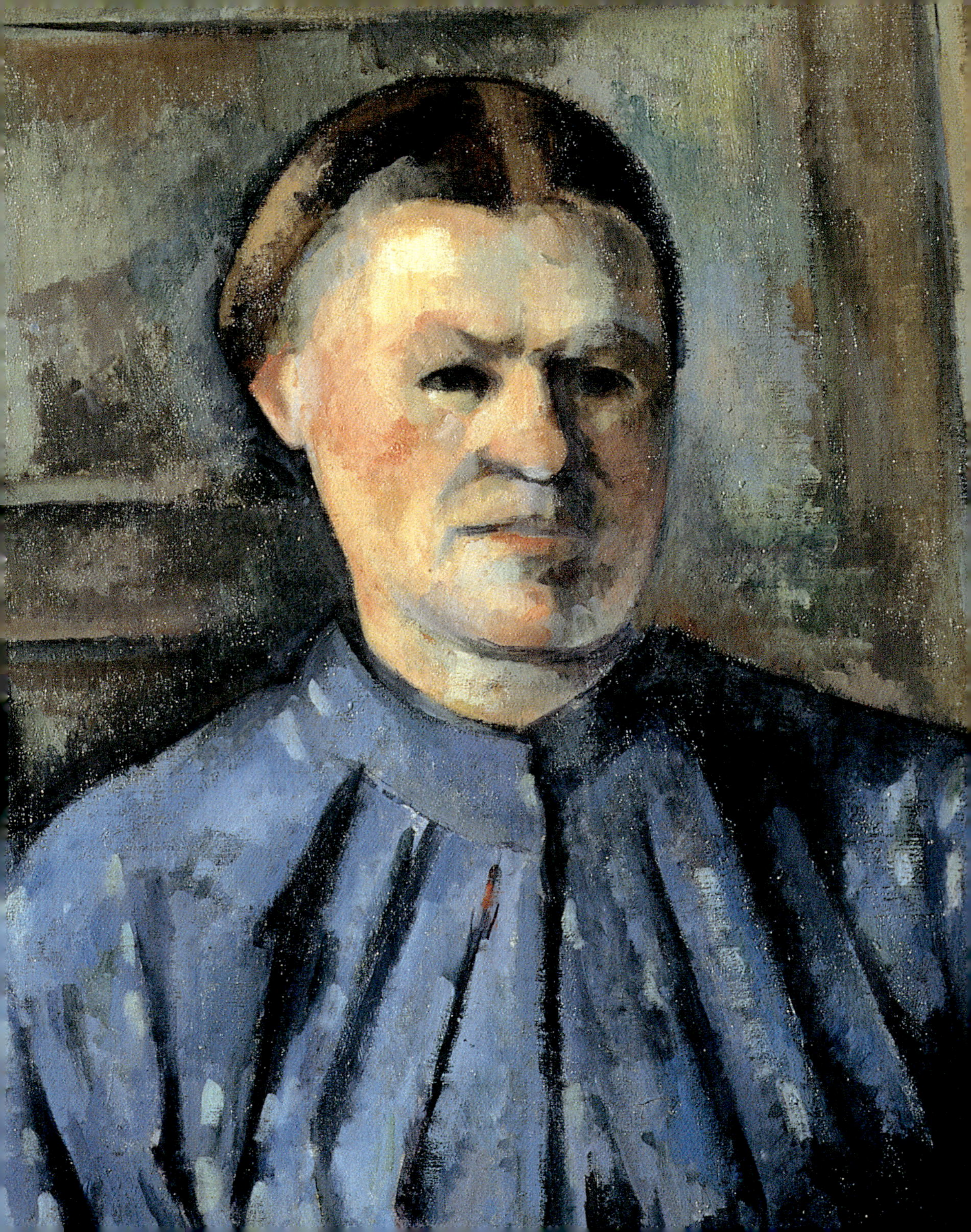

The Masterpieces

Woman with a Coffee Pot
(detail), *c.* 1895
Paris, Musée d'Orsay

Sorrow – *or* The Magdalen

1865–1868

Oil on canvas, 165 × 124 cm

Paris, Musée d'Orsay

This painting of a deeply sorrowful Mary Magdalen crying over a lifeless body was included in the decorations of the salon of the Jas de Bouffan, the residence of the former governor of Provence, which Cézanne acquired in 1859. It was painted next to his four decorative panels of the *Four Seasons* (1860–1862), a *Bather* inspired by a painting by Courbet, and a *Christ in Limbo* inspired by a work by Sebastiano del Piombo.

The subject was dear to the seventeenth-century painters whom Cézanne studied assiduously at the Louvre during his first stays in Paris. The scene is charged with strong symbolism in much of his early production (for example, *The Abduction* and *The Negro Scipio*). The strong, masculine body of Mary Magdalen seems to catalyze, with new expressive power, the tangible tension of her anguish and contrition as well as the bitter and obscure sense of death. Cézanne gives the dense color, applied in wide, doughy expanses, the task of building the figures and making them emerge forcefully from an indistinct and alienating ground that encompasses everything.

The whirls of the brush and the vivid luminosity of the whites reveal the extent to which Cézanne had learned the chromatic lessons of the sixteenth-century Venetian masters, Rubens, and Spanish painters of the fifteenth century which, with Gustave Courbet, Édouard Manet, and Honoré Daumier, provided the artist with his principal sources of inspiration during these years of intense artistic experimentation.

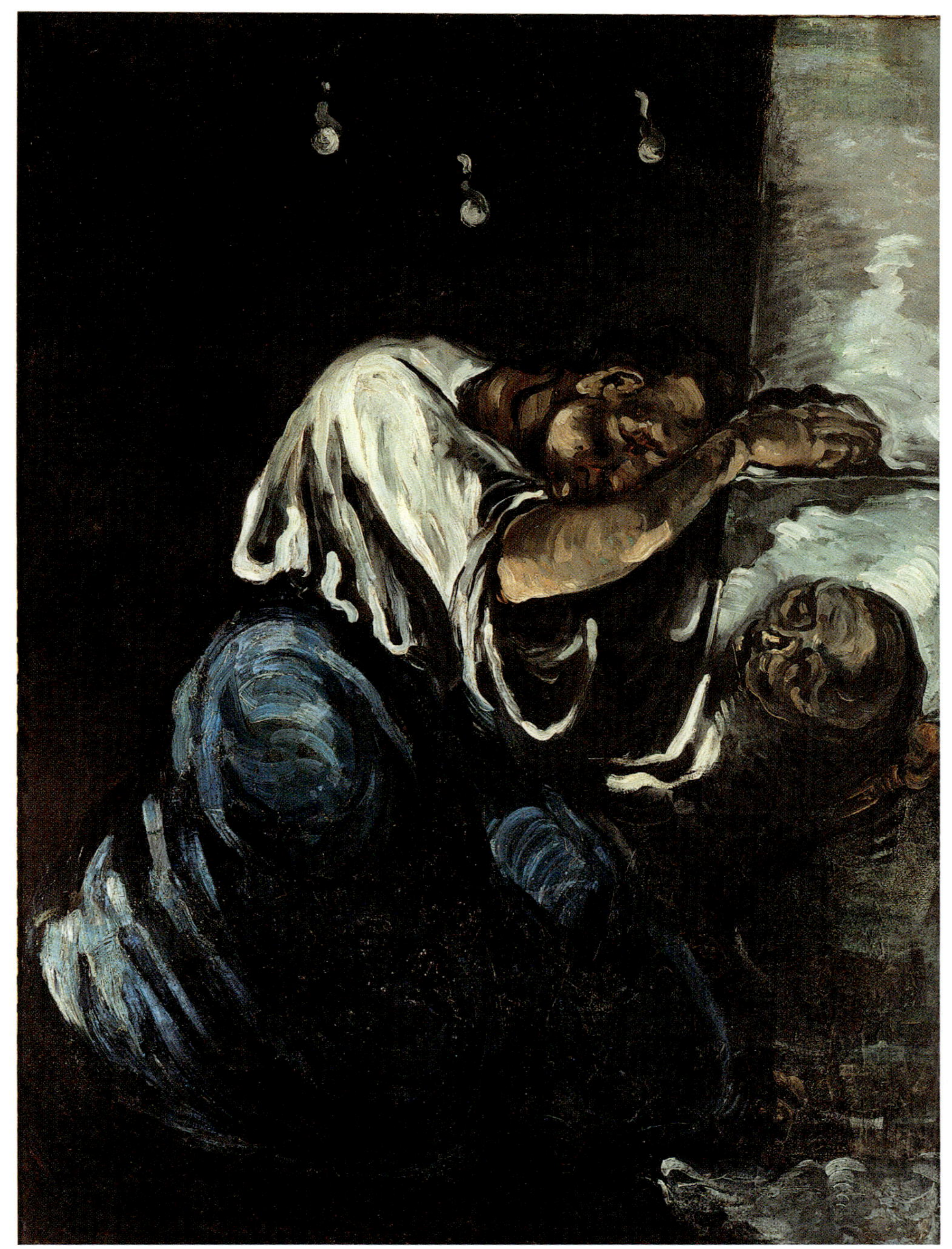

Still Life (Sugar Bowl, Pears and Blue Cup)

c. 1866
Oil on canvas, 30 × 41 cm
Paris, Musée d'Orsay (on deposit at the Musée Granet, Aix-en-Provence)

Three pears, a sugar bowl, and a blue cup are placed on a table of neutral color and stand out against the black background thanks to the artist's dense impasto. This was one of Cézanne's first experiments on a traditional theme, one that was always dear to him: the still life. After setting out his objects with care, the artist worked impulsively using a palette knife to spread the paint thickly and irregularly and build the forms with vigor. Cézanne loved strong, light-filled colors: the intense blue of the cup, the greens, the yellows, and the oranges of the pears, which he transformed into repositories of sumptuous impastos and then used again in the designs that decorate the sugar bowl. The painting's chromatic splendor clearly reveals the sources of inspiration of the artist, who was still searching for his own style. On the one hand we see an original interpretation given to the colorism of Édouard Manet—who in Paris in 1865 exhibited his superb still lifes by Alfred Cadart—but, on the other, the attention the artist paid to the light was derived from his frequent visits to works by fifteenth-century Spanish artists that he had opportunity to admire in the Louvre.

This small painting appeared in *Louis-Auguste Cézanne Reading L'Événement*, one of the artist's first portraits of his father. Cézanne depicted his father reading a liberal newspaper (though he was in fact a convinced conservative) and added an image of this small still life behind the armchair-cum-throne on which his father is seated. It thus became an emblem of his inalienable desire to dedicate himself to painting despite the firm opposition of his father.

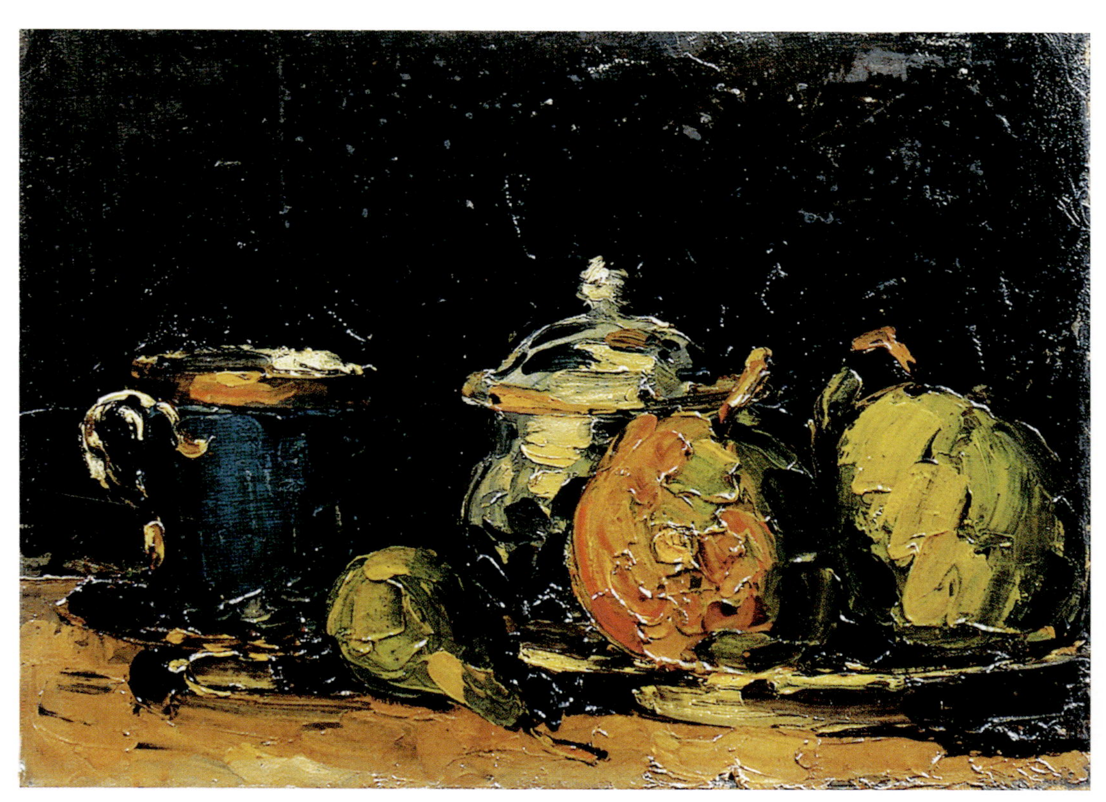

Portrait of Achille Emperaire

1867–1868
Oil on canvas, 200 × 122 cm
Paris, Musée d'Orsay

"On one occasion, in the shop belonging to Père Tanguy, the paint dealer on Rue Clauzel, I saw [...] the *Portrait of Achille Empéreire* [sic], the painter and friend of Cézanne. [...]. In the portrait painted by my old master, he is shown seated in a large armchair wearing a bathrobe; his slender hands hang down from the arms of the chair, his half-open robe reveals two thin legs covered only by long johns; he has his feet on a footrest. Cézanne painted him as he was after taking his morning bath. His head, larger than is natural, is fine and expressive and with long hair. Moustache and goatee beard adorn his lips and chin, his huge eyes and heavy eyebrows are heavy with weariness. The painting was sent to the Salon, probably after the war, but rejected. I discovered it beneath a heap of very mediocre canvases by Julien Tanguy, who told me its story. He had to hide it from Cézanne, who often came to his house, because he had decided to destroy it." This is Émile Bernard's account of the magnificent portrait that Cézanne made in 1867 of his dear friend Achille Emperaire, a delicate painter known at the École Suisse in Paris. He was affected by dwarfism and was a great connoisseur of Venetian painters.

Using a new and courageous artistic vocabulary, which vigorously expressed its originality, Cézanne built the figure of Emperaire using brutal and original color combinations that help him to imbue the sitter with a sense of monumentality and a forceful expressiveness. The face, bony knotted hands and fragile legs on the footrest are bathed with a uniform white light that pitilessly reveals everything and displays the reality of the man, warts and all. In the features of Emperaire's face and the "magnificent cavalier head in the style of Van Dyck" (Joachim Gasquet), Cézanne focuses his artistic skills and these aid in giving the sad, melancholic figure of his friend an unequalled dignity.

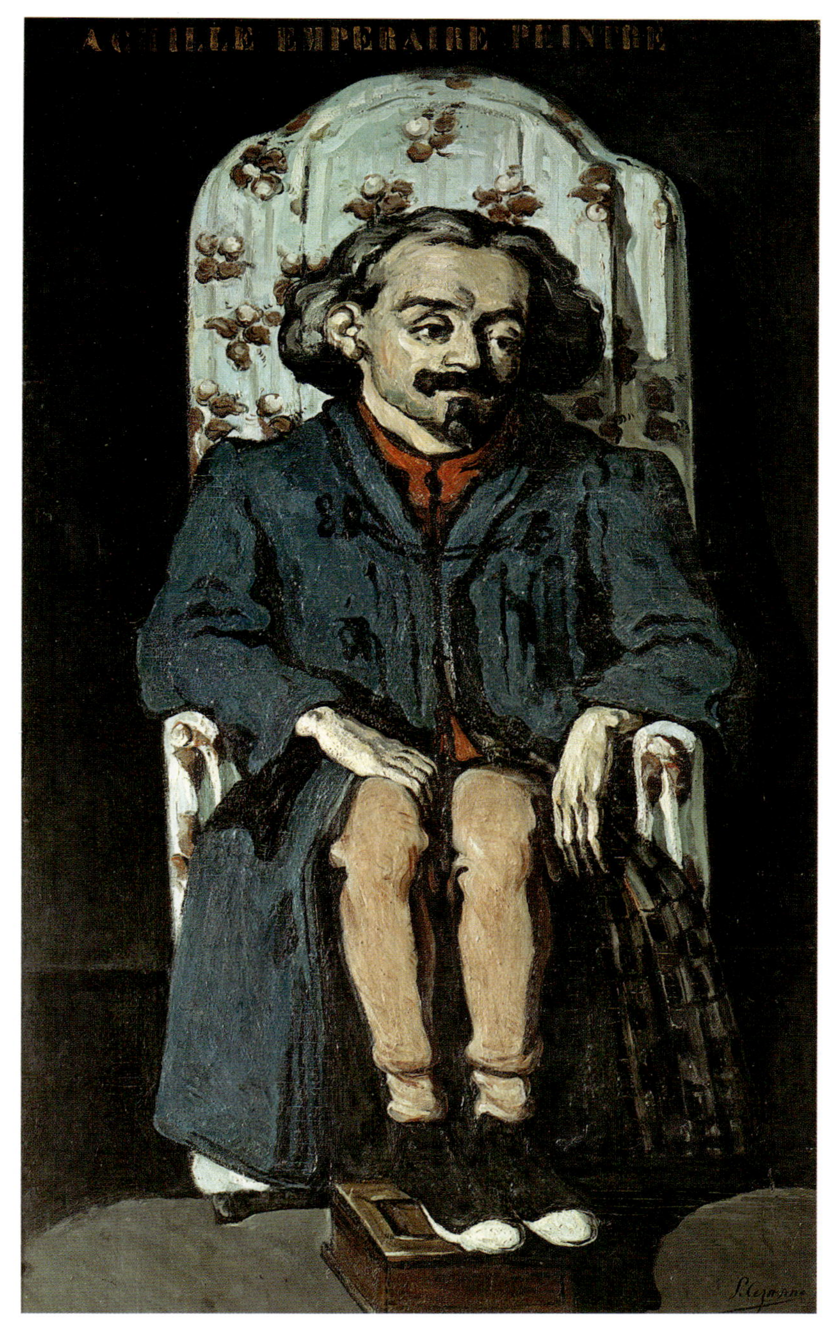
ACHILLE EMPERAIRE PEINTRE

Still Life with Green Pot and Pewter Jug

1867–1869
Oil on canvas, 64 × 81 cm
Paris, Musée d'Orsay

The fruit and familiar utensils offer Cézanne a rich repertoire of forms that provide him with the opportunity to analyze reality. The painter greatly enjoyed setting out these docile, reassuring objects and, after observing them for a long time, depicting their various muted but beautiful forms on the canvas. His kitchen table was very humble, and humble too were the things he arranged on it. His model lacks the elegance of Manet's tables because Cézanne was uninterested in objects for what they were: his concern lay in their form and volume. Though he picked up the strident contrasts of black and white from Manet, his simplified and expressive still lifes in this period are more reminiscent of the classical serenity of those by Chardin, an artist whom the young Cézanne much admired.

This apparently unordered and makeshift painting clearly shows its static, composed character, its tendency to immobility and silence. The objects in the picture plainly exhibit the force of their volumes and impose themselves as pure forms invested with a steady, strong light though the power of color. Cézanne used heavy impasto to build his thick shiny surfaces and added black outlines to give them greater presence. He worked with care on the form of each piece of fruit and set them out on a dazzlingly white tablecloth that contrasts strongly with the black knife. Everything emanates a sense of stillness and concentration that is surprising when compared to his compositions of dynamic and troubled figures of the same period.

The theme of the still life seemed to be particularly congenial to Cézanne because it obliged him to make direct contact with his model. Confrontation with the reality of things—the truth inherent in the objects—helped him to curb his visionary imagination, and taught him the value of careful, scrupulous observation of nature.

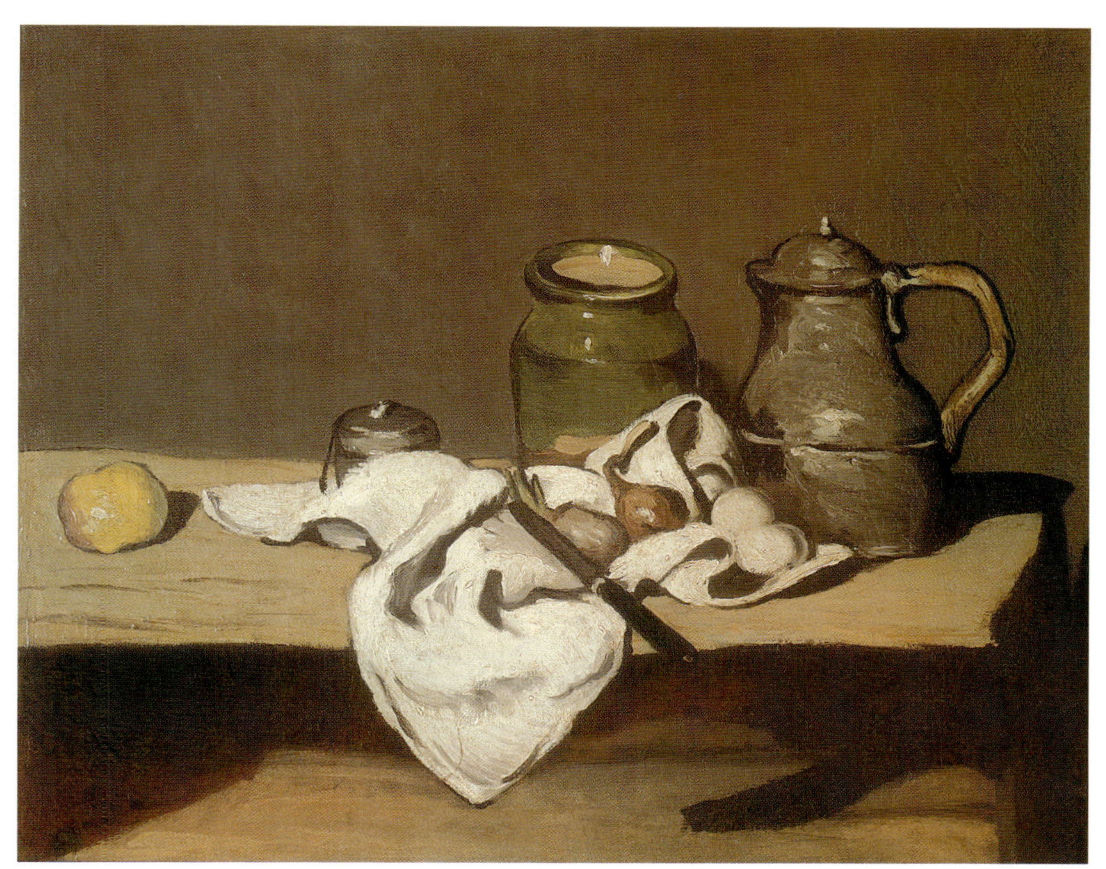

Young Girl at the Piano – Overture to Tannhäuser

c. 1869

Oil on canvas, 57 × 92 cm
St. Petersburg, The State Hermitage Museum

A middle-class interior. A young girl at the piano (perhaps the artist's beloved sister Rose Cézanne) and a woman seated on a settee sewing. The painter chooses the intimacy of a provincial house to stage his deep fascination with the music of Richard Wagner; he offers a modest but poetic tribute to *Tannhäuser*, the opera by the German composer which was performed in Paris for the first time in 1861. Cézanne shared his love for the turbulent, passionate music of Wagner with Baudelaire, the painter Bazille, and many French intellectuals. In Paris he attended the concerts conducted by Jules Pasdeloup, sometimes participating in the evenings organized by Commandant Lejosne, an ardent supporter of the composer. Cézanne's friendship with the German musician Heinrich Morstatt also helped to intensify his enthusiasm for the opera and, in December 1865, Cézanne invited Morstatt to Aix where he asked him fervently to "make our acoustic nerve vibrate with the noble accents of Richard Wagner."

In 1866 Cézanne made his first draft of a painting titled *The Overture to Tannhäuser*; this was followed by a second which he decided to abandon. "I tried to paint an evening spent with the family but I did not at all manage it," he wrote to Zola, "anyway I'll keep trying and another time it may come right." The third and final version was produced at the end of the 1860s, in which this subdued intimate scene represents the contrast between the monotony of provincial life and the insuppressible aspiration to art represented by the girl at the piano. Cézanne offers a symbolic representation of the ferocious dualism of the flesh and the spirit, the earth and heaven, in which, in Baudelaire's opinion, lay the profound significance of Wagner's opera and which was so admirably anticipated in the overture.

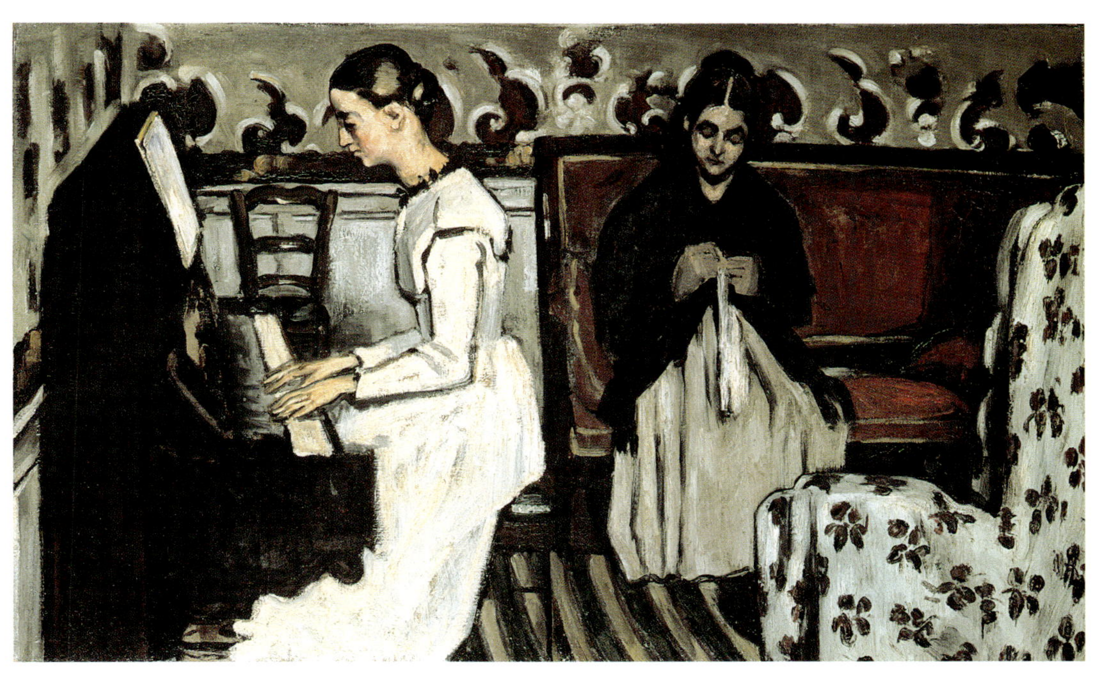

Paul Alexis Reading to Émile Zola

1869–1870
Oil on canvas, 130 × 160 cm
São Paulo, Museu de Arte

Long forgotten, this painting was only recognized as a work by the master in 1927. Hidden in the attic of Médan castle—Émile Zola's luxurious residence on the banks of the Seine—it became part of the writer's collection of Cézanne's works during his years of close friendship with the artist.

The painting is of Paul Alexis, a journalist and Zola's secretary, reading a manuscript while his friend curled up on a divan listens to him with close attention. Alexis and Zola probably met in Paris in September 1869. A productive artistic partnership began that culminated with the contribution by Alexis to the collection of short stories called *Les soirées de Médan*, which summarized the meetings organized by Zola in his summer residence and became the manifesto of the French Naturalist school.

Cézanne had already tackled this subject in a painting of the time (now in Zurich) which shows Alexis and Zola intent on reading in a bourgeois interior. In this second version, Cézanne chose intimacy and outdoor light, portraying the two friends in the garden of Zola's house in Rue de La Condamine in Paris, which the novelist used as a meeting and study place for the young avant-garde artists of the capital.

Painted with summary brushwork that plays on the contrast of vivid blacks and whites in the manner of Manet and Daumier, the painting was never completed by the artist. In August 1870, after the outbreak of the Franco-Prussian war, he decided to take refuge in Provence with Zola and left the canvas in Paris. With the exception of the head, the figure of the writer remains in the draft stage.

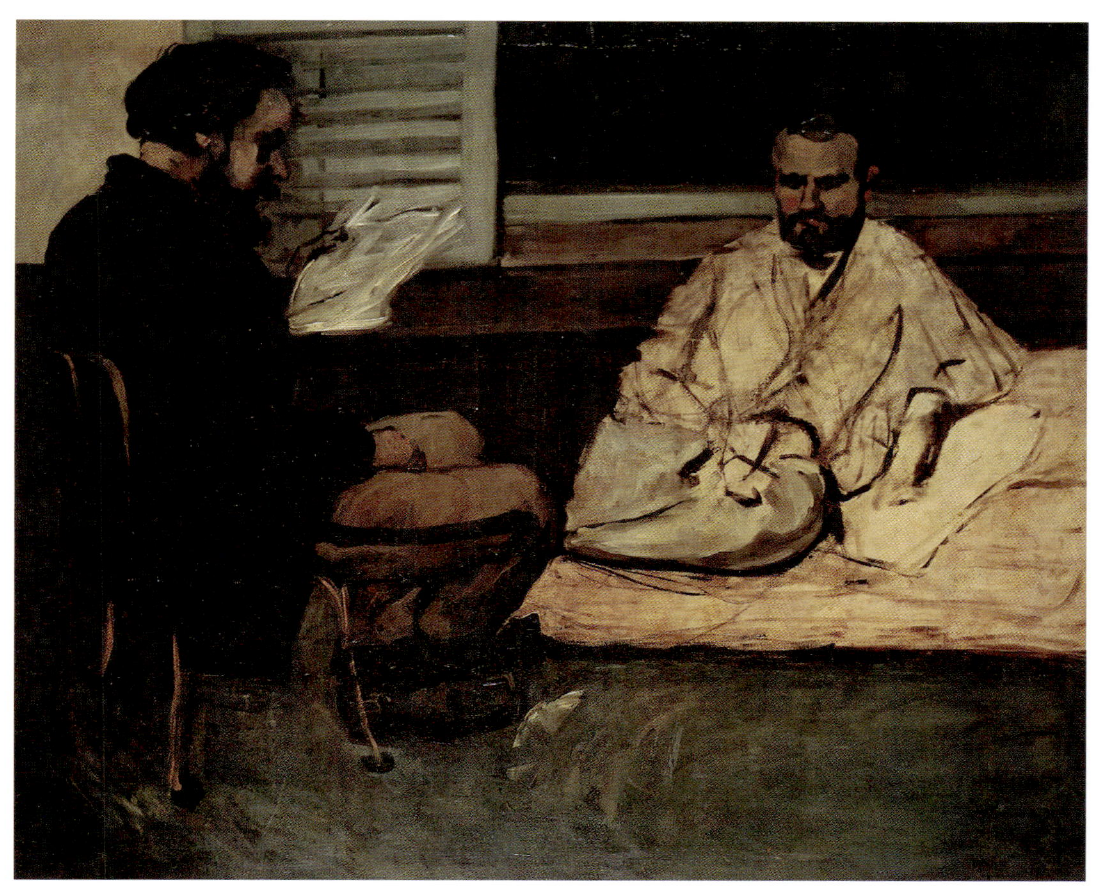

The Railway Cutting

1870
Oil on canvas, 80 × 129 cm
Munich, Neue Pinakothek

Painted near the Jas de Bouffan, this landscape demonstrates Cézanne's close contact with the painting of the impressionists, which he had the opportunity of studying during his first stays in Paris. The colors on his palette became lighter, more luminous and clearer but he did not give up on the use of a heavy impasto, which he had learned from the realist painting of Gustave Courbet.

Cézanne used broad, definite brushstrokes that give the painting great expressive intensity and formal precision. The material nature, forms, and volume of everything in the painting is apparent, nor is the painting at all flaky as was typical of the impressionist works of the same period. The careful arrangement of the visual elements on parallel planes helped the artist to impose order on the observer's vision and to guide the eye to the center of the painting, toward the railway cutting that slashes through the landscape like an open wound. The painting represents a veiled attack on the "benefits" brought by modernity. Unlike Zola and his impressionist friends, Cézanne had a harsh opinion on man's aggressive alterations to the countryside and on several occasions stamped his firm disapproval of iron, machines, and the irrational eagerness for the new, all of which insinuated their way into nature violating its majestic beauty.

The Railway Cutting also marked the first appearance of Mont Sainte-Victoire in Cézanne's works. In the later years of his intense artistic career it was to become his favorite motif.

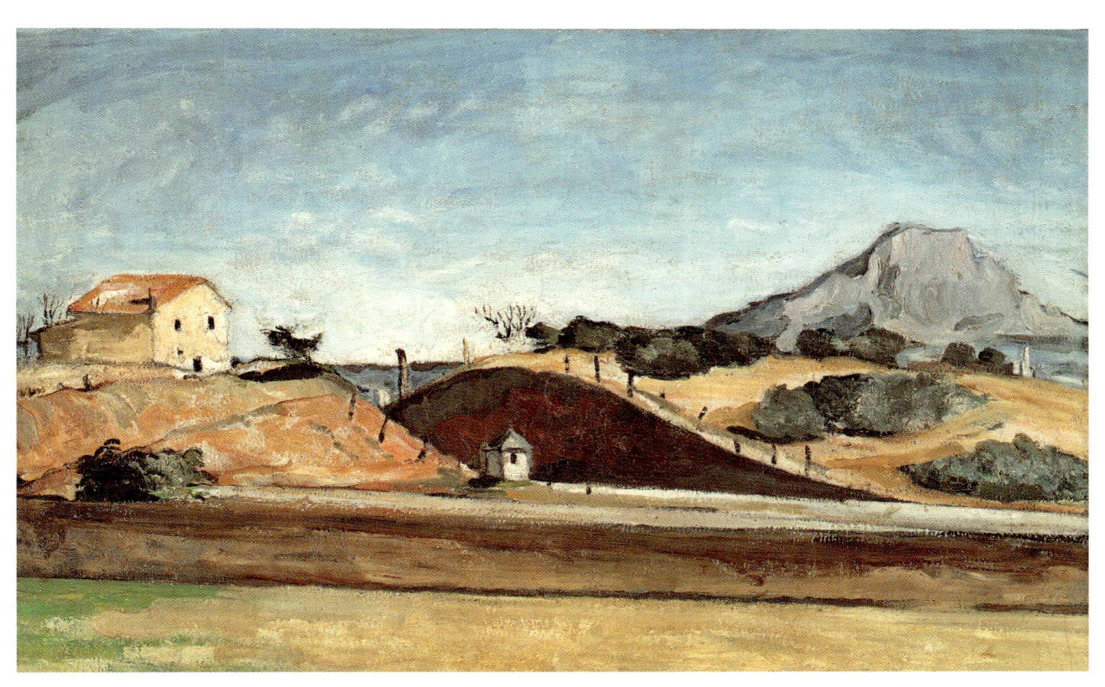

The Robbers and the Donkey

1870
Oil on canvas, 41 × 55 cm
Milan, Civica Galleria d'Arte Moderna

In his paintings of the 1860s and early 1870s, Cézanne often drew on literature for his subjects and this dense, disquieting work is an example. Taken from *The Golden Ass* by Apuleius, it shows the moment in which Lucius, who has been turned into a donkey by a spell that went wrong, is freed from the clutches of the robbers who had "stolen" him thanks to the fiancé of the girl with whom he shared his captivity.

The young man, who in reality wished to become a bird, had only just taken the potion that turned him into a donkey when he was stolen and hidden by the thieves; this prevented Photis, the girl he loves, from bringing him the rose petals that would have restored him to his normal appearance. This is the beginning of a long and difficult attempt to return to being a man. He is blocked by strange, unforeseen adventures that have prompted Apuleius's text to be read symbolically as an account of the difficult journey of the soul toward liberation from our earthly form.

Cézanne's painting is an interpretation of the imaginary situation narrated in the story. His characters are set in an unreal, windswept landscape created using dark tints and thick, violent brushwork. On the left are the robbers, whose faces are deformed by cruelty and greed; in the shade beneath the tree perhaps stands the young man who freed him; in the background, apparently uninterested by what is happening around him (the ignorance of humanity?), sits a man smoking; and at the center facing away from the observer is poor Lucius, illuminated by the sun as he starts out alone on his wanderings that are only interrupted by divine intervention.

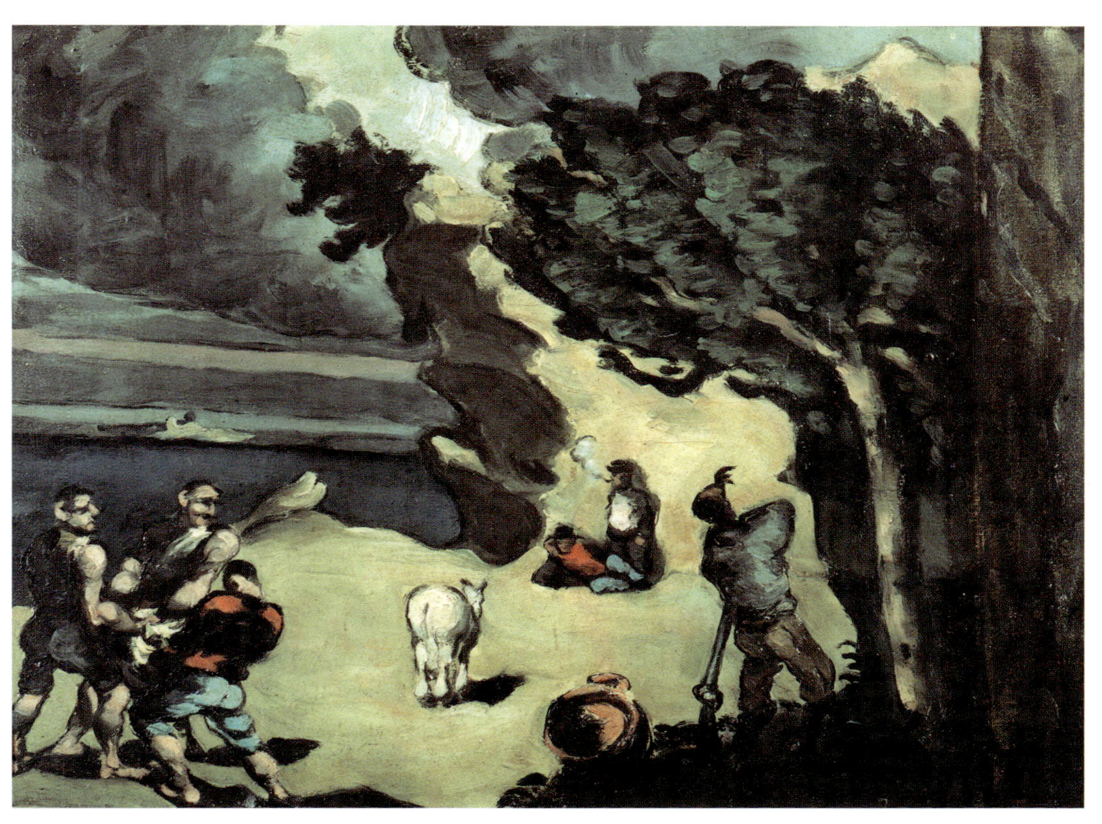

Pastoral

1870
Oil on canvas, 65 × 81 cm
Paris, Musée d'Orsay

This is a generic and conventional title for an enigmatic work painted by Cézanne in the early 1870s. Art historians such as Robert Rosenblum have often pointed out the strong autobiographical element in the work which provided Cézanne with the opportunity to evoke the erotic dreams of his free and passionate youth. The painter almost certainly identifies himself with the man lying on the grass (though at the time he was perhaps older and already losing his hair) and resting his head on his hand like in Delacroix's *Death of Sardanapalus*. Immobile, he orchestrates the scene calling on voluptuous but deformed women's bodies to exhibit themselves. Distractedly, they display themselves to his gaze and that of the bystanders. The painter is accompanied by two men in city clothes who probably represent his childhood friends Émile Zola and Jean-Baptiste Baille, with whom he went on youthful expeditions into the solitary and wild ravines of the Provençal countryside. The scene is permeated with a charged atmosphere. The bright colors—the deep blue of the sky and the dark green of the large expanses of grass—contribute to emphasizing the air of mystery, suspense and hallucination that was completely extraneous to the works that Cézanne was using during this period as figurative points of reference, such as Manet's *Déjeuner sur l'Herbe* and the *concerti campestri* (paintings of fully-dressed male musicians playing in the open, listened to by nude females) by early sixteenth-century Venetian artists exhibited in the Louvre. Despite the chaotic emotional atmosphere and the idea of an unreconciled conflict, what remains firm in Cézanne is the intention to restore order to his vision. The painting is constructed around the long diagonal that cuts the composition in two, accentuated by the horizontal pose of the painter and mysterious bather lying on the grass. This oblique movement is balanced by the vertical rhythm of the boat's sail and the bottle on the grass, the latter emphasizing the rise of the tree in the distance.

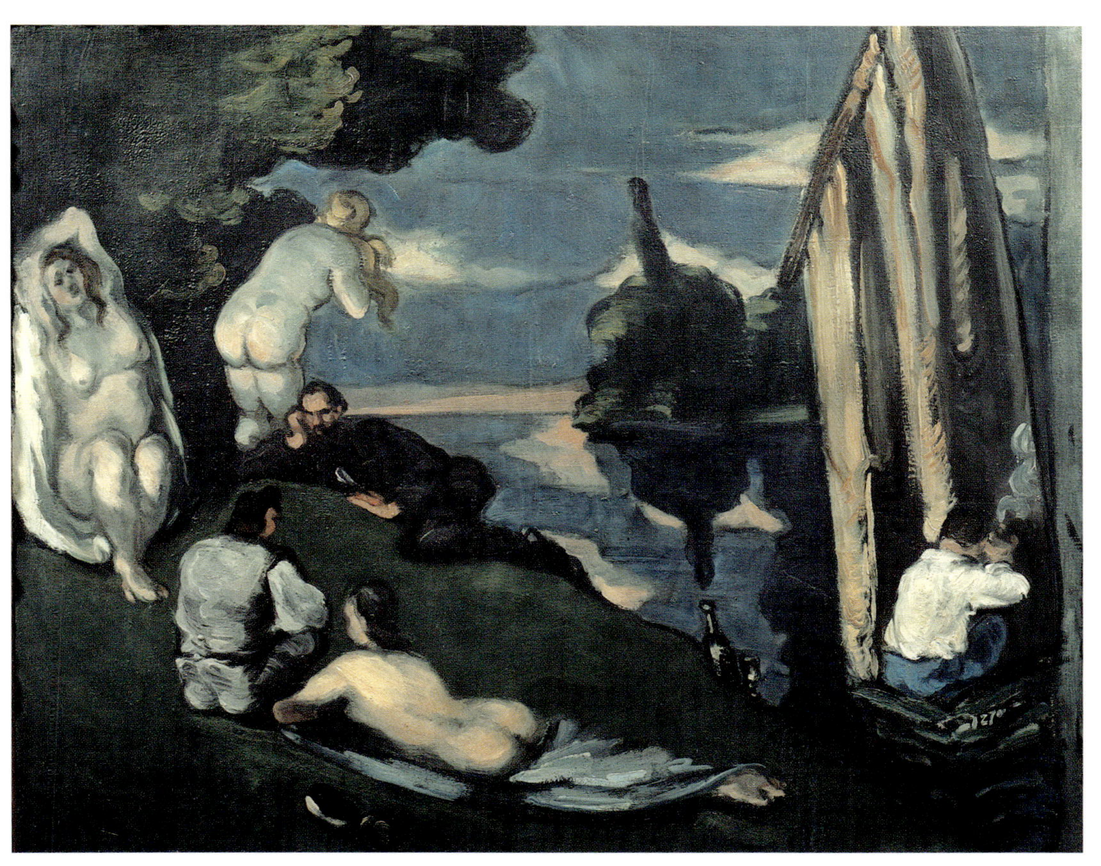

The House of the Hanged Man

1872–1873
Oil on canvas, 55 × 66 cm
Paris, Musée d'Orsay

Displayed at the first impressionist exhibition in the studio of the photographer Nadar with *Modern Olympia* and a view of Auvers-sur-Oise, *The House of the Hanged Man* was the outcome of new experimentation into the relationship of light and color carried out by Cézanne in 1872–1873. The painter had accepted Camille Pissarro's invitation to paint *en plein air* in the countryside around Pontoise in the Île-de-France. It was here that, following the advice of his colleague, he learned to lighten the colors of his palette and leave behind him the dark, gloomy tints of his paintings of the 1860s. With Pissarro he discovered the delight of painting *d'après nature* and understood that only direct contact with the subject could bring truth and freshness to his art. The impressionist technique of short strokes of color aligned beside one another helped him to discipline the violence of his brush-work in earlier works and to aid him in his analytical approach to depicting what he saw. Unlike the painters of Batignolles, Cézanne was not at all interested in creating an *impression* of what he saw but in making the painting a means of research into the stable and eternal forms of nature. In *The House of the Hanged Man*—in fact no-one had ever been hanged here—these presuppositions are already clearly made explicit. Cézanne constructed his view with great precision, resorting to a slow, flat brushstroke that cleanly defines the volumes of the house, tree, and valley, making them slide heavily against one another. His brush gives a material solidity to every element of the view: even the cobalt blue sky of the Île-de-France, a favorite motif of Monet's airy paintings, is transformed into a heavy mass of color, but, even by itself, this succeeds in creating the impression of light.

Although the impressionist exhibition did not enjoy success, and in spite of the mockery and sarcastic comments it aroused, Cézanne managed to sell his painting to the collector Armand Doria for three hundred francs.

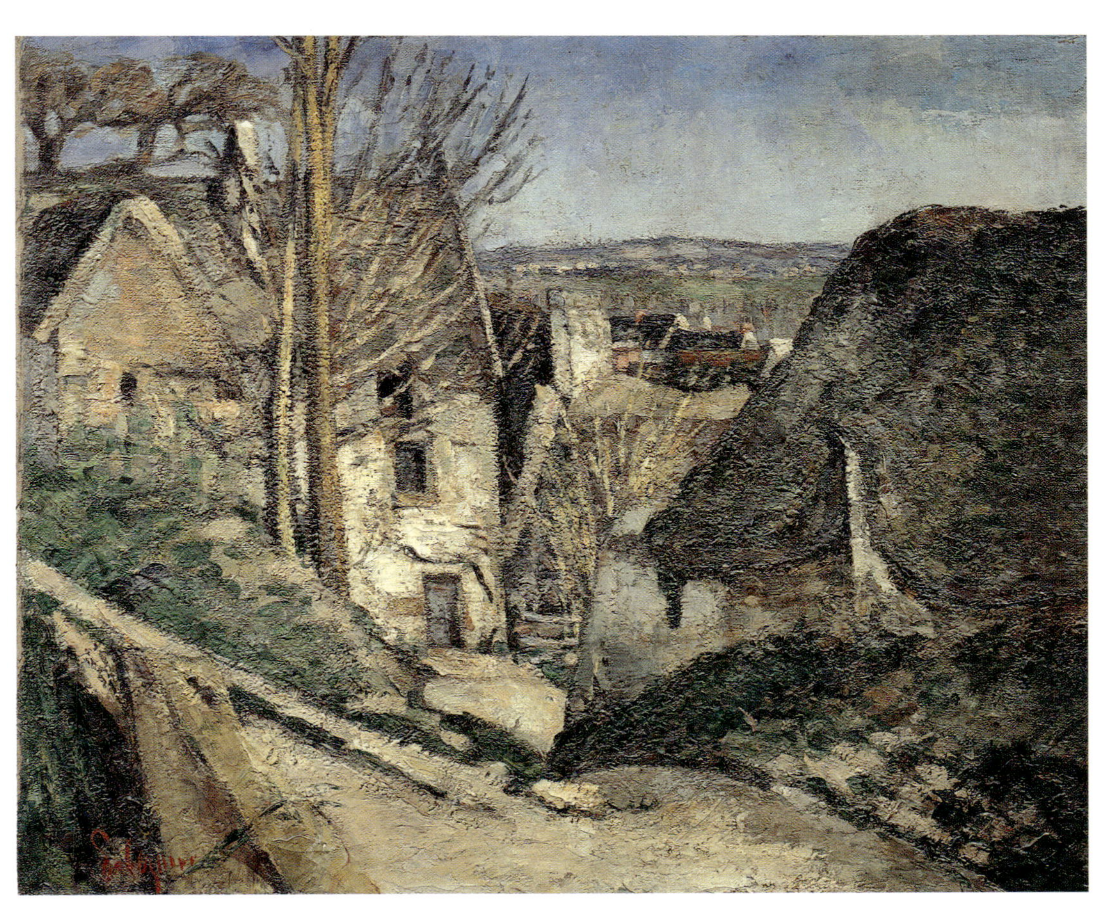

The House of Dr. Gachet

1872–1873
Oil on canvas, 46 × 38 cm
Paris, Musée d'Orsay

Dr. Paul-Ferdinand Gachet, a socialist and military doctor during the Commune of 1871, as well as an oddball and art lover, moved to a house in Auvers-sur-Oise close to Pontoise in 1872. A supporter of "modern" painters, he often received in his house those artists attracted by the gentle countryside of the Île-de-France and who worked *en plein air* in the environs. A favorite destination of Daubigny and Corot, and later of Pissarro and Van Gogh (Gachet had Van Gogh stay in his house during the final tragic period of the artist's life), Auvers-sur-Oise also attracted Cézanne enough for him to spend a fruitful period there in 1873. In doing so he struck up a friendship with Dr. Gachet, who became a passionate supporter of his personal aesthetic. Cézanne painted this fascinating view of the doctor's house which, like *The House of the Hanged Man*, is constructed around the new understanding of space, light, and color. He adopted the compositional scheme dear to Pissarro—the motif of a road that curves away in the distance and around which the landscape wheels—but Cézanne achieved very different results from his impressionist colleague. "His docile apprenticeship at the Impressionist school," wrote the Italian critic Renato Barilli, "now seems to have ended; or better, the theme remains typical of Pissarro, based around the motif of a small road and the interpenetration of houses and branches, but that same motif of the road becomes revealing of 'another viewpoint': instead of disappearing according to the canon of convergence, it rises before our gaze and falls forward, determined not to leave us too soon, and even to annul the receding effect of the curve with its obstinate frontality." Cézanne depicts the landscape in solid forms built using a dense and compact, though luminous, impasto that was the fruit of slow, meticulous work. What he has succeeded in doing is to extend our vision and to reveal to the distracted and fallacious eye of humans things that we do not usually see.

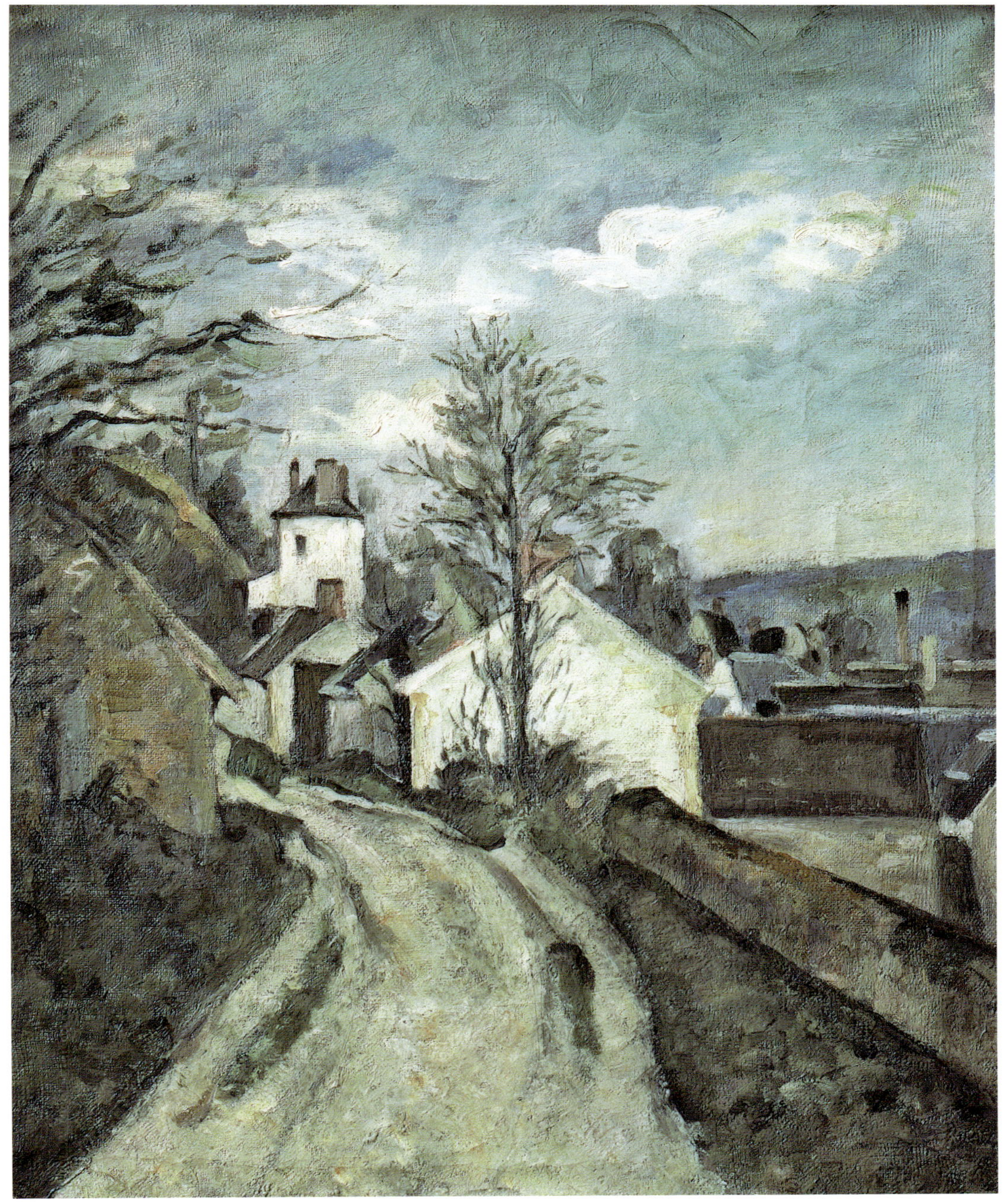

A Modern Olympia

1873–1874
Oil on canvas, 46 × 55 cm
Paris, Musée d'Orsay

Executed ten years after Manet's *Olympia*, Cézanne's *A Modern Olympia* was painted in Auvers-sur-Oise in 1873. Paul Gachet, the son of Dr. Gachet, who was a close friend of Cézanne and the first owner of the painting, recounted that the idea of producing a painting in open competition with Manet's came to Cézanne following an animated conversation with the doctor. In reply to Gachet's admiration for Manet's painting, Cézanne is supposed to have promised argumentatively that he could paint a new, more daring version of the theme.

Behind the drawn curtains of a room in a *maison de luxe*, Cézanne's *Olympia* is seen by her observers as an apparition. As her servant reveals her, she curls up in an unusual pose and fixes her eyes on her lover who trembles with anticipation. A man in city clothes, barely defined by the few though vigorous brushstrokes, contemplates her from his seat on the sofa. This is undoubtedly the artist himself who, once more, decided to let a painting make an unequivocal statement on his complex personal relationship with women.

In 1874 Cézanne decided to exhibit the painting in the first impressionist show organized in Nadar's studio and consequently received the "attention" he expected. The painting received a storm of mocking comments, which was judged by the official art critics to be the nebulous result of delirium tremens. The subject and pictorial *ductus* were both scandalous, the brushwork broken and approximate, and the chromatism excessive with improbable combinations of black and white. "Alas, go and look at it!" wrote the art critic Louis Leroy in *Le Charivari*, "A woman folded in two from whom a Negro girl is removing the last veil in order to offer her in all her ugliness to the charmed gaze of a brown puppet. Do you remember the *Olympia* painted by M. Manet? Well, that was a masterpiece of drawing, accuracy and finish compared with the one by M. Cézanne!"

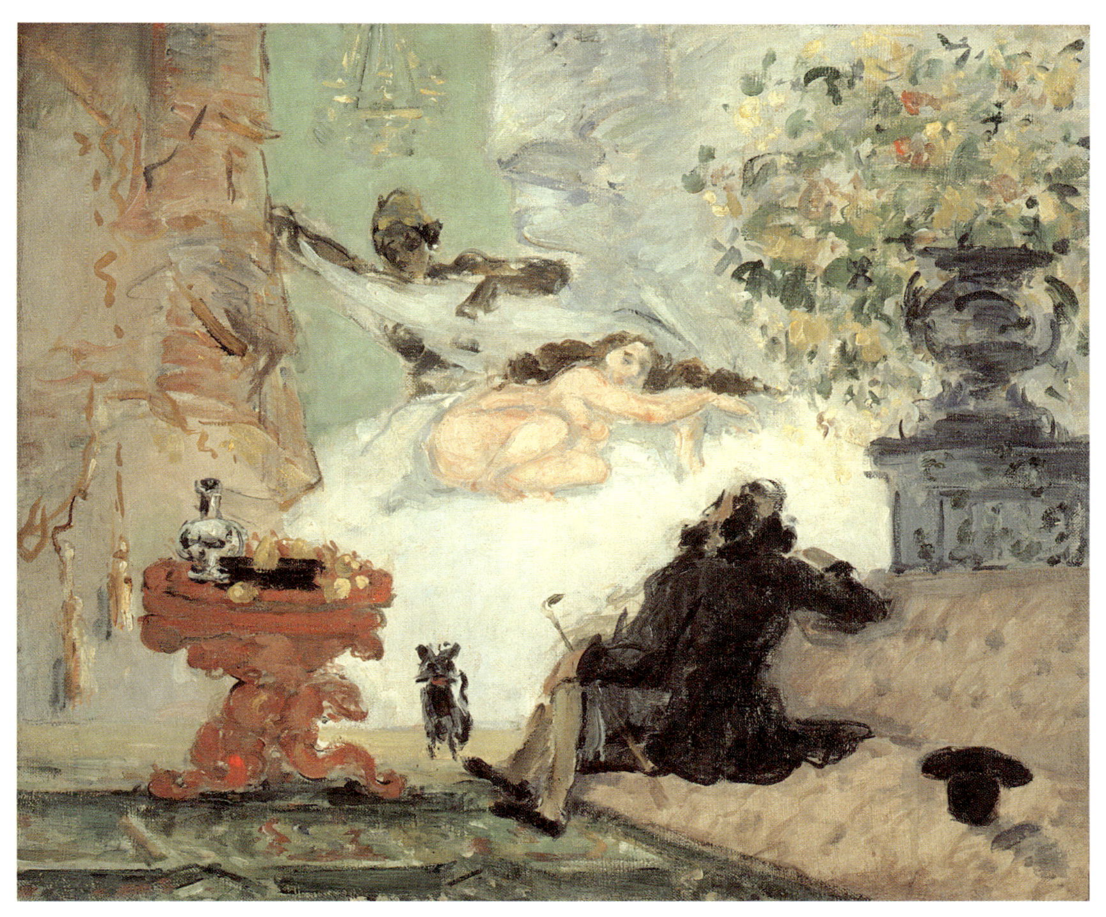

Three Bathers

1874–1875
Oil on canvas, 19 × 22 cm
Paris, Musée d'Orsay

The study of the nude body in a natural setting, the theme of the *Bathers* was a constant in Cézanne's work from the 1860s. The painter used the nude as a "docile instrument for probing the spatial cavity" (Renato Barilli). The nude could be arranged in any manner, subjected to any kind of interpretation and liberty that clothed figures—which are obliged to yield to the logic of convention and custom—do not permit.

Cézanne took the theme of the nude from conventional painting and made use of it in his intricate experimentation with form. He made frequent visits to the classical statuary in the Louvre and returned to the lessons he had learned on drawing models at the École des Beaux-Arts in Aix.

The premise on which his experimentation is based is already clear in this tiny painting. The composition appears heavy and condensed. Nature provides the solid setting for the three enormous female figures that stretch, twist, and bend to reveal their massive bodies and muscles and to impose their solid presence on the space. Hints of the painting of Raphael and Michelangelo can be gleaned in the poses of the figures and the way that Cézanne handles their volumes. Judged harshly by nineteenth-century art critics, Cézanne's *Bathers* are in fact some of his greatest contributions to the evolution of modern art. Henri Matisse, who owned another version of the *Three Bathers* that was painted a little later (about 1875) and now in the Petit Palais, remembered with feeling, in a letter to the conservator, Raymond Escholier, at the Musée de la Ville de Paris, to whom he wished to donate it, the time he spent in rapt study of Cézanne's tiny painting, which had been bought thirty-seven years earlier by Vollard. He said it had been for him an essential "moral support at critical moments in my adventure as an artist."

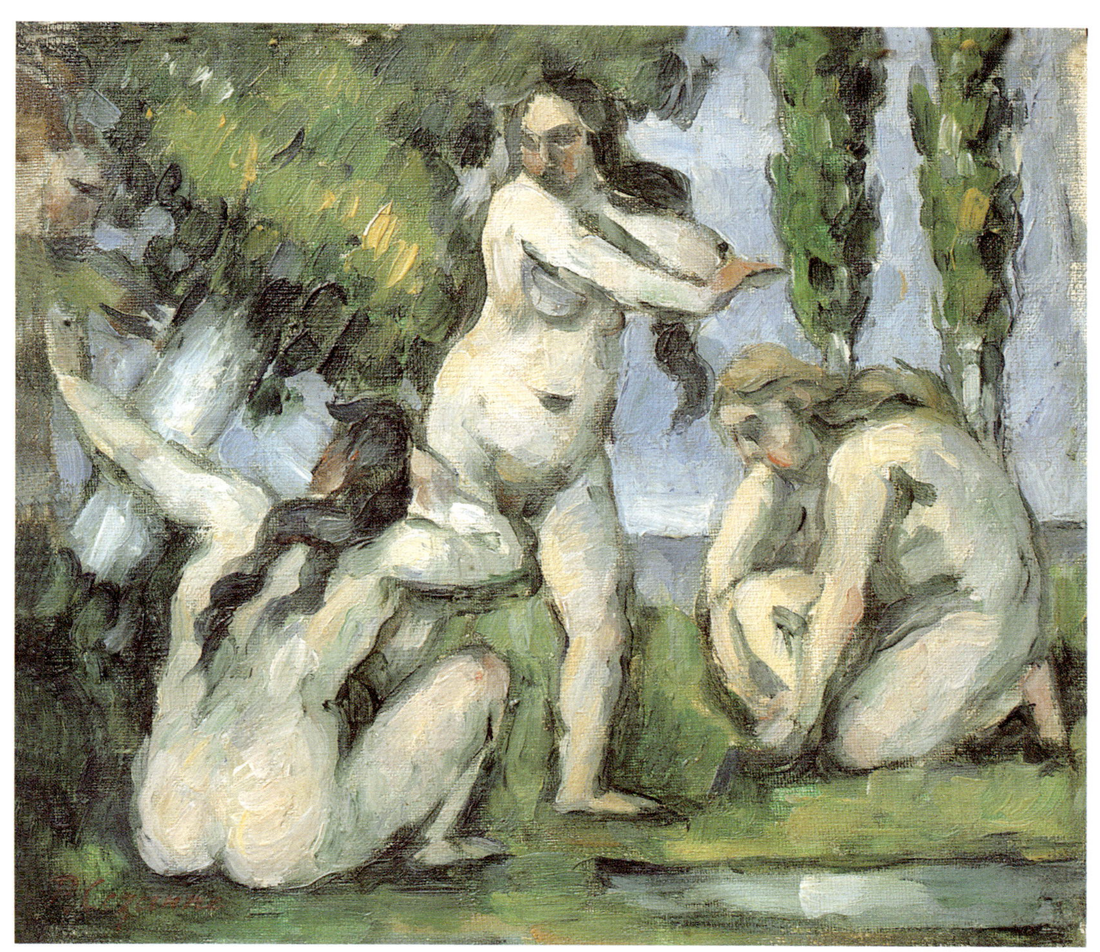

Self-Portrait in a Casquette

c. 1875
Oil on canvas, 53 × 38 cm
St. Petersburg, The State Hermitage Museum

"He was tall and thin, with knobbly joints, a strong bearded head, a very thin nose that was lost between the bristles of his moustache, small clear eyes … great tenderness at the back of his eyes. He had a strong voice … he was slightly round-shouldered and had a nervous twitch that was to become chronic." This is how Émile Zola described Claude Lantier in his notes for *L'Œuvre*, his 1886 novel that marked the end of his friendship with Cézanne. Lantier was a failed painter, devoured by insecurity and ambition, who chose suicide when the weight of his creative inadequacy became too heavy to bear. Cézanne recognized himself in this brief portrait and it cannot be excluded that Zola had his friend in mind, whom he had several times reproved for his hesitation toward his relationship with art ("Is painting only a fancy that you took into your head one fine day when you were bored?" he once asked Cézanne peremptorily).

Zola accumulated ideas for his novels during the feverish days of the early exhibitions organized by the impressionist group. When this self-portrait was painted it is undeniable that there were parallels between the writer's words and this powerful, introspective portrait in which Cézanne is depicted deep in thought, his gaze evades that of the observer, and his sunken features are hidden by his long thick beard. The painter is viewed close up and his face emerges from the indistinct background owing to the heavy impasto that builds the forms layer on layer. Although the black of his cap, beard, and jacket is the dominant color in the painting, the artist's face is illuminated by vivid touches of blue, yellow, violet, and red that produce intense variety in chromatism. The rapid and approximate *ductus* brings to mind Cézanne's contemporary experimentation on the relationship between form, color, and light which he carried out *en plein air* alongside Pissarro.

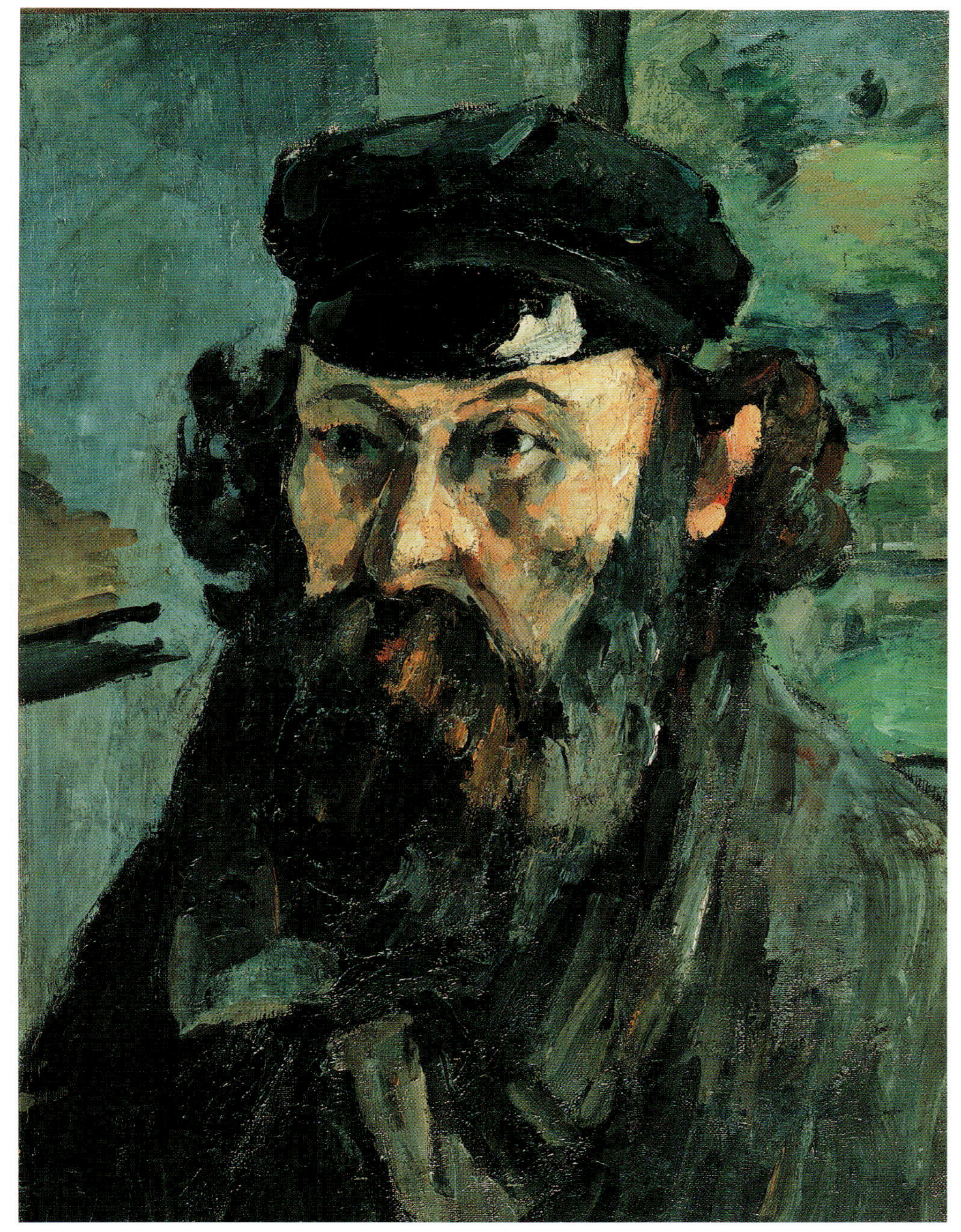

The Temptation of Saint Anthony

1875–1877
Oil on canvas, 47 × 56 cm
Paris, Musée d'Orsay

"See the complexion of my radiant body; Anthony, and do not resist seduction. Do not resist, I am all powerful! The forests tremble at my breath, the waves stir at my jumps. Virtue, courage, compassion dissolve at the scent of my mouth. I accompany man step by step, and on the brink of the tomb it is to me that he turns!" These notes were written by Cézanne on a preparatory watercolor to the small, fascinating painting in the Musée d'Orsay executed between 1875 and 1877 and inspired by *The Temptation of St. Anthony* written by Gustave Flaubert and published in 1874. The sumptuous atmosphere evoked by the French writer, the harsh, sun-baked landscapes of the Thebaid, the magnificent retinue surrounding Luxury who was sent by Satan to tempt Anthony, and the hermit in search of God are treated by Cézanne with a composition of great expressive power that revolves around the nude body of the temptress. In the form of an apparition she dominates the scene which is bathed in a diaphanous, diffused light. As though driven by the wind, her escort of full-bodied putti scurry around her, while Anthony, overshadowed by Satan, attempts vigorously to resist her blandishments.

Cézanne attempts to represent the difficult theme of sexual slavery through his fragmented and energetic brushwork, and the energy inherent in the whites, greens, and blues. He also refers to his own complex relations with women, something he had expressed in paintings in the 1860s, such as *The Orgy* (circa 1868) and dealt with in greater detail in *A Modern Olympia* (1873) and *The Eternal Woman* (1875–1877).

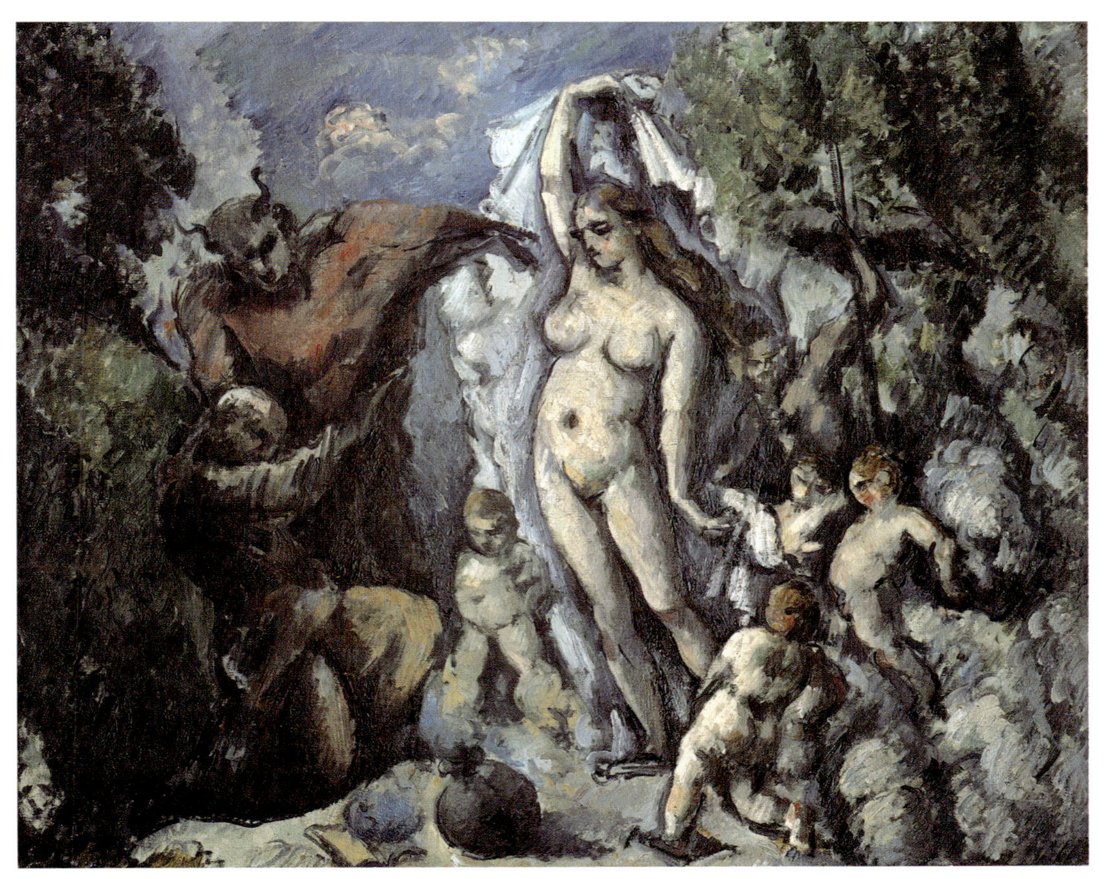

Portrait of Victor Chocquet

1877

Oil on canvas, 46 × 38 cm
Columbus (Ohio), Columbus Museum of Art

It was through Pierre-Auguste Renoir that Cézanne came to know Victor Chocquet in Paris. Chocquet was a modest clerk at the Ministry of Finance but a refined collector of modern works and an enthusiastic supporter of impressionist painting. While visiting Père Tanguy's shop one day, Chocquet noticed a *Study of a Nude* by Cézanne and was so struck that he bought it on the spot. He felt a sincere sympathy and esteem for Cézanne from this moment on. The two also shared a heartfelt admiration for the art of Eugène Delacroix.

In 1876 Chocquet commissioned Cézanne to paint two seaside views and it is to this same year that the first of the three portraits of him dates. This portrait was exhibited at the third Impressionist exhibition but won the decided disapproval of Degas, who commented that the work was the effigy of a madman painted by a madman.

According to Georges Rivière, the portrait in Columbus was painted by Cézanne in the dining room of Chocquet's Rue de Rivoli apartment in Paris. Seated on a Louis XVI armchair, the elegant collector—without a tie and wearing slippers—gazes directly at the observer. A series of paintings by Delacroix, Corot, Courbet, Manet, and, of course, the younger generation of artists, Renoir, Monet, and Pissarro hangs behind him.

Cézanne's handling of the portrait is deft and powerful. He constructs the figure of Chocquet through a vivid and orderly mosaic of colors, at times following a horizontal trend, at others vertical. The desire to bring all the surfaces into foreground—despite Chocquet's left foot, which seems to break through the space between the scene and the observer to suggest depth—is all concentrated by the painter in the collector's left wrist, which becomes the imaginary meeting point of five different planes.

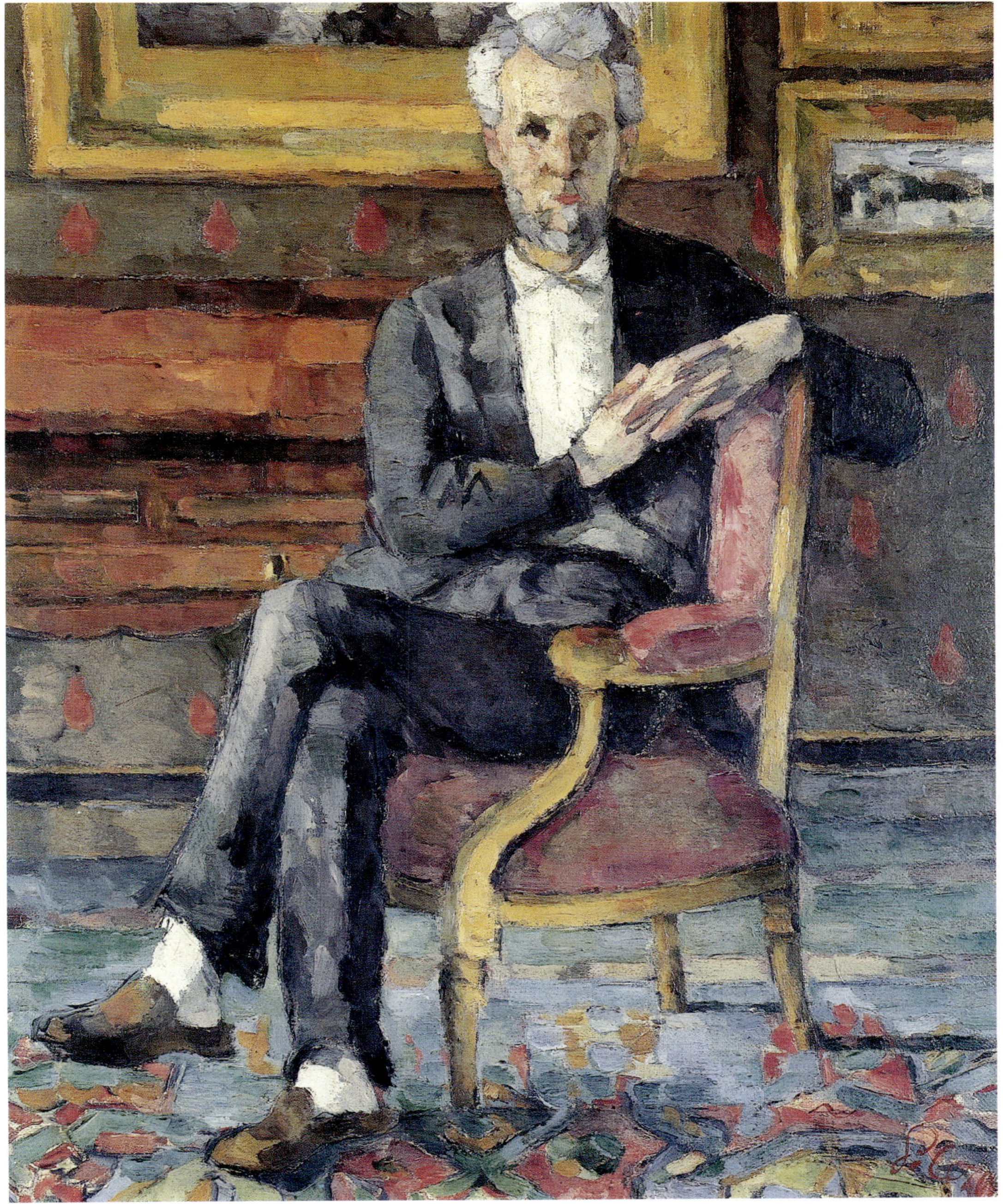

Farmyard in Auvers

c. 1879
Oil on canvas, 65 × 54 cm
Paris, Musée d'Orsay

When it entered the Musée du Luxembourg as part of the bequest of the painter Gustave Caillebotte, the painting bore this title. Dr. Gachet's son claimed that it was painted near Pontoise during one of Cézanne's stays in the Île-de-France at the end of the 1870s.

Built up by tiny, contiguous applications of the palette knife, this anonymous corner of the French countryside provides confirmation of the progress the painter was making in these years in his depiction of the landscape and the way he viewed his subject. Turning his back on the airy, spacious vistas typical of impressionist painting, Cézanne frames his view with two solid sections of wall that each throw a heavy shadow on the foreground. A sloping road winds sharply to the right and runs straight into the farm buildings. At the center stands the small red-roofed farmhouse and shed that seem almost suffocated by the intrusion of the wall on the right; in addition the wall seems to accentuate the movement of the entire painting toward the foreground and its tendency to become flattened. The different planes of the road, house, and walls all slide up against one another heavily, removing the suggestion of depth; they draw up their masses and volumes and project them toward the real space occupied by the observer. The view is congested yet it is luminous thanks to the painter's tiny light-filled touches of color. The clear blue sky flecked with white gives space to the landscape, which seems to draw respite from the presence of the tree in front of the house. This pulls the eye toward the hill behind the farmhouse and suggests the presence of wider, more spacious areas.

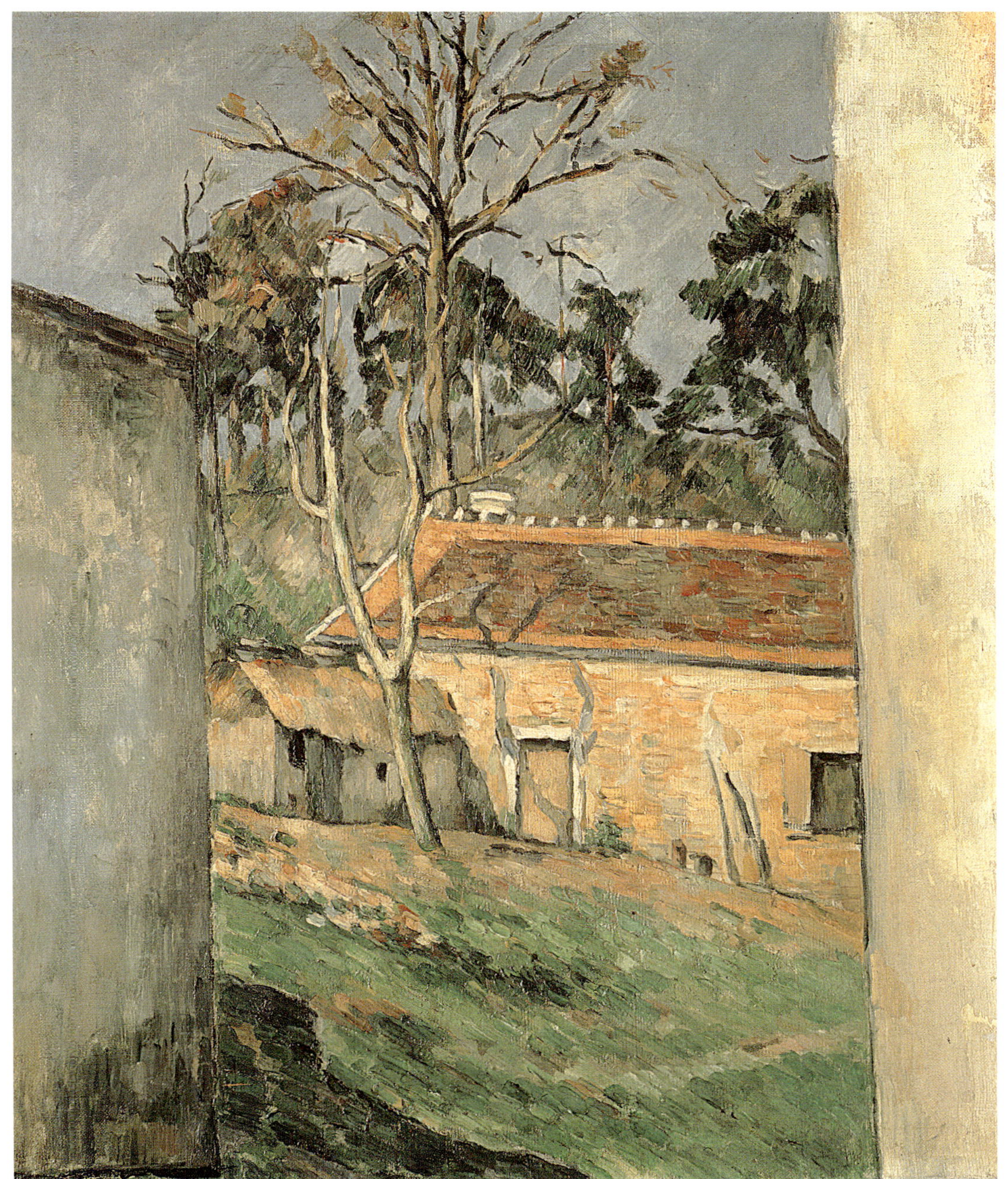

Poplars

1879–1880
Oil on canvas, 65 × 80 cm
Paris, Musée d'Orsay

This light-filled painting is of a corner of the park belonging to Marcouvilles castle in the hamlet of Patis not far from Pontoise. It was painted during one of Cézanne's stays in the town where his friend Pissarro lived.

The entire aim of the work is to capture the clear light of a summer day and the sedate beauty of the countryside in the Île-de-France. The painter worked carefully to construct the landscape with little touches of color using a small palette knife that helped him find the required precision. The touches of blue, green, and bright, luminous yellow run in all directions to suggest the movement of the wind in the trees and the gentle atmosphere of the peaceful, silent scene.

A long, sinuous curve suddenly moves away from the foreground with aggressive brushwork but then stretches gently into the distance. It helps to establish the dynamics of the space and divide the painting into two broad, counterbalancing areas. The left side, dominated by the field and flooded by sunlight, is open and clear, whereas the right side—in which the poplars, the central feature of the painting, stand out against the sky with their strong verticality—was used by the painter as a structural element in the painting.

Although it was from Pissarro that Cézanne derived the spatial schema that revolves around a road curving away into the distance, there seems to be a dramatic tension in his paintings. The luxuriant vegetation, crystalline light, and joyous abundance of green links the landscape of Marcouville with the high points he achieved in works like *The Bridge at Maincy*.

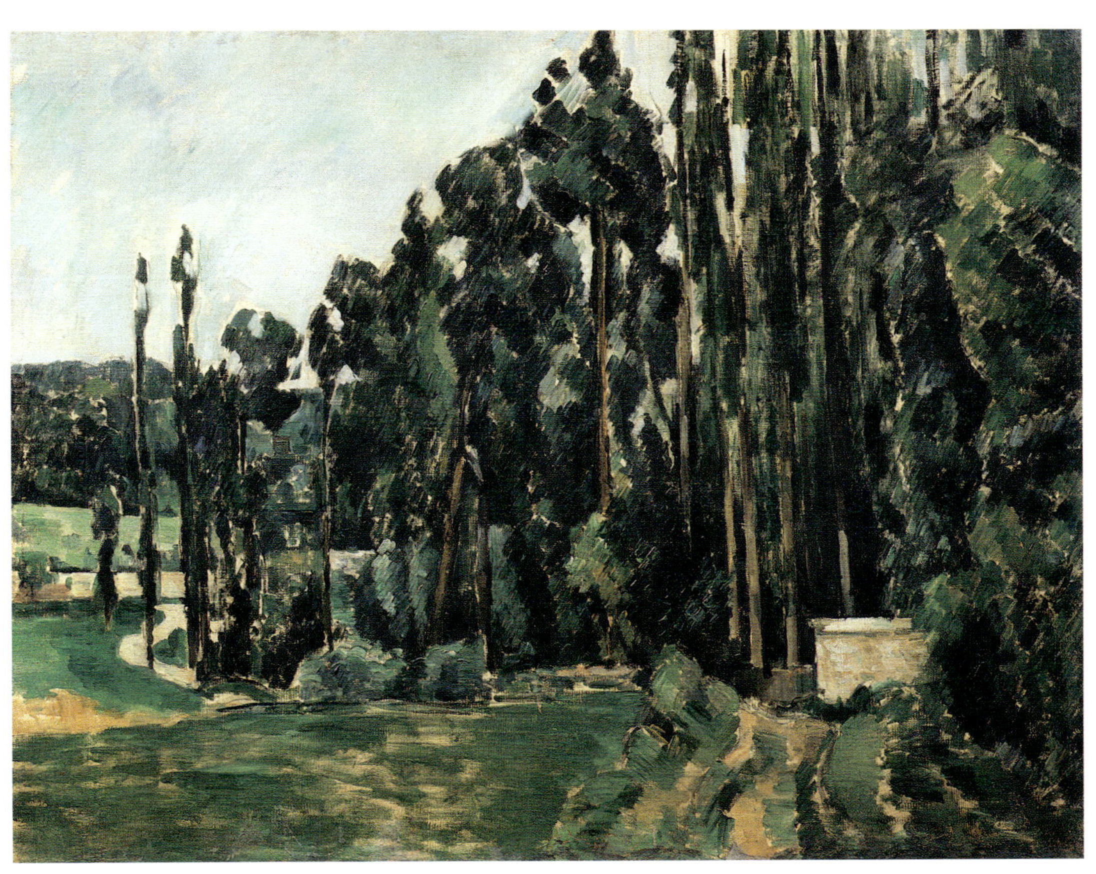

The Bridge at Maincy

1879–1880
Oil on canvas, 60 × 73 cm
Paris, Musée d'Orsay

This painting, which has been given various dates by art historians, has now been ascribed to the years 1879–1880 due to a photograph taken in 1958 that once and for all established the site where the painting was executed. The place was Maincy, a hamlet near Melun, where Cézanne stayed in the spring and summer of 1879.

The work is of extraordinary freshness. The painter used short but solid touches of the brush to define the space from the foreground—signaled by the firm verticality of tree trunks—and the background, occupied by the dense curtain of vegetation. Everything has been constructed with precision and absolute structural rigor: the touches of color give concrete definition to the form of the bridge, branches, and leaves and in an orderly manner catch the light and mobility of the reflections on the water of the river Almont. These, too, are represented in tiny limpid patches of color but, unlike in the paintings of Monet, Cézanne does not force color to fade away, preferring to maintain all of its constructive and structural power.

The Bridge at Maincy seems to contain an echo of the early landscape studies Camille Corot painted in Italy (1825–1828) which, in views like *Tiberina Island* and *The Bridge at Narni*, succeeded in finding the underlying essence that linked conventional compositional rigor to the empirical candor of *en plein air* painting.

The clarity of the scene suggests a highly limpid atmosphere; Cézanne allows the light to circulate freely across the surface of the water and among the branches and leaves, and he employs the range of greens, browns, and yellows to describe the natural beauty of the countryside around Melun.

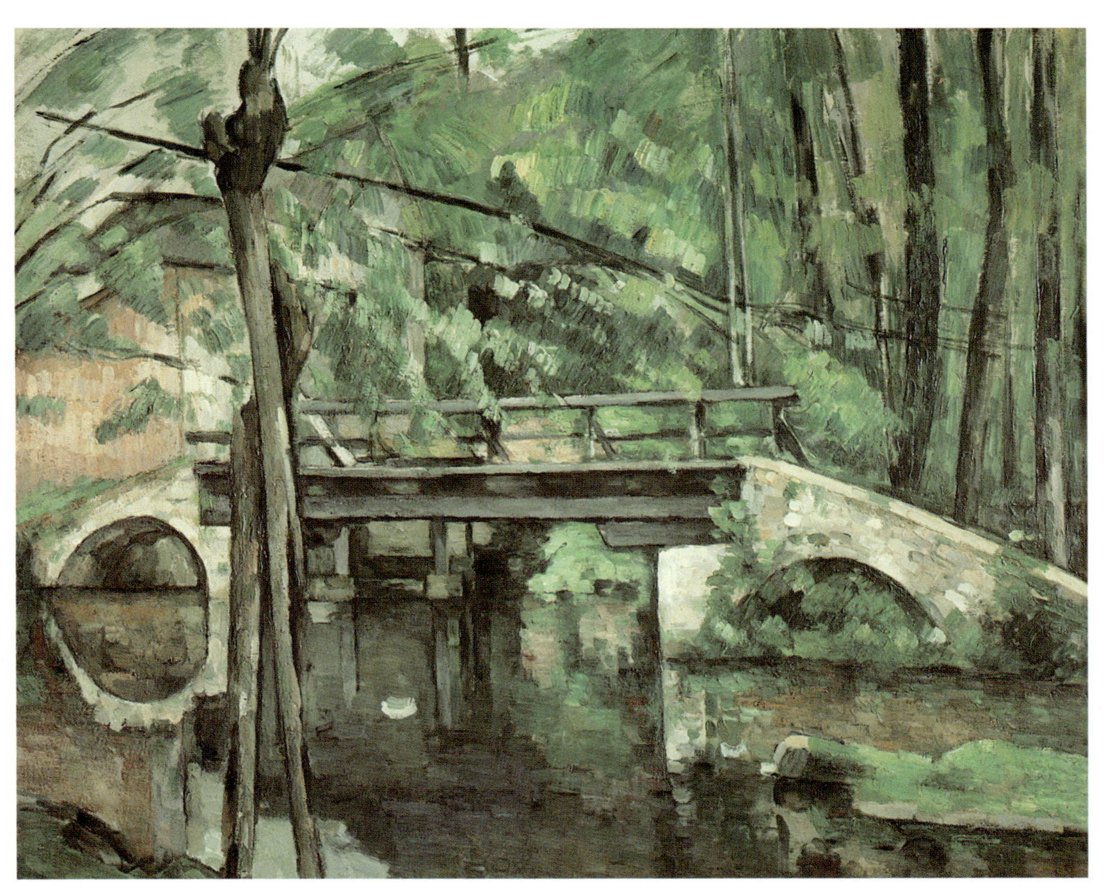

Melting Snow, Fontainebleau

1879–1880
Oil on canvas, 76.6 × 100.6 cm
New York, The Museum of Modern Art
Digital image © 2003 Florence, The Museum of Modern Art, New York/Scala

Cézanne spent the winter of 1879–1880 in Melun (a small village not far from Fontainebleau forest). It was particularly cold and the painter was undoubtedly forced to paint indoors. Obliged to abandon his *en plein air* studies, he opted for a method that was widely used by landscape painters: that of painting from a photograph. This was recounted by Maurice Denis in 1899 after having seen this painting on sale as part of the Doria collection, and it was confirmed by Duret in 1906, who claimed that *Melting Snow, Fontainebleau* was painted *à l'intérieur.*

Fontainebleau forest, with its thick, wild vegetation, was a favorite spot to paint for the Barbizon school artists, in particular for Camille Corot, the "father" of the French landscape painters for whom Cézanne held great esteem. The forest also enchanted the Provençal artist, who dedicated to it this canvas now in New York.

The intricate interplay of lines and planes offered by the landscape, which was already reduced to two dimensions by the photograph, allowed the painter to study and freely define the complex spatial problems presented by the view. With a series of small touches of the palette knife, applied diagonally and with great vigor, Cézanne forces the path through the forest to rise steeply in the foreground and lead the eye into the distance. Where the tones are darker he used a thicker impasto (in particular on the trunks and branches) to define their forms more cleanly, whereas they seem lighter and more delicate where he wants to create the "liquid" effect of the snow melting. His lovely palette of yellows, pale blues, and greens in the sky are made to stand out by contrasting them with whites and blacks.

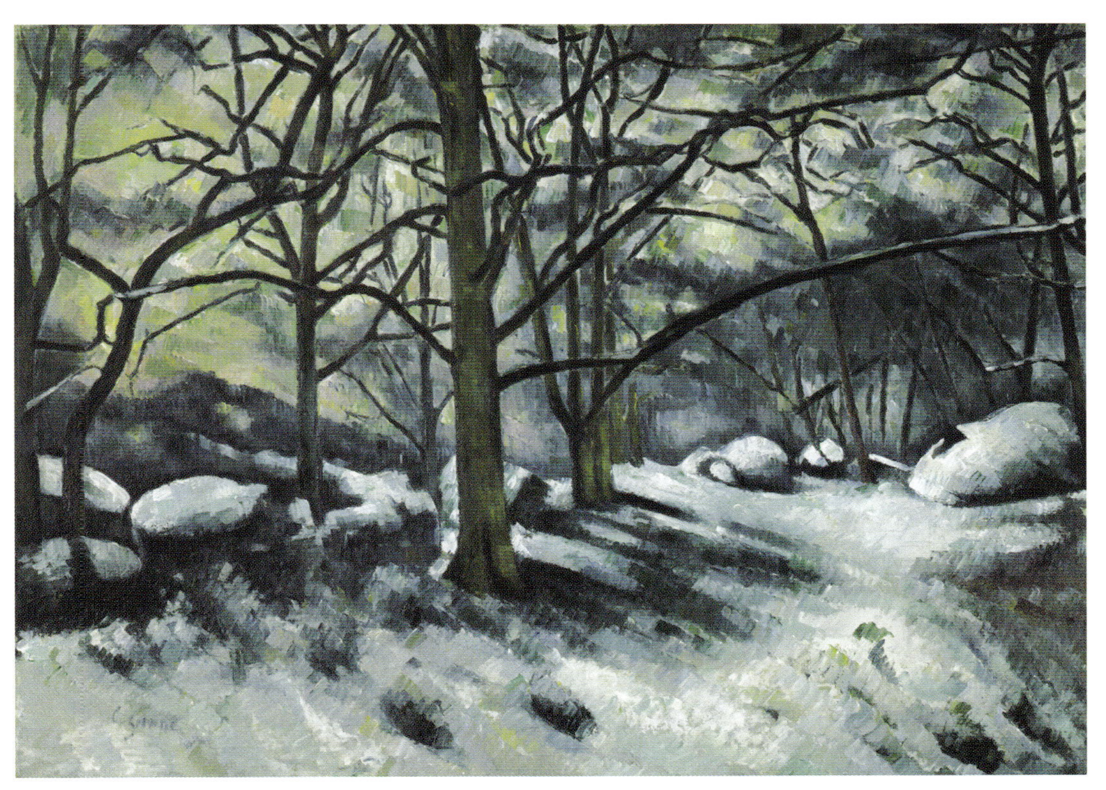

Self-Portrait with Hat

1879–1880
Oil on canvas, 65 × 51 cm
Bern, Kunstmuseum

"When Cézanne painted a self-portrait," claimed Westheim, "he transposed the immense weight of creation, the task of which was to transform chaos into order, into melancholic features. We see the man that advances silently in his time, that places himself above the problems of his contemporaries, in awful solitude because he understood the creation of his essence, an extreme synthesis of divergent elements. In such a description of the self there is nothing of Cézanne that his contemporaries knew, nothing of the *petit bourgeois* that led his life so pedantically." Although the painter had always placed little importance on his physical appearance, he felt the need to portray himself forty-six times throughout his artistic career. This particular painting suggests the anxiety he caused himself through his self-analysis and the assertion of his personality despite his general incomprehension, and the need for a more intimate relationship with his most patient model—himself.

This hypothesis seems supported by his pensive, unassuming attitude and his serious, frowning expression. The figure of Cézanne stands out strongly against the background dominated by the right-angles of the door and window that accentuate the impression given by the painting of general severity. The strong features of his face are dashed in with thick broken brushwork and seem almost sculpted out of wood, as though to give an idea of fixity and stubborn immobility that only the intensity of his gaze diminishes. The impression of austere composure is stressed by the clothes the painter chose: a heavy brown jacket with a thick outline along the left shoulder, and his "shapeless old hat," which often provoked derisive comments from his refined colleagues in Paris.

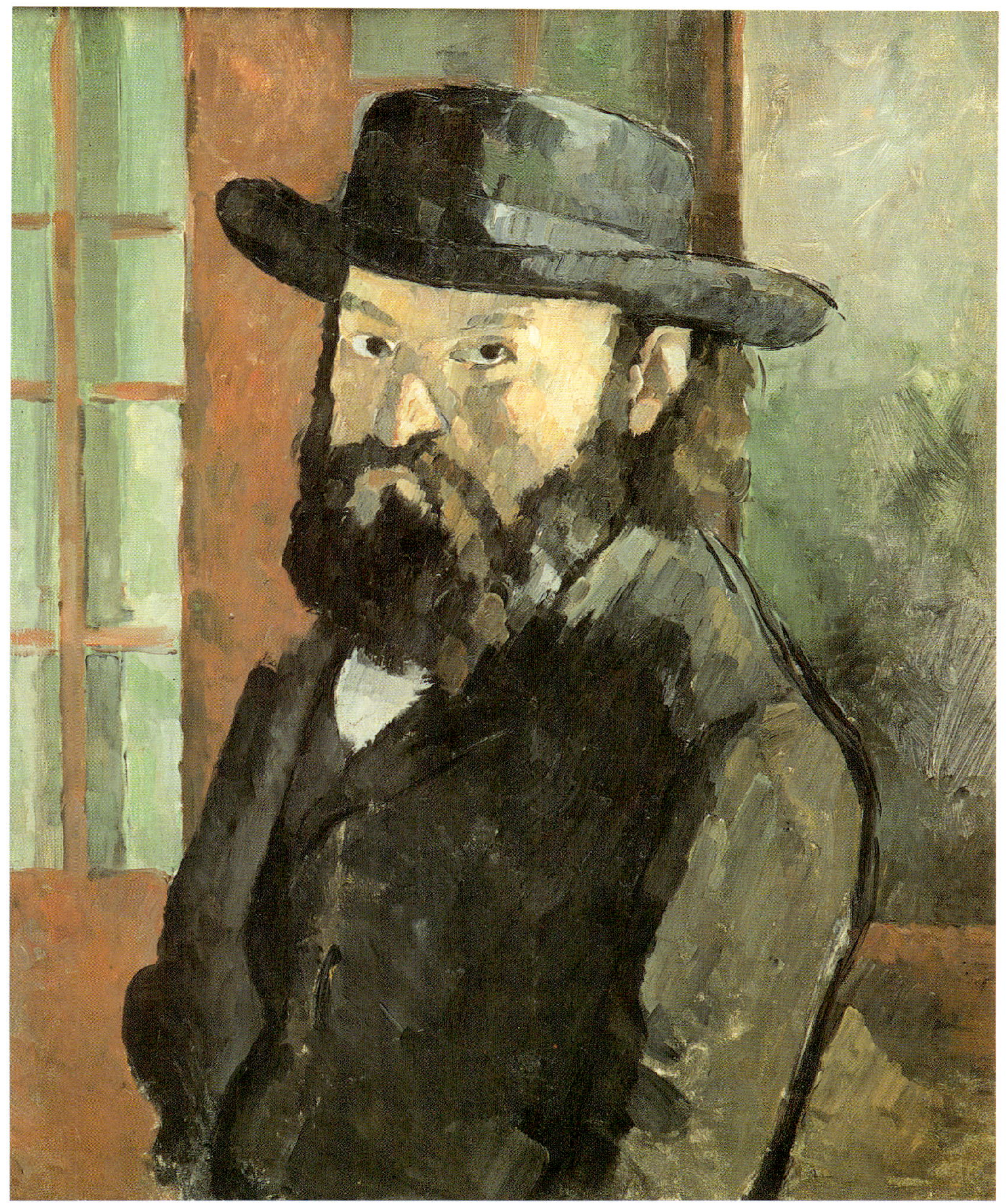

Self-Portrait

1880
Oil on canvas, 26 × 15 cm
Paris, Musée d'Orsay

At the very end of the 1870s Cézanne painted another self-portrait that, though left unfinished, remains strongly expressive. This was a difficult period for the painter following the closure of the third impressionist exhibition to derision and sarcastic comments that exacerbated his insecurity and deep sense of inadequacy. He was beset by serious disappointment but he continued his work on nature indefatigably. He sought refuge in Provence in search of peace and concentration. A sense of seriousness and dignified composure emanates from this painting, in which we meet the lively but oblique stare of the artist; his lips are closed, his expression absorbed, almost sulky, and his round head is marked by advanced baldness. Our eye dwells on the nuances of color in his beard and hair, on the light reflected on his forehead and the reddish tones of his cheeks and nose that are shown up strongly by their contrast with the cooler tones of the backdrop.

With the exception of his head, the painting has remained no more than a draft, allowing us to understand a little more about Cézanne's technique which, during these years, built form using color which he applied to the canvas with a palette knife over thin pencil marks, building up the lines one at a time until the desired tone was achieved.

Pissarro, to whom the portrait belonged, wrote enthusiastically in a letter to his son that Cézanne had painted "unfinished but superb" heads of great pictorial power and with unprecedented expressive vitality.

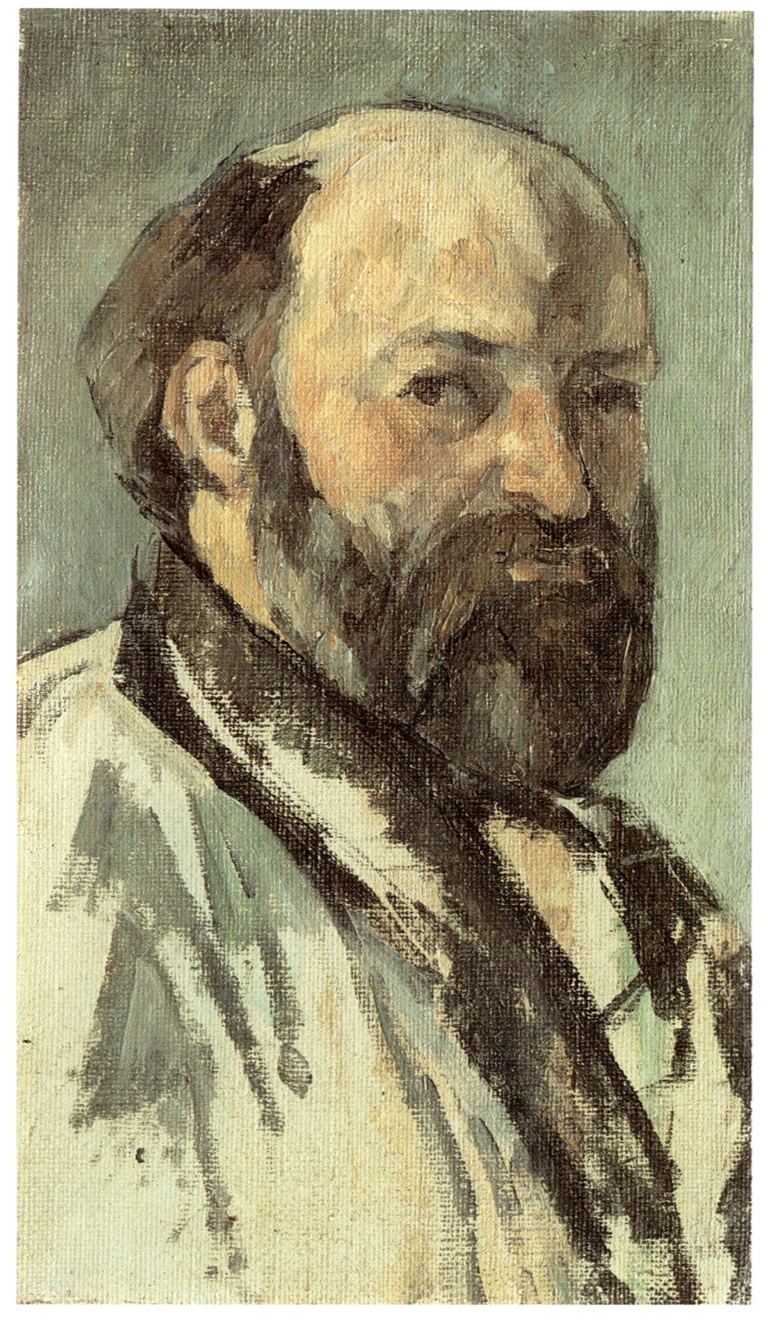

Self-Portrait

c. 1882
Oil on canvas, 46 × 38 cm
Moscow, The Pushkin State Museum of Fine Arts

Painted in the 1880s, this self-portrait gives an impression of deep melancholic concentration. The composition appears busy because little space is given to the background and the face of the painter is able to fill almost the entire canvas. A weave of small but even brushstrokes "builds" the artist's shirt and jacket and is then transformed into a denser and thicker impasto on the beard. With the exception of Cézanne's broad and smooth forehead, which catches and reflects light throughout the painting, the dominant tone of the work revolves around a range of dark colors that bring out the silent, intense atmosphere of the painting. The confident brushstrokes follow the profile of the nose linearly and the outline of the nose gives the face of the artist an almost "orientalizing" appearance (as John Rewald noted), which is completely at odds with his other self-portraits. Exhibited in the Museum of Modern Western Art in Moscow after the October Revolution, it was particularly admired by members of the Russian avant-garde.

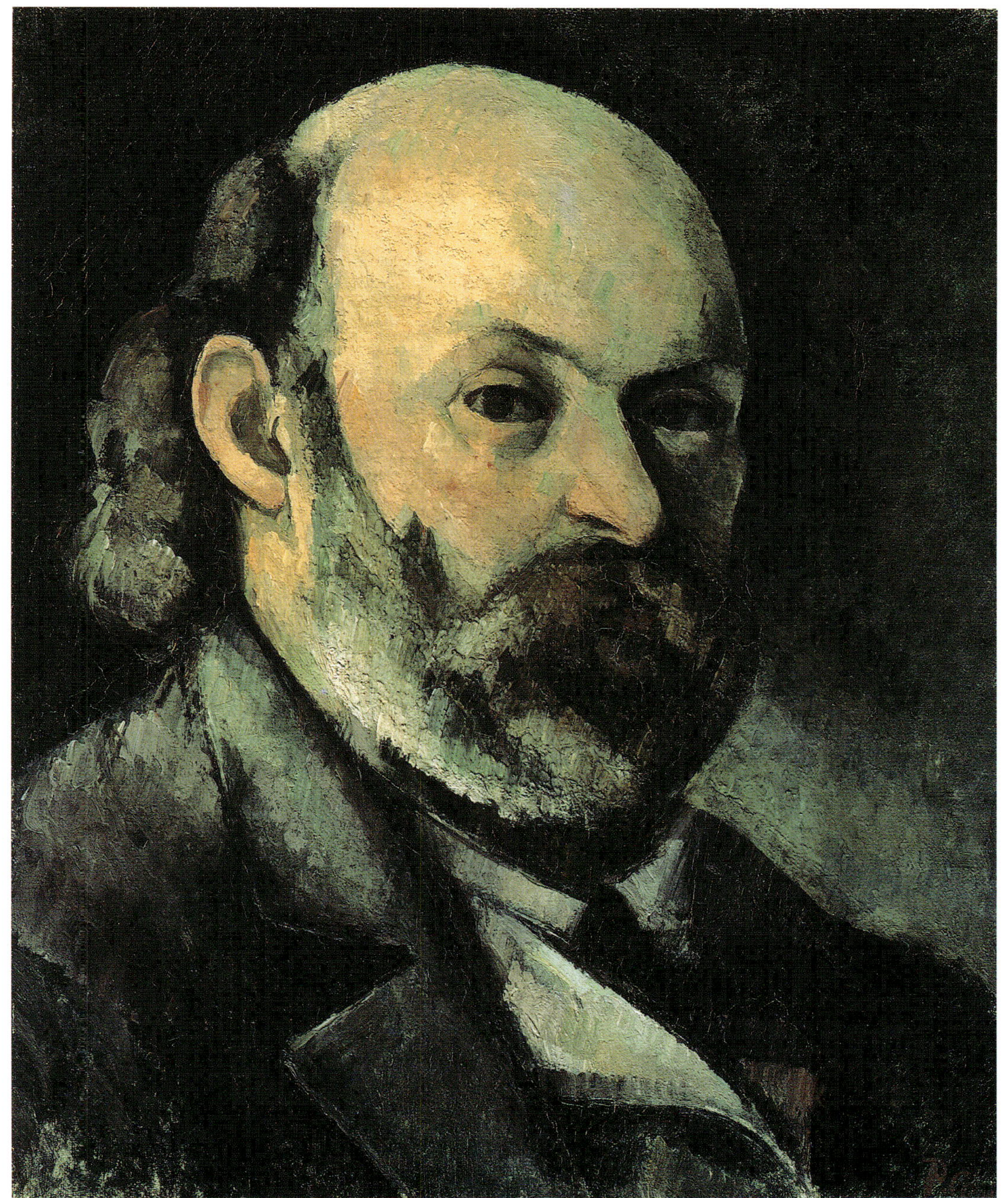

L'Estaque

1882–1885
Oil on canvas, 65 × 54 cm
Paris, Musée d'Orsay

Writing to Pissarro in 1876, Cézanne described L'Estaque, a small fishing village overlooking the Bay of Marseille, as follows: "It is like a playing card. Red roofs against a blue sea [. . .]. There are olives and stone pines that never lose their leaves. The sun is so frightening that it seems that objects were silhouetted not only in black and white, but also in blue, red, brown and violet." The area's sun-kissed and even landscape and the energy of the vegetation so fascinated Cézanne that he decided to stay there to paint *en plein air*. The result was a series of views of great beauty that so pricked the curiosity of Renoir that he went to L'Estaque to paint with Cézanne in 1882.

In this work the painter divides the scene into four distinct bands: one each for the earth, sea, mountains, and sky. His brushwork is fired by extraordinary power, taking in the dense vegetation that overlooks the sea in a mosaic of colors that follow the energetic diagonal of the coast. For the sea he chose a dense and uniform impasto of intense blue that he endowed with slight movement by touches of violet and green. The mountains in the distance are represented as compact volumes constructed using a mosaic of colors that range from blue to green to yellow following an extremely regular *ductus*. The painting derives its strength from chromatic contrasts: the luminous field with patches of red, orange, and green stands out against the cobalt blue sea and its static, majestic presence. The painting's dynamic character aroused the admiration of Gustave Geffroy, who summarized his impression of Cézanne's canvas as follows: "Southern sea, heavy blue water, rocky hills, the stupor of the things under the sun, landscape built with rare strength, attention and freshness."

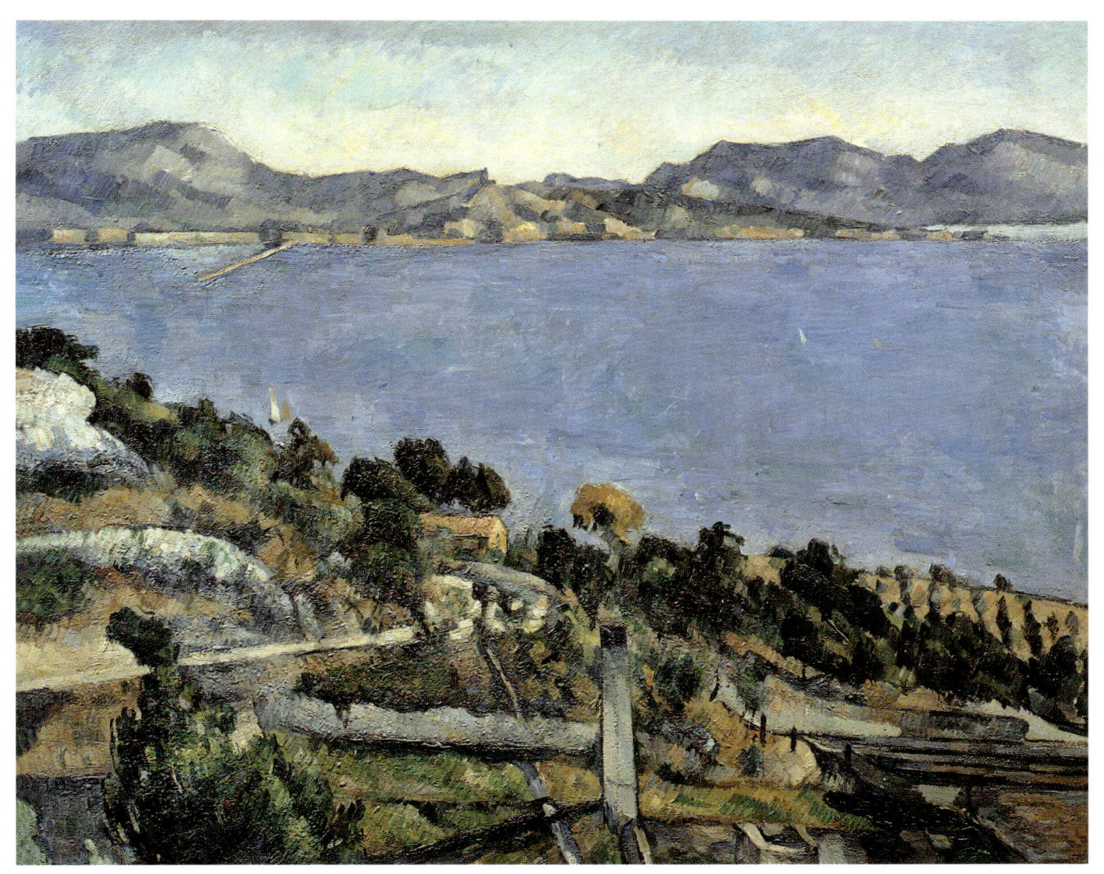

Farmhouse and Chestnut Trees at Jas de Bouffan

c. 1884

Oil on canvas, 92 × 73.7 cm
Pasadena, Norton Simon Museum

Enveloped in deep solitude and surrounded by the affection of only his family and a few friends, Cézanne enjoyed spending time at the Jas de Bouffan, the family home, with its avenues of chestnut trees and stone basins filled with water. The ravines and attractive corners created by the harmonious combination of architecture and nature fascinated him and over the years became one of his favorite themes, the one on which he worked most persistently in peace and with absorption. He painted the family estate in both summer and winter, dwelling on the relationship between the clean geometrical lines of the buildings and the dense rows of trees in search of new, delicate harmonies.

A silent, engrossed air is suggested by this sunny summer view of the chestnut trees and the farmhouse at Jas de Bouffan, painted about 1884. Cézanne chose the vertical format and framed the buildings with two large chestnut trees whose thick foliage throws a heavy shadow onto the foreground. The observer's gaze then moves across the sunlit grass to the farmhouse which, with its regular, geometric lines, is easily transformed by Cézanne into a simple linear set of parallelepipeds illuminated powerfully by the sun to emphasize their abstract regularity. The balance in this painting between curves and straight lines, compact masses and insubstantial foliage reaches absolute perfection.

Until 1943 the work belonged to Fannie Toure, a servant at Jas de Bouffan. According to Mme Toure, the master gave it to her when she was obliged to return to her family during a cholera epidemic that struck France between June and October 1884. Cézanne chose this picture because Mme Toure's daughter loved to walk among the chestnut trees.

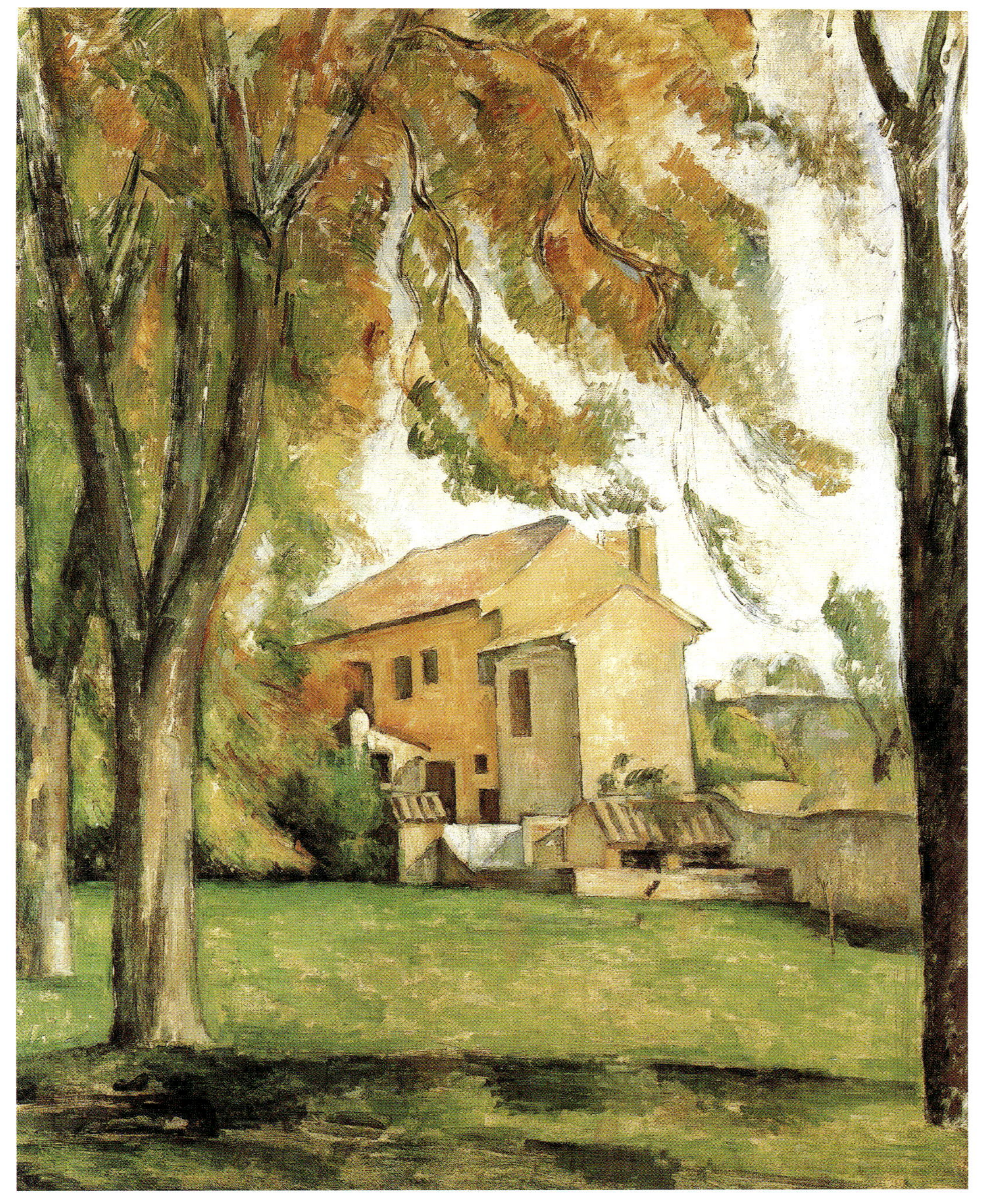

The Bather

c. 1885
Oil on canvas, 127 × 96.8 cm
New York, The Museum of Modern Art

"The statue of a pensive man in a landscape." This was Meyer Schapiro's pithy but apt description of Cézanne's lovely *Bather* in the collection of the Museum of Modern Art in New York. It was painted in the 1880s when the artist's experimentation with figures and his ambition to render nature in solid forms were well developed.

The figure of the solitary *Bather* moves surely toward the observer, with physical freedom, unconstrained by trees or plants, leaning slightly forward as though he were subjected to "a sort of flattening, of being pulled on either side that makes him broader than normal" (Renato Barilli). Completely absorbed, with his eyes looking down on where he is going, the bather seems intimately wedded to his setting, a natural part of it.

His body has the same tones as the ground; "his" blues are the blues of the water, sky, and mountain in the distance, almost as though Cézanne is referring to the common origin of all things and demonstrating his neutrality with regard to all the "objects" found in nature. The artist's analytical eye is as concerned with the landscape as it is with men and women, apples or trees, all of which are equal members of the world of forms.

A monumental figure, *The Bather* derives further power from the fact that he is the only vertical element in a setting of horizontals, in particular the mountain in the distance and the flat line of the ground. The interplay of perpendiculars dominates the spatial arrangement of the canvas which is given greater energy by the diagonal represented by the man's arms which, if extended, would meet the diagonal of the profile of the mountain behind at the center of the canvas.

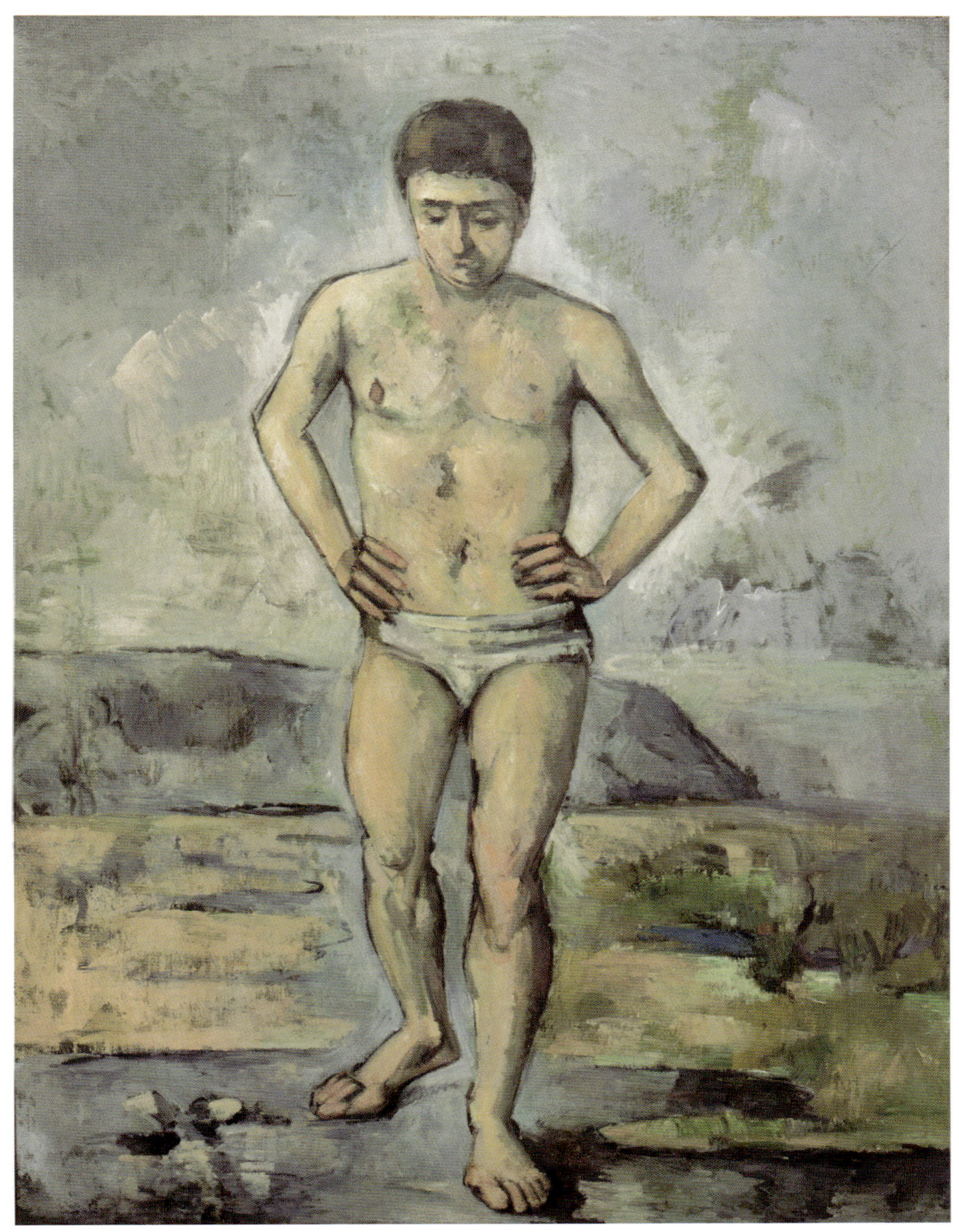

Chestnut Trees and Farm at Jas de Bouffan

c. 1886
Oil on canvas, 72 × 91 cm
Moscow, The Pushkin State Museum of Fine Arts

Jas-de-Bouffan was the name of the artist's family home in the countryside of Provence. With its simple, regular buildings and rows of leafy chestnut trees, Cézanne painted unforgettable views of this place that he knew so well. In the 1880s, when his self-imposed "exile" in the Midi was felt more intensely, he returned with particular interest to this subject. He was specially attracted by the interpenetration of architecture and nature, the relationship of volumes and the effect of the strong Provençal light, which together, offered a vast range of possibilities of expression. In the south it was easier to employ the intensity of the sun to build space with colors, while at the same time meeting the need to restore order to nature and allowing the landscape to reveal itself through sophisticated color combinations.

The Moscow version of the Jas de Bouffan opens with the brusque rise of the road in the foreground, carrying the eye toward the grass and the houses in the distance. The tall chestnut trees with their dense foliage stand on the right, created by the painter with light touches of the brush in a modulated range of greens, while the wall on the right leads the eye to buildings illuminated by the clear southern light. The sky has been rendered magnificently with an extraordinary selection of blues flecked by white and gold to give movement to the clouds and suggest the wind through the branches. The passage from the shaded areas beneath the trees to the strongly lit yellow and green field was an ambitious development, which exhibits once again the success Cézanne had achieved during this period in his experimentation with the relationship between light and color.

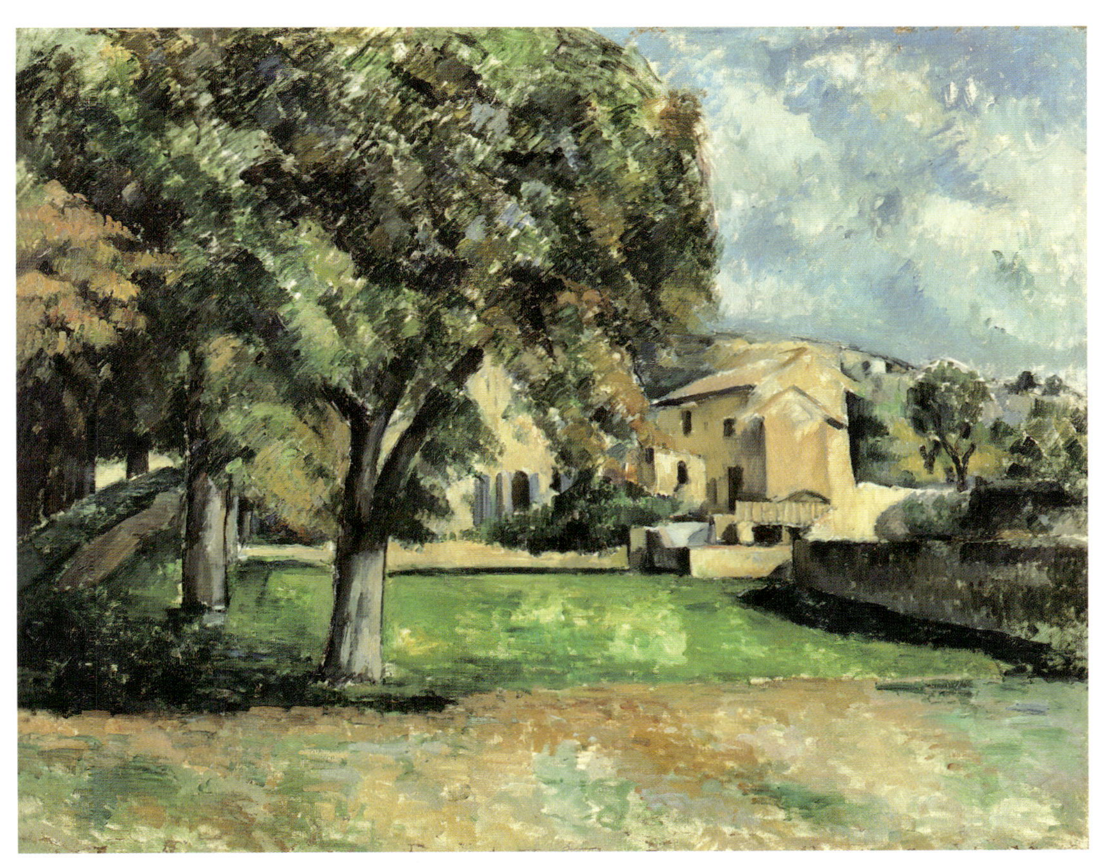

Pierrot and Harlequin (Mardi Gras)

1888

Oil on canvas, 102 × 81 cm
Moscow, The Pushkin State Museum of Fine Arts

The Commedia dell'Arte, which was imported to France in the sixteenth century, became very popular in the country at the end of the nineteenth century. The bizarre characters that had inspired artists like Watteau in the eighteenth century continued to remain favorites and Pablo Picasso also made use of them for his "exercises" on the human figure and color.

After years working almost exclusively on landscapes, still-lifes and the motif of the bathers, Cézanne embarked on a new direction in the treatment of the human figure by drawing on the wide range of characters offered by the Commedia dell'Arte. He did this in four canvases, all painted during his stay in Paris in 1888 to 1889 in the studio in Val-de-Grâce.

In this painting, composed by the artist in front of a heavy curtain with a floral motif, Cézanne's son Paul and Paul's friend Louis Guillaume posed for him as though in movement. Like two puppets manipulated by the eye and brush of the artist, Harlequin and Pierrot do not tell us anything of their deeds and adventures; instead, like lifeless masks, they display simply their volumes as figures. The painter studied their forms in a purely mental space, using the motif of the lozenge to create the architectural solidity of Harlequin's body and a series of folds in Pierrot's costume that project it towards the observer like a pure volume. The contrast between the warm red and orange and the cool blues of the background helped Cézanne emphasize the difference in depth of the planes. He often used color for reasons of perspective, in particular, blues to suggest or accentuate a sense of depth.

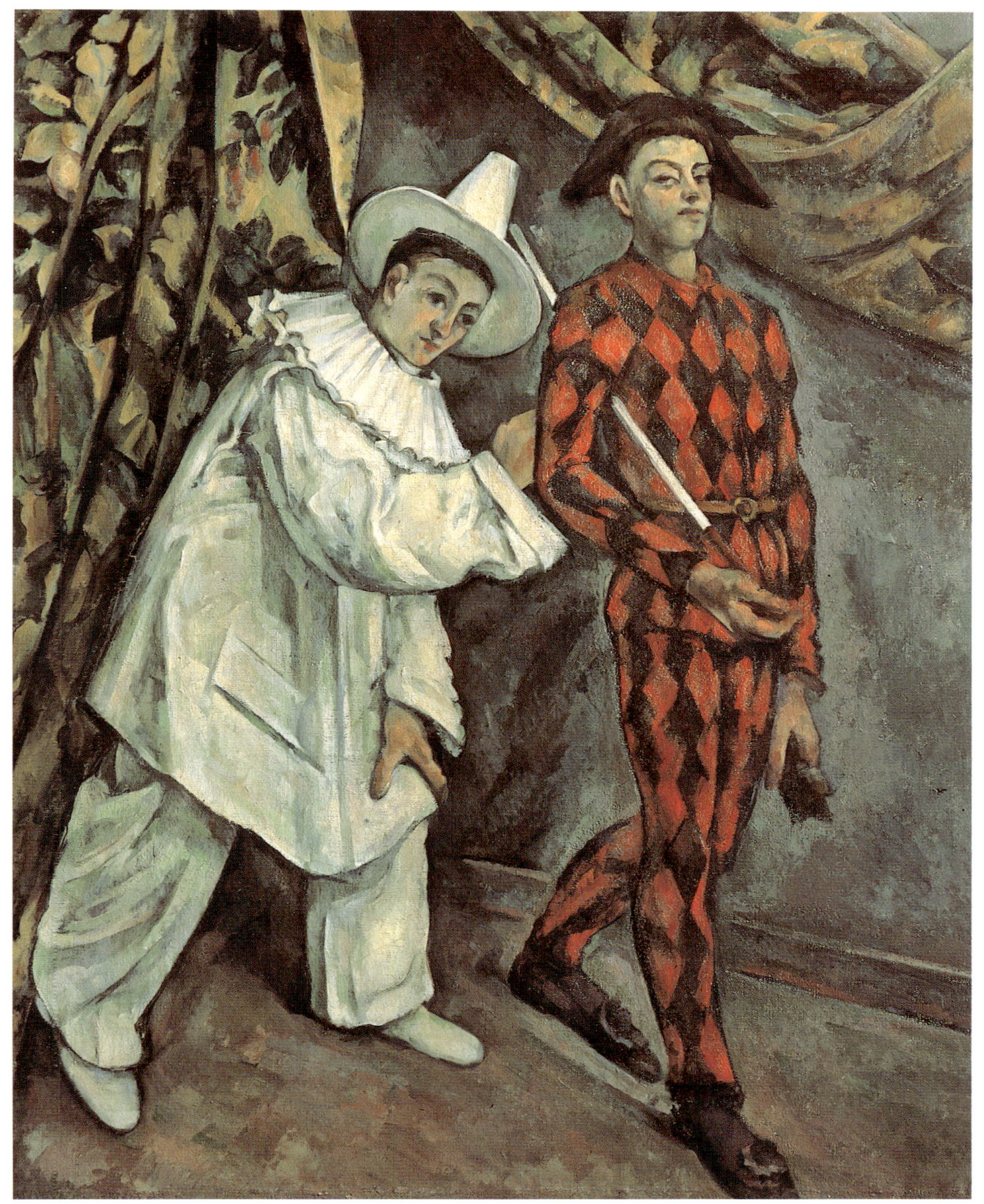

Madame Cézanne in a Yellow Chair

1888–1890
Oil on canvas, 81 × 65 cm
Chicago, The Art Institute of Chicago

A beautiful woman with chestnut hair and large dark eyes, Hortense Fiquet met Paul Cézanne in Paris in 1869 when she was nineteen years old and earning her living as a model. The young painter must have been very attracted to her despite his shyness and terror at physical contact, but Hortense's calm, unassuming character must have encouraged him. The two began a relationship they kept secret so as not to incur the anger of the disapproving Louis Cézanne. It was only in 1886, after the death of his father, that Cézanne decided to formalize their relationship. The birth in 1872 of their only child, Paul, may have put a distance between them. Hortense was not at all fond of the monotony of life in Aix and preferred to spend most of the year in Paris. Cézanne was looked after by his mother and unmarried sister, Maria, who looked after the family house.

Cézanne painted twenty-four portraits of the lovely Hortense and made a number of drawings. She was certainly his favorite model, the most patient and the one that best tolerated the long hours in a pose required by her husband.

Executed when the studies made by Cézanne on form were reaching extraordinary simplification, this painting does not convey the breadth of Hortense's attractiveness or the delicacy of her features. The artist has transformed his model into a series of volumes that excludes his wife's emotional dimension. Her body is cleanly defined against the chair on which she is seated by the strong chromatic contrast between her red dress and the yellow upholstery. Her head is a perfect oval and the cylinders of her arms and hands reflect the intense chromatism of the painting. Cézanne painted the portrait using vigorous brushwork in an attempt to imbue the entire composition with light, and the projection of the figure into the foreground gives the model a monumental quality.

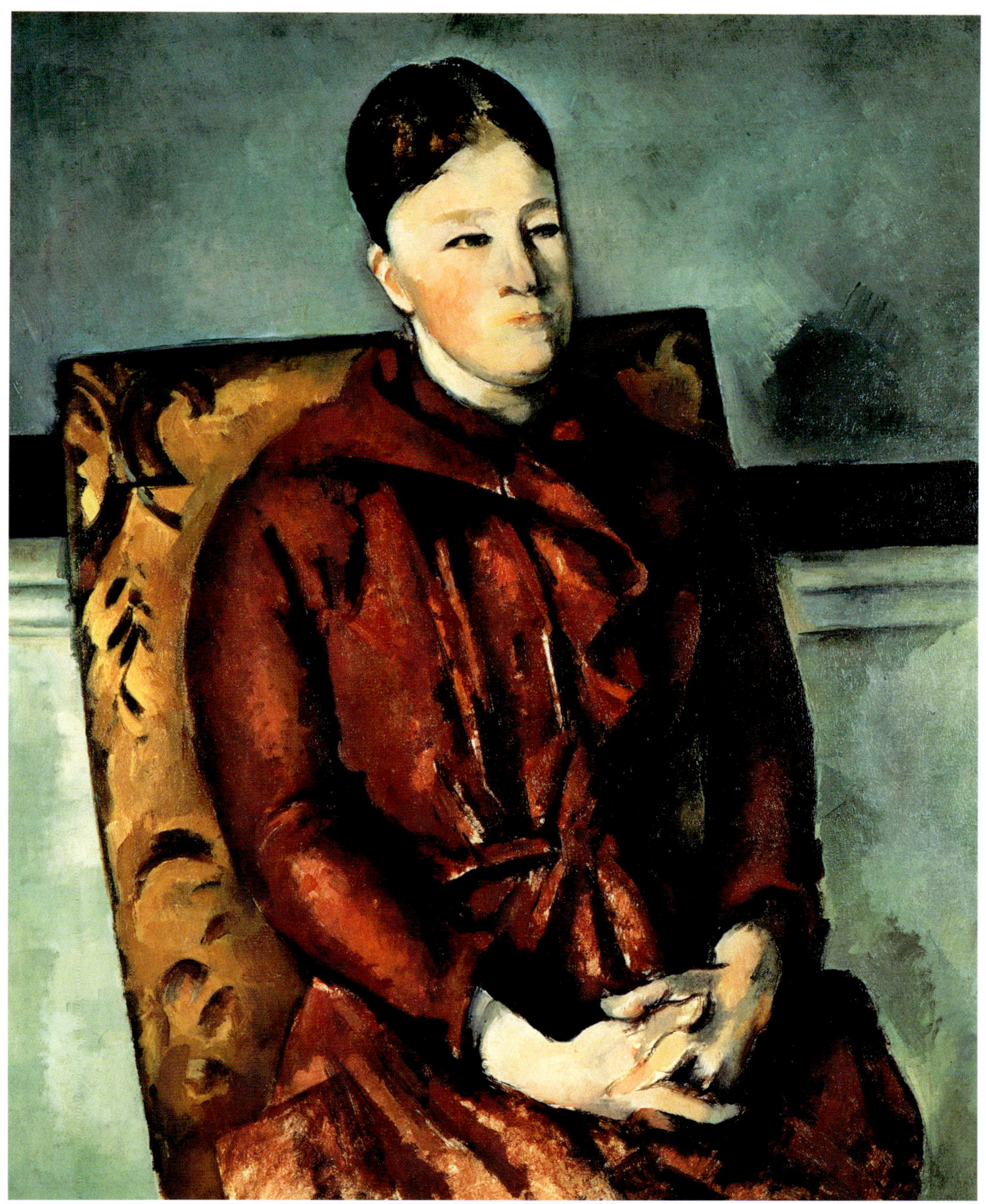

Boy in a Red Vest

1888–1890
Oil on canvas, 79.5 × 64 cm
Zurich, Bührle Foundation

During the years 1888 to 1890 Cézanne left his self-imposed exile in Provence to live in Paris with his wife, Hortense, and son, Paul, in an apartment on the Île Saint-Louis at 15, Quai d'Anjou. During this brief but productive stay in the capital he spent a lot of time on studying the human figure and, extraordinarily, he decided to hire a professional model for a small series of paintings. When painting portraits he usually used people near to him who were prepared to put up with the long hours needed to pose, but this time, thanks to a large inheritance following the death of his father in 1886, he chose to use a young model of Italian origin named Michelangelo di Rosa.

Cézanne made four intense portraits of the boy in different poses, which allowed him to study the relationship between the figure and space. In this lovely version in Zurich, Cézanne portrayed the boy in the traditional pose of melancholy with an engrossed and distant expression, though one filled with unprecedented tenderness. Using color Cézanne builds the forms through the juxtaposition of bright patches of color: the brilliant red of the boy's vest and the violets, greens, and transparent whites of his sleeve. With his whole body leaning forward, Michelangelo's figure is contained within a series of diagonal lines (the seat, table, curtain and his left arm) that help to render his image distant and detached.

It was this absorbed melancholy with which Cézanne permeated his characters that struck a deep chord in the aesthetic imagination of Amedeo Modigliani who, after visiting the large retrospective that the Salon d'Automne and Bernheim-Jeune gallery dedicated to Cézanne in 1907, reproduced the version of the *Boy in the Red Vest Standing* from memory.

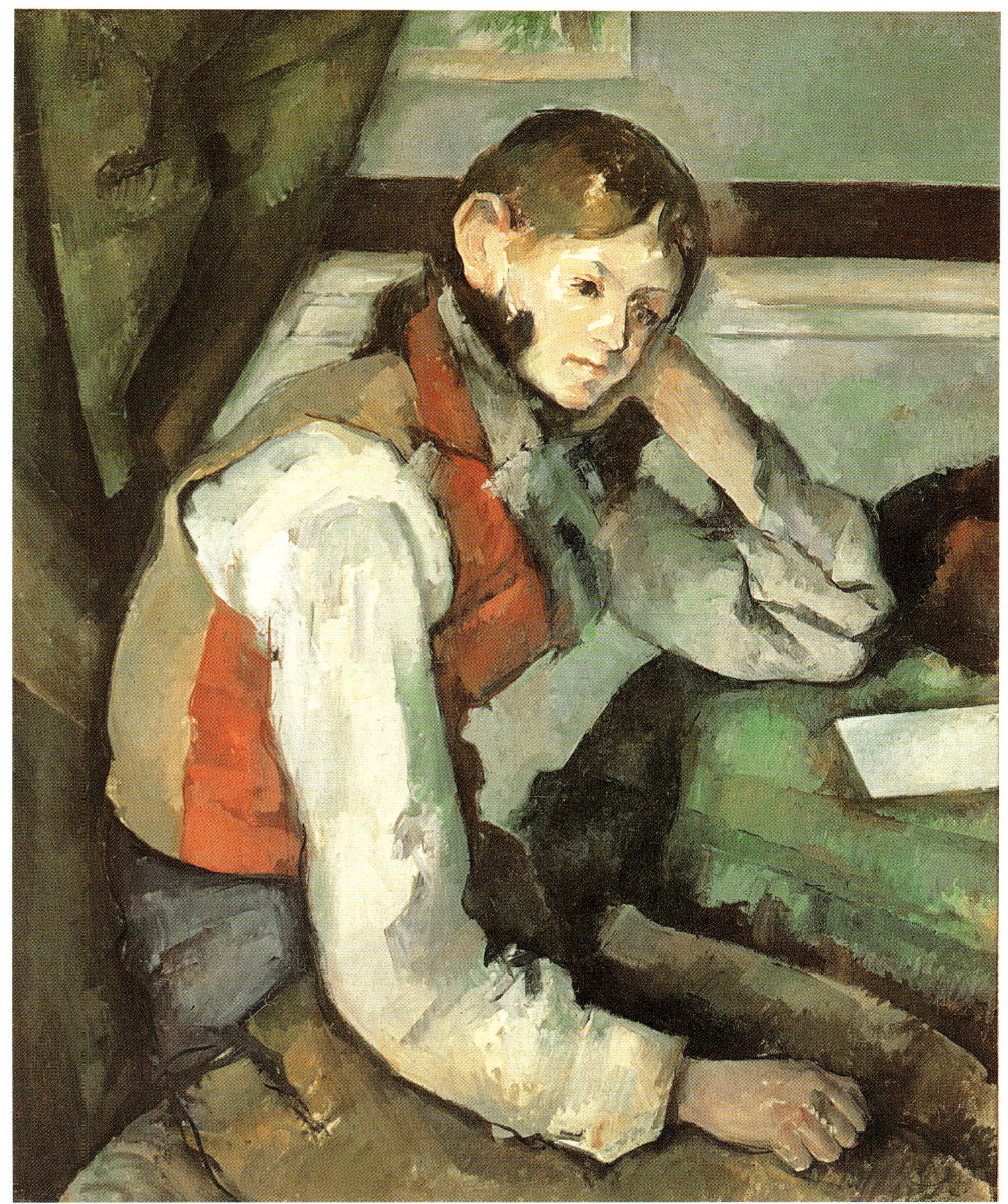

The Banks of the Marne

1888–1890

Oil on canvas, 65 × 81 cm
St. Petersburg, The State Hermitage Museum

Between 1888 and 1890 Cézanne lived in Paris with his family and seemed to spend most of his time studying the human figure in his studio, yet the desire for direct contact with nature continued to be of great importance to him and, during the summer months, he went out into the countryside along the banks of the Marne (one of the rivers that flows through the Île-de-France) to paint *en plein air*. During this period he painted intense, transparent views of the riverbanks with their thick, wild vegetation and cool, silent corners. This painting in the Hermitage represents one of these spots: the painter set his easel on the riverside so that he could paint the other bank where the dense foliage of the trees seems almost to embrace a country house. The painting exudes peace and quiet and it gave Cézanne a further chance to study color and the way in which objects are reflected in the water. A favorite theme of the impressionists, who found the mobility of water a perfect motif to emphasize the value of the impression or the fleeting vision they were portraying, a landscape with a sheet of water helped Cézanne to test his ability to give structural order and stability to the canvas. In this painting, Cézanne captures the reflections and effects of transparency given off by the river through refined use of chromatism and translates them into pure volumes. In so doing he gives the transient reflections consistency and order and imbues the impression with structure and persistence. This carefully studied and precise procedure does not invalidate the freshness of the view: the scene maintains its charm and allows itself to be filled with light through color. In this painting blue is the heart of Cézanne's vision. With it he manages to "sound the tonal bell that liberates his mute poetry" (Colin Eisler).

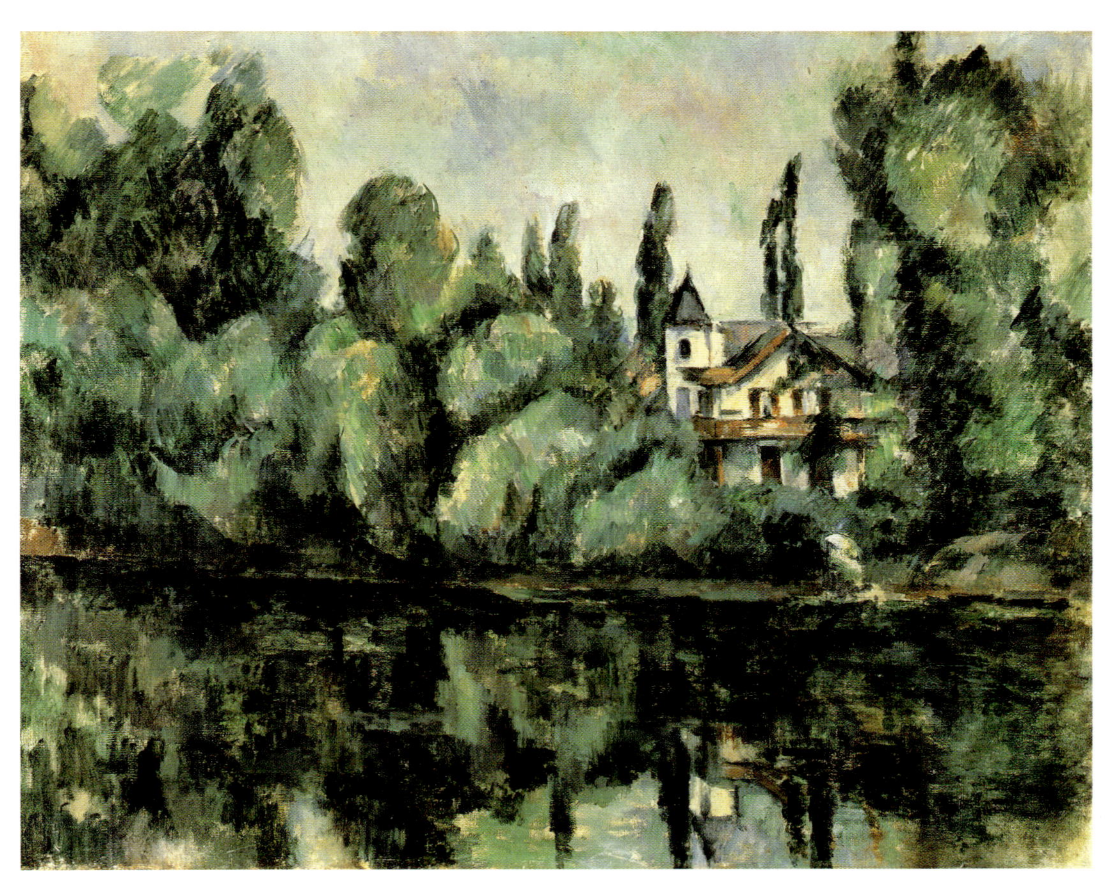

The House at Bellevue

1890
Oil on canvas, 60 × 73 cm
Geneva, Musée d'Art et d'Histoire

Around 1855 Maxim Conil, who in 1881 had married Rose Cézanne, the painter's sister, purchased the property of Bellevue near Aix. Frequent visits to Rose offered the artist the chance to find new motifs to study: Conil's property, which consisted of buildings of different heights, was particularly congenial to Cézanne's analytical eye, and he studied its articulation in space carefully. He made very simple studies of the pigeon tower, which he saw in simplified linear forms, but in this painting he concentrated on the entire set of buildings, lingering over their varied volumes. Cézanne viewed Bellevue from below, following the diagonal of the road that leads to the houses and enhanced by the row of trees in the middle distance. Walls and sections of building follow one another in order, bathed by the strong, liquid sunlight of Provence. The scene is dominated by a sense of harmony and order, and reveals the slow, meticulous work of the painter, who gradually builds up the picture with small touches of a rich range of greens, yellows, ocher, browns, and blues with painstaking concentration. Although the painting gives the impression of complete interpenetration of architecture and nature, Cézanne underlines the difference between the stone and nature by treating them in different ways: whereas the approach he uses for the buildings is regular and rhythmical, his treatment of the trees and bushes seems more dynamic as a result of his energetic and irregular brushwork.

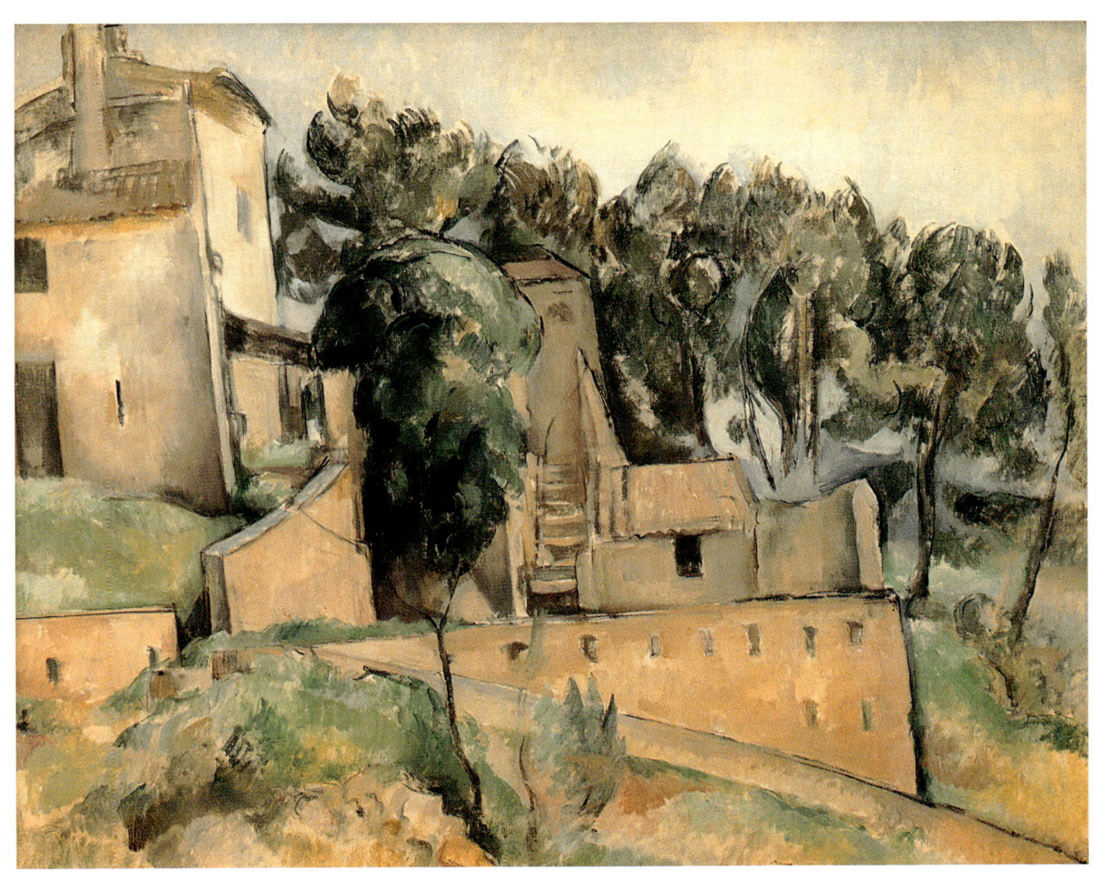

Sugar Bowl, Jug and Plate of Fruit

c. 1890
Oil on canvas, 61 × 90 cm
Moscow, The Pushkin State Museum of Fine Arts

"People think that a sugar bowl has no physiognomy or spirit," said Cézanne to his friend Joachim Gasquet, "but even sugar bowls change every day. You have to be able to handle them, tame them. [...] I have given up on flowers. They soon wither. Fruits are more faithful. They like having their portrait painted." Fruit was one of Cézanne's favorite themes throughout his painting career. Central features of his still lifes, he chose them carefully, preferring those with simple rounded forms (apples, peaches, pears, and onions) and placed them with meticulous care, supporting them with wood or books so that their pictorial potential was expressed to the full. They force themselves on the observer's attention as pure forms and vivid colors imbued with chromatic values captured by the aesthetic eye of the painter. Cézanne responds to the provisional character of reality with a new harmony, one that his eye has intuited and that the tools of his trade (brush, palette knife, colors, etc.) have reproduced in all its tenuous nature.

A constant theme of the artist's pictorial work between 1890 and 1900, his still lifes became complicated. The objects increased in number and Cézanne took particular care over the placement of the objects in his compositions to ensure that the pieces of fruit were as expressive as possible. This painting in the Pushkin Museum is a perfect example: it features a sugar bowl, a hexagonal pitcher (also used in other compositions) and a plate of fruit placed—as usual—on a white, red-striped tablecloth. Arranged on a small wooden table, the objects crowd into the foreground and almost out of the canvas. This forward movement is further emphasized by the daring diagonal of the baseboard, which follows a different perspective and crosses the horizontal plane of the table as though it wished to force it outside the picture.

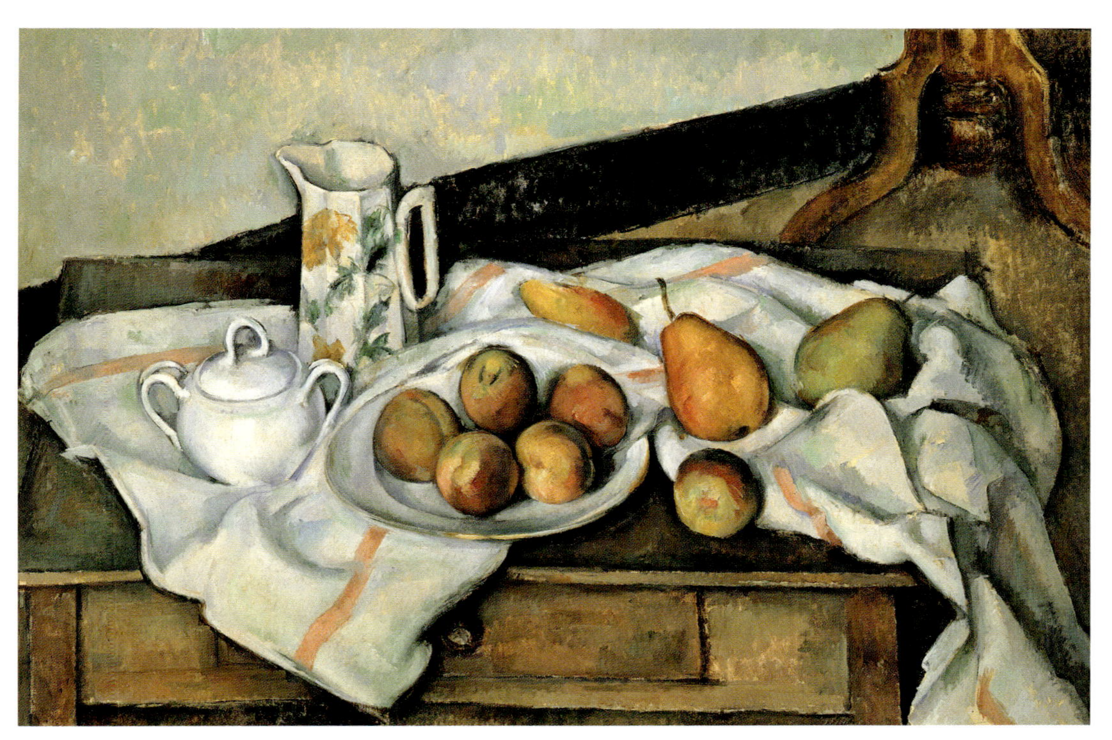

Bathers

c. 1890
Oil on canvas, 60 × 81 cm
Paris, Musée d'Orsay

This was the largest painting Cézanne dedicated to the subject of bathers, particularly the theme of male bodies in free movement in space. It is certainly the most complex in composition, with nine figures in a natural landscape.

Cézanne made many preparatory drawings for it that reveal his interest in the treatment of the male nude by Renaissance masters and, above all, in Michelangelo and the famous cartoon made for the *Battle of Cascina*, which was practically a manual of poses and an indispensable study for knowledge of the male anatomy.

The painting conveys the idea of order and monumental calm. Cézanne defines the space by creating the diagonals of the triangle in which the other figures exist in the two bending figures on the extreme left and right of the picture. Symmetry reigns throughout the composition: there is interplay between the figures, for instance, between the nude facing away from us and holding the cloth in one hand and the man with his arms folded in the background. Another example is the pairing of the energetic figure in shorts in the foreground with the nude with raised arms in the background.

The poses and positions of the bodies are generally taken from classical statuary (the man with the cloth is taken from the *Roman Orator* in the Louvre) and were studied carefully by the painter Malevich. In his manual written for the Bauhaus (*Die Gegenstandlose Welt*, Munich, 1927) he observed how Cézanne had proceeded methodically toward the abstraction of natural bodies, which his analytical eye had reduced to pure surfaces and pictorial volumes.

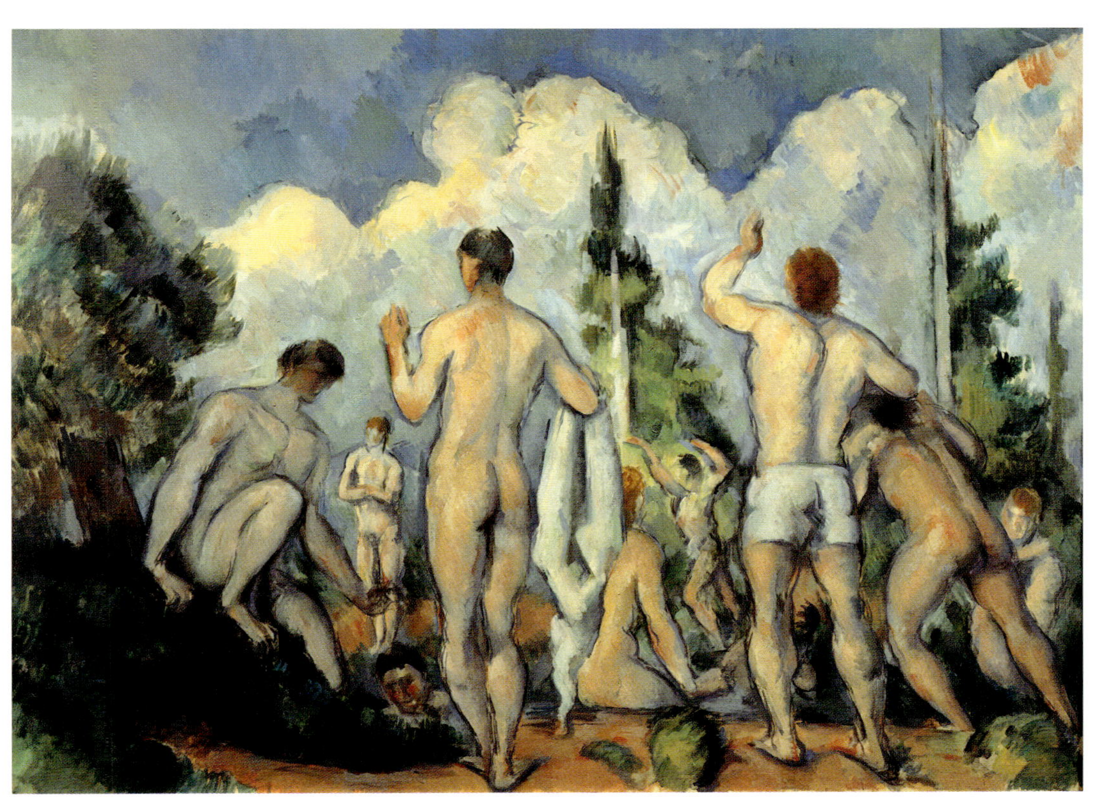

Portrait of Madame Cézanne

c. 1890
Oil on canvas, 81 × 65 cm
Paris, Musée de l'Orangerie

Of the portraits of Madame Cézanne made by the artist, the ones characterized by such evident frontality and symmetry are rare. He preferred a three-quarter or profile view that allowed him to play on forms and volumes and unexpected shifts of planes.

In the portrait in the Orangerie, however, Madame Cézanne stands out against an indistinct background and looks peremptorily at the observer. Facing fully forward, she seems endowed by a monumental force that makes her appear almost hieratical despite the small size of the painting.

Cézanne employed a free and advanced technique in painting this portrait: he built the figure by juxtaposing small patches of bright colors. Much attention was paid to the face, which wears a severe, almost forbidding expression and has tightly closed lips. Cézanne composed the face with great care, adding brushstroke on top of brushstroke and concentrating on the reflected light. The same treatment was given to the dress using different tones of blue, which are lit up by darts of white that underline the light. Though painted only a short while after *Portrait of Madame Cézanne in a Yellow Chair* (Art Institute, Chicago), this painting reveals the artist's experimental character and his constant study of the relationship between form and color that was to lead him to the extraordinary modern attributes of his later works.

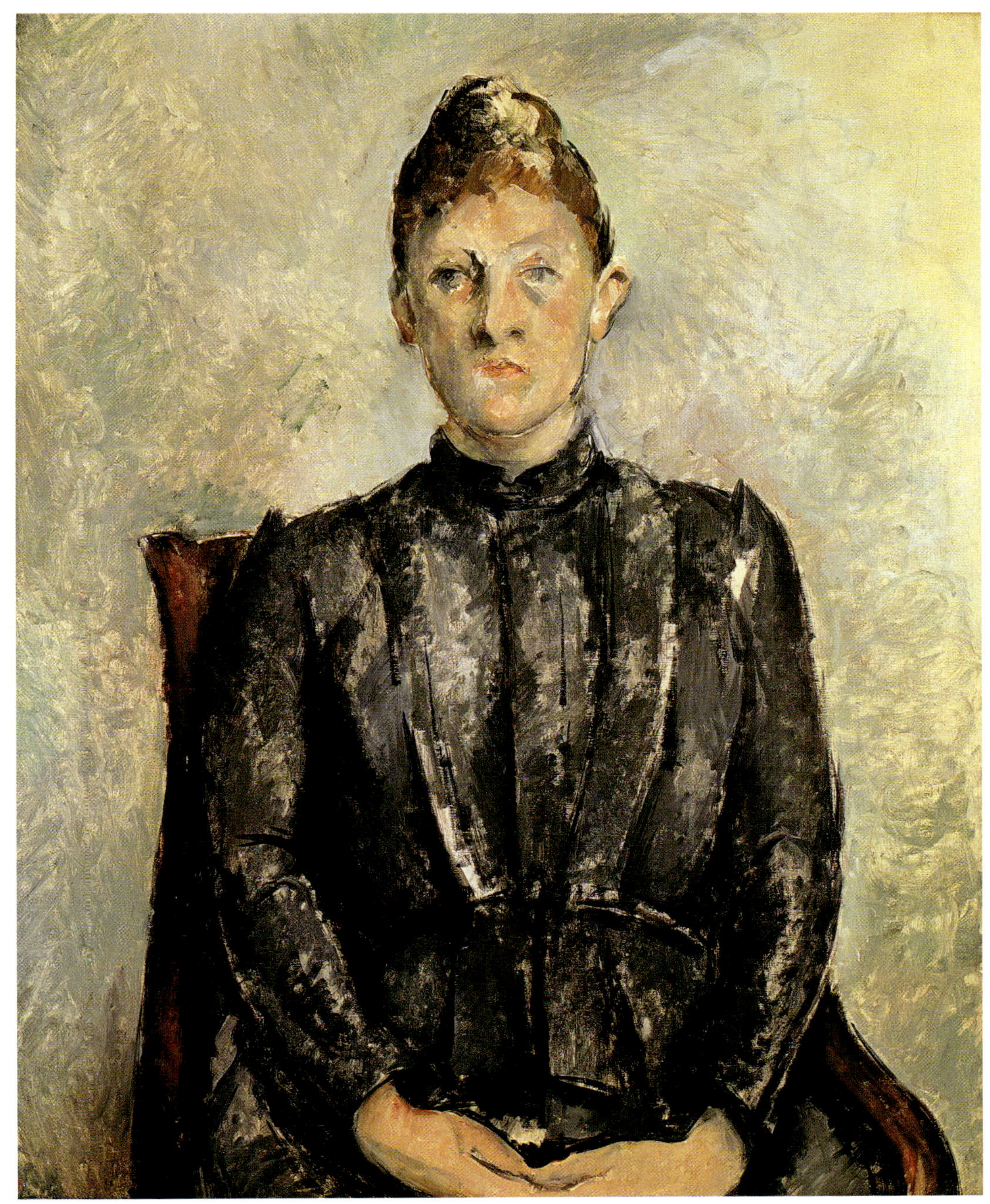

The Smoker

c. 1891
Oil on canvas, 91 × 72 cm
St. Petersburg, The State Hermitage Museum

Cézanne dedicated three canvases to this young farm laborer with a tanned face who worked for his family at Jas de Bouffan. He chose him as the figure for paintings executed during the same period as the small series dedicated to card players; this man was a card player as well and a frequent visitor to the brasserie in Aix.

The young man poses patiently in the painter's studio in the family home, his face expressing a pleasant tranquility. Behind him are paintings by the eccentric artist, Monsieur Cézanne, the strange man who wandered round Aix stained with paint and whom people made fun of. It is difficult to recognize the paintings: the largest one, the only one that can be discerned, is a still life of a bottle and fruit on a mauve background, certainly one of the earliest painted by the artist.

With his arm resting on a table, his head supported by his right hand, wearing the hat typical of the Midi and with his white clay pipe in his mouth, the farm laborer posed for the master of Aix for just a few coins. The painter diligently constructed the man's figure with refined modulations of color that include greens, mauve, ochers, reds, and bright blues all treated with a skilful and meticulous *ductus*. Attention centers on the man's face, his absorbed expression, the wide curve of his shoulders, and naturally on his strong, calloused hands that attest to long days of manual labor. Cézanne seems to linger over the left hand and highlights it with spots of red to give it greater three-dimensional substance. The diagonal of the curtain behind the man's shoulders is reflected in the man's right arm and helps to bring the figure forward into the foreground until he is almost pushed out of the space of the canvas.

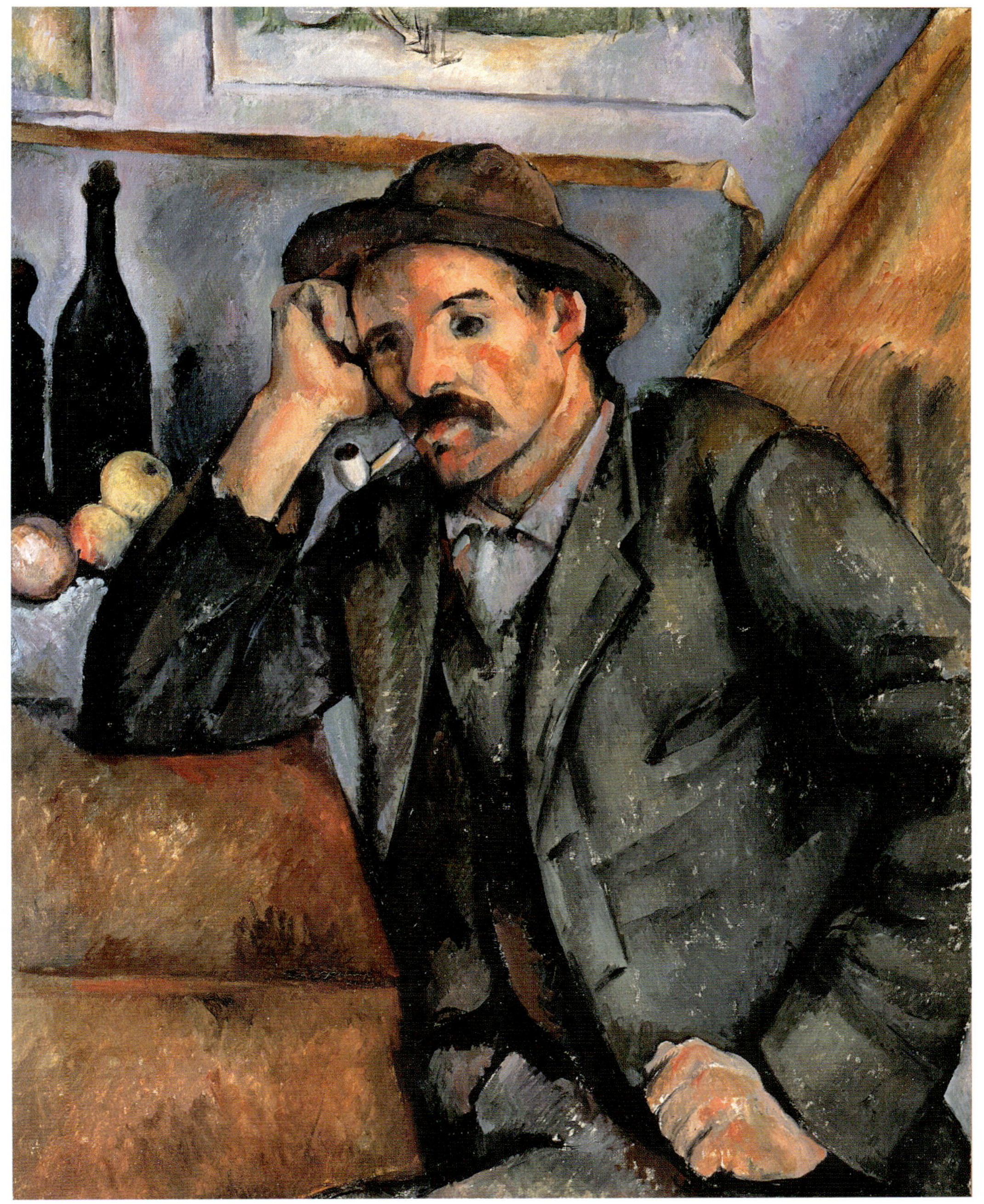

Card Players

1893–1896
Oil on canvas, 47 × 56 cm
Paris, Musée d'Orsay

Between 1892 and 1896 Cézanne painted a small series of works dedicated to card players that may have been influenced by Louis Le Nain's *Card Players* (1635–1640), now in the museum in Aix. Cézanne produced five versions, one with five figures, another with four, another with three, and two versions with a pair of players, all in a short period of time. He spent a long time studying the subject and preceded the paintings with a large number of studies. Some experts claim that he simplified the composition as he progressed, starting with five figures and finishing with two, but there are those who argue that Cézanne worked on several paintings simultaneously.

This painting is the smallest of the series and probably one of the later ones. It conveys the sense that it is the result of great concentration by the painter and of a long, close study. The two perfunctorily described players are seen facing one another in a cramped setting, intent on the game. The positions and poses of the players are perfectly symmetrical and their faces are completely devoid of any psychological dimension. The scene betrays an atmosphere of suspense.

"The fixity of the player waiting," wrote the art historian Giulio Carlo Argan, "is defined by the cylindrical form of his hat, which is repeated in his sleeve, by the straight line of the seat back, and by the touches of white in his pipe and collar," whereas the "psychological mobility of the other [the player on the right] is given by the paler, reflective colors in his jacket, hat and face, and by the less rigid and wavier lines [that describe his form]."

Cézanne made color the real "substance of the pictorial space": it is no longer a "local tint connected to things" but transforms the painting "into a weave of colors to which small touches give a density and autonomous direction compared to the form of the objects."

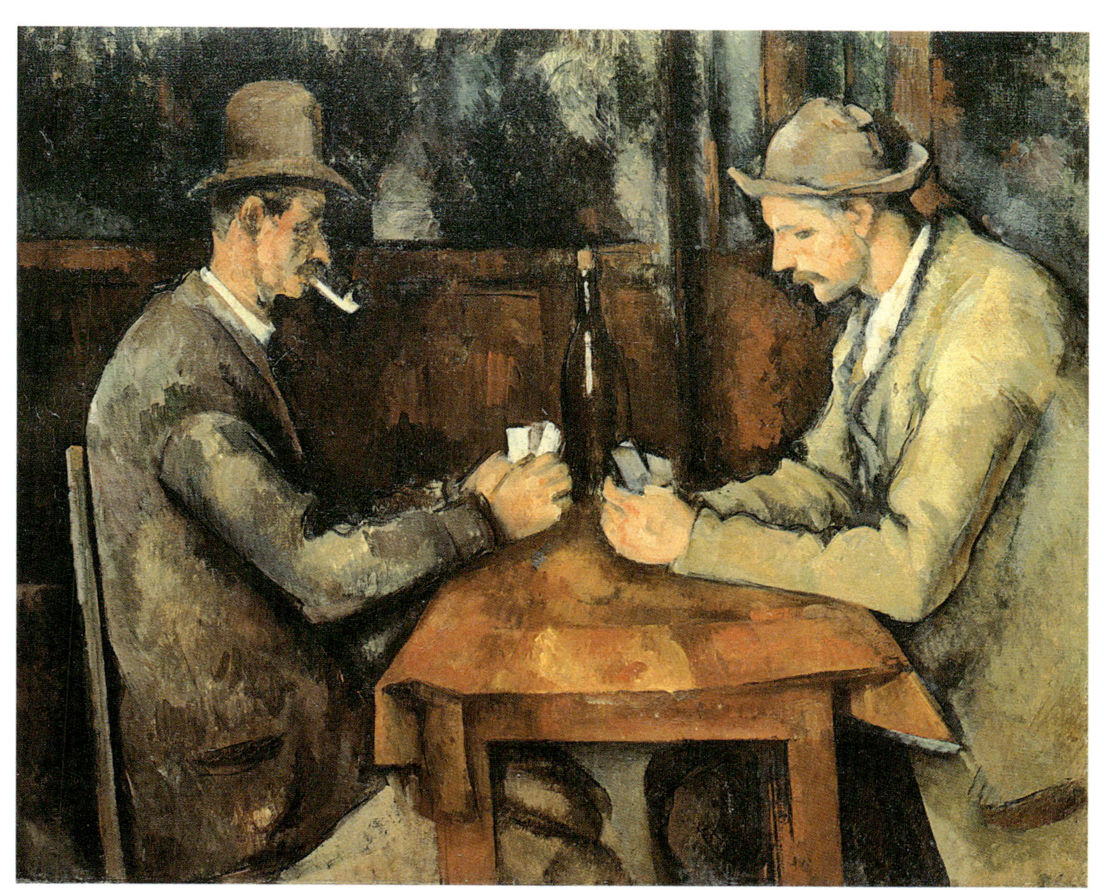

Man with Pipe Resting on a Table

1893–1896

Oil on canvas, 91 × 72 cm

Moscow, The Pushkin State Museum of Fine Arts

After the version of *The Smoker* now in the Hermitage Museum, Cézanne painted two more versions of the young farm worker at Jas de Bouffan: a half-length which is in Mannheim and this full-figure portrait in the Pushkin Museum in Moscow. The works have been dated by experts to the same period as the *Card Players* with which they share many characteristics in terms of theme and style.

Once again Cézanne decided to portray the man in his studio at Jas de Bouffan. A portrait of a woman that hangs carelessly on the wall of the little room with the edge curled has been identified as the portrait of Madame Cézanne in Detroit. Like in the painting in the Hermitage, the young farm laborer here sits tiredly on a seat, his left hand resting on one leg, his right hand supporting his head in a melancholic pose. He wears the same clothes and has his white pipe in his mouth. He looks distractedly at the painter, perhaps waiting to be told that this umpteenth and tiring session is over. And Cézanne, as in the other painting, proceeds slowly. He uses a series of delightful colors: the apparently restricted palette is in fact very rich, making use of variations of greens, blues, ochers, browns, and reds that all contribute to conferring an unexpected monumental power on the painting. Although the body of the young man is rather slender, his figure imparts a notable degree of plastic power that has prompted the art historian Lionello Venturi to comment, "The peasant depicted by Cézanne is as individual as a portrait, as universal as an idea, as solemn as a monument, and as firm as a clear conscience."

Gertrude Stein also admired many of Cézanne's paintings of farm laborers and had one in her apartment in Rue de Fleurus in Paris; it was the preparatory watercolor to the painting in Mannheim that so aroused the admiration of his painter friends, Henri Matisse and Pablo Picasso.

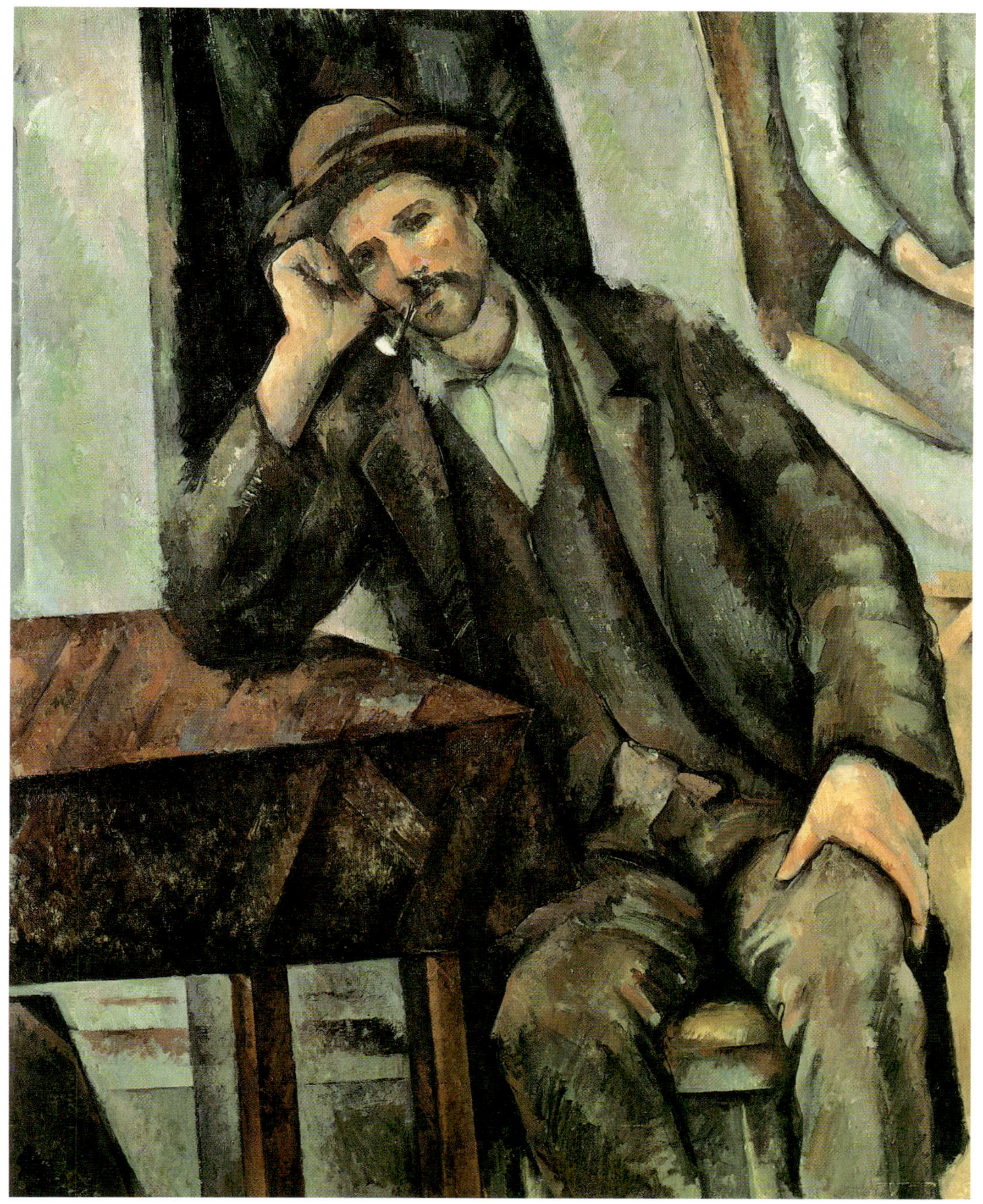

Woman with a Coffeepot

c. 1895
Oil on canvas, 130 × 97 cm
Paris, Musée d'Orsay

The core of Cézanne's artistic experimentation lay in his desire to impose formal order on his internal perceptions, and to study the underlying structure of things and their eternal quality that lies within the transience to which everything is subject. In the series of portraits he concentrated on during the last years of his career, the desire to impose stability on what is naturally in continual change became insistent and reached a level of great expressive power. The model being painted had no value in herself—what Cézanne was interested in were the volumes her body represented and the way in which she occupied space. Thus even the face of his maid, and her body made heavier by her age, could become the motif and object of a study. In this painting the woman poses for Cézanne on an invisible seat and leans slightly to her right. She appears to be held up by the straight vertical line that runs from her neck down through her skirt and which seems to flatten her against the narrow rectangular panels behind. In spite of seemingly posing in an atmosphere of calm and silence, her figure suggests she is exceedingly restless. This is intimated by the fact that her hands resting heavily on her legs appear about to move and by her furrowed brow, illuminated by mosaiclike touches of color.

Yet her most outstanding quality is that of immobility, which Cézanne stresses with the addition of the still life on the table. Cup, teaspoon, and coffeepot recreated in pure, summary forms subject the entire painting to a rigid imperative of verticality and the geometrical order Cézanne imposed on his subjects. Suspended in their own universe, the touches of his brush, the lines and forms sing in unison as they build unprecedented harmonies carefully orchestrated by the mind of the painter.

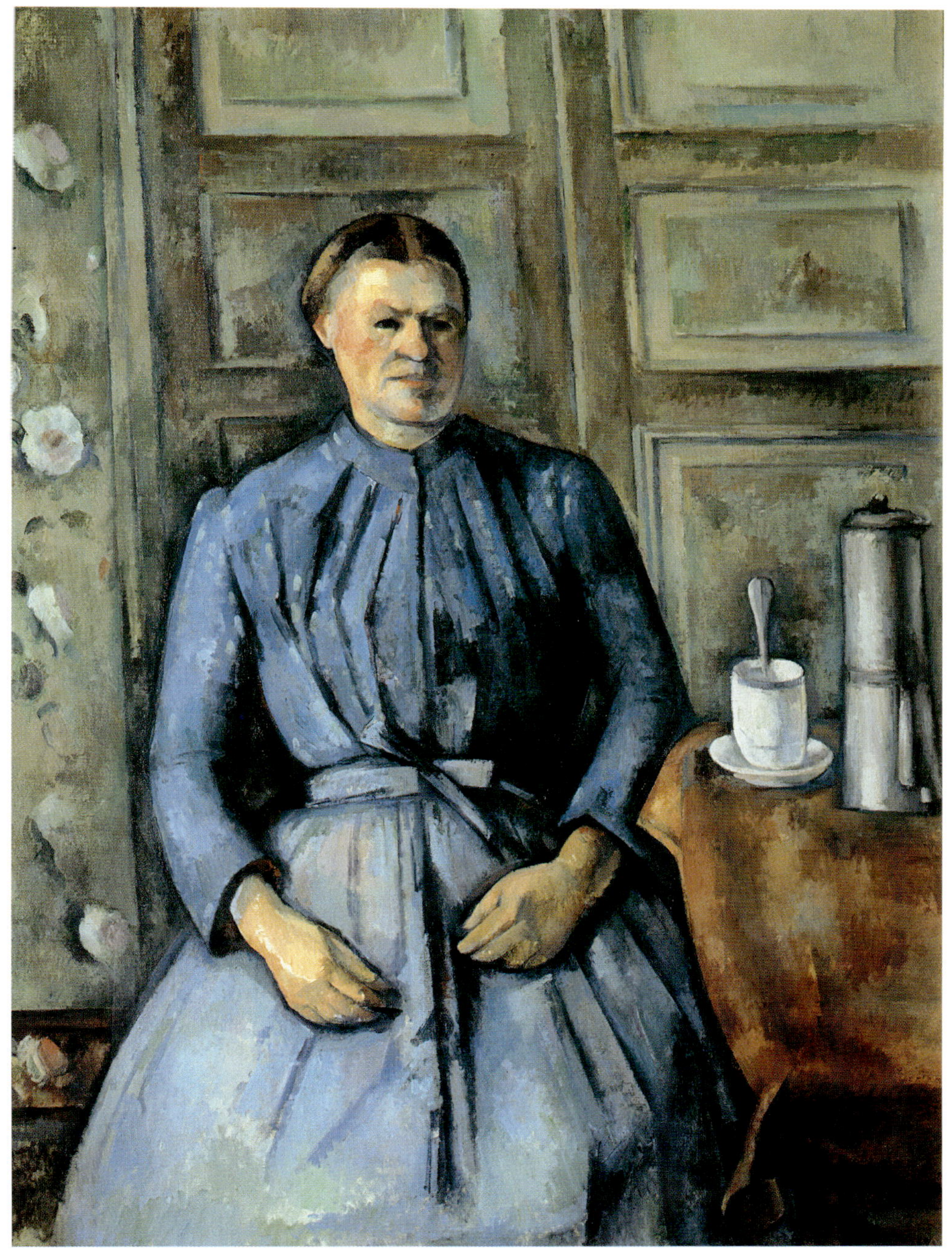

Bridge Over the Pond

1895–1898

Oil on wood, 64 × 79 cm
Moscow, The Pushkin State Museum of Fine Arts

The view of a pond crossed by a bridge and the thick and intricate vegetation in a corner of a forest reflected in the water offer Cézanne the opportunity to experiment with the subject of vision. In this painting Cézanne takes a fragment of nature and subjects it to a process of decomposition and recomposition to give mental and visual order to what is naturally subject to a continual process of change. The pond occupies much of the space of the canvas and aggressively invades the foreground. The vegetation is invasive and the painter depicts it by means of bands of vertical, horizontal and densely interwoven brushstrokes across the entire surface. He gives few indications of a macrostructure, in fact, we are only just able to make out the bridge on the left side of the painting from the colorful mosaic whose task it is to translate the chaotic and transient into order. Cézanne builds "a powerful architecture of planes, buttresses, archways, intersections and refraction" (Renato Barilli) using only color. Filled with light, its expressive possibilities are multiplied by the incredible variety of tones the painter employs. But the vast range of greens, ochers, yellows, and blues, all employed to create this powerful symphony of trees and plants, can only furnish a provisional description of the scene, as the painting is barely able to contain the vista in the narrow limitations of the canvas.

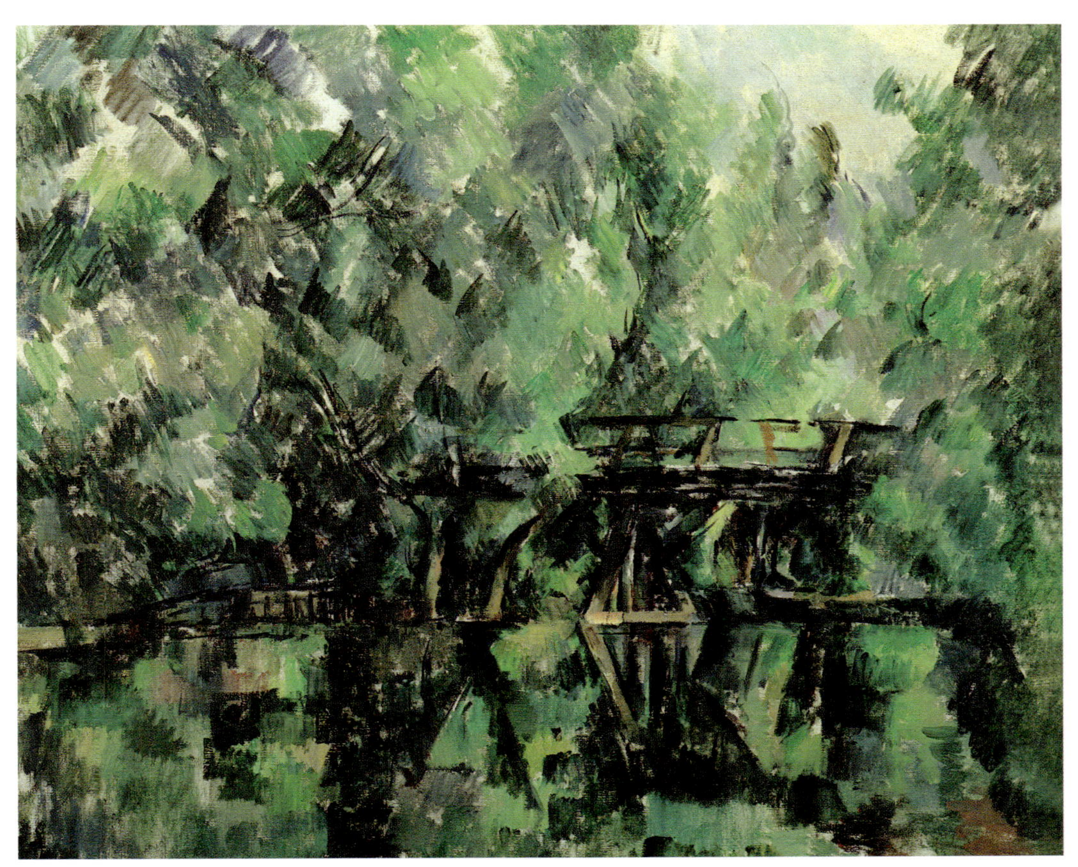

Still Life with Apples

1895–1898
Oil on canvas, 68.5 × 92.7 cm
New York, The Museum of Modern Art

Cézanne told his friend Gasquet that man-made objects, like natural ones, change every day. Apples that do not seem like apples, and which were always on the point of rolling around on the table, were for the artist a unique opportunity to investigate the subtle relationship between objects and space. Vertical lines are opposed to horizontals, and diagonal lines to circles and ellipses. The warmth engendered by reds and yellows is contrasted by the severity of blue and gray outlines. The painter chose these objects for their capability to suggest the broadest range of tactile and visual sensations, then he arranged them so he could represent those sensations using traditional pictorial means. Nothing is haphazard; everything seems meticulously organized as though it were its own universe, a reflection of secret harmonies captured by the investigative eye of the artist.

Cézanne set out his apples on the simple table. On the left a heavy floral drape acts as a backdrop and draws the eye toward the solid verticality of the hexagonal pitcher on the right, which he described with broad, clearly visible brushstrokes. Its strong linearity engages in a dialogue with the curves of the fruit and ellipse of the plate, enlivening the interplay of simple pared down forms. The chromatic power of the composition revolves around the bright reds, greens, and yellows of the different fruits depicted in their magnificent essentiality. The other tones are neutral and applied with delicate, sometimes rotating brushwork that confers a slight note of movement on the immobility that Cézanne imposes on his forms.

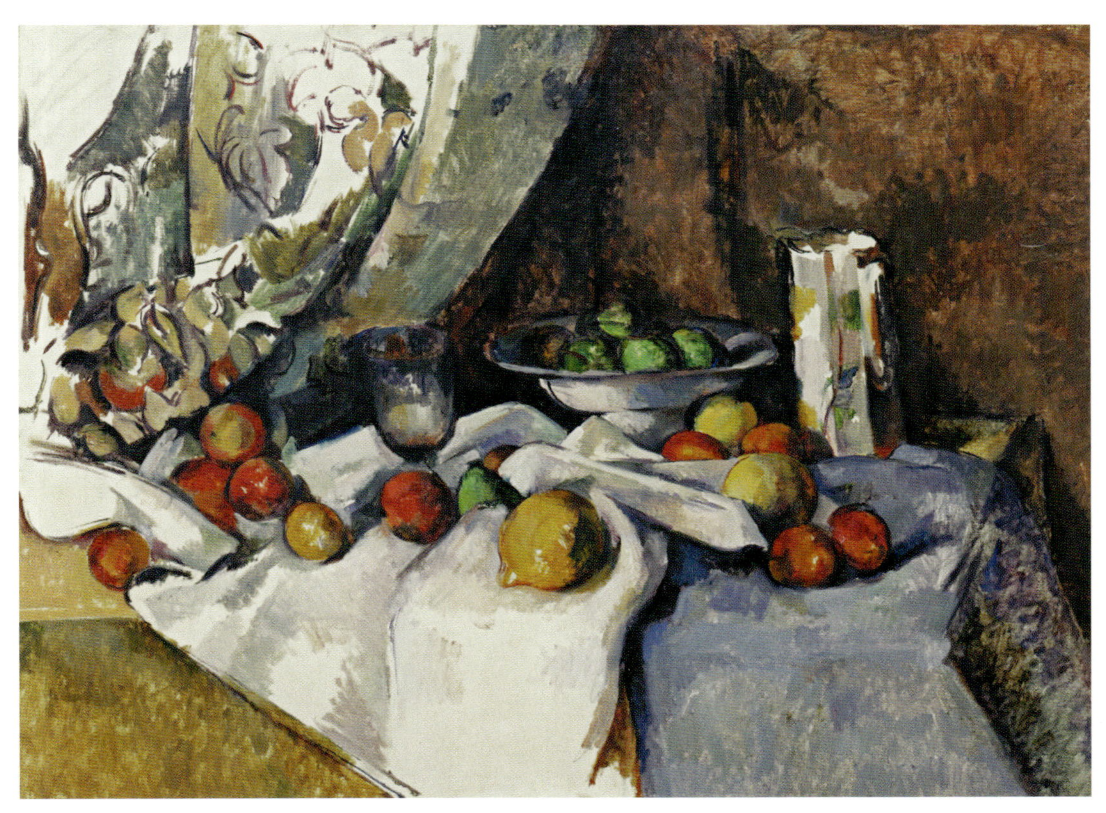

Still Life with Red Onions

1896–1898
Oil on canvas, 66 × 82 cm
Paris, Musée d'Orsay

This painting in the Musée d'Orsay is undoubtedly one of the most interesting results of Cézanne's experimentation with still lifes. In this case he took onions as his subject as they have a more complex structure and were therefore particularly suitable to his artistic research during these years, and for their "greater linear flexibility and above all for their more open and wavy form" (Meyer Schapiro).

The center of the composition is plainly set on the left side of the canvas and is given an unexpected thrust toward the observer by the slight but effective projection of the knife from under the plate. Apparently placed at random, the sequence of curves represented by the onions is countered by the sharp angles of the table in a very subtle balance of forces: the former is centrifugal and expansive, the latter containing and constructive, almost as though to underline Cézanne's constant attempt to impose order on the chaotic movement to which all things are subject.

Using delicate modulations he carefully interprets all the shades of color that his observation of nature suggests to him: employing pinks, reds, blues, and oranges he skillfully builds the forms of the onions, then dwells on the transparency of the glass, which he emphasizes by means of the play of the reflections and the faintness of its outlines. The paint has been applied thinly and the delicacy of the effects of light betrays, once again, Cézanne's interest in Spanish painting of the seventeenth century. Even the wall—perhaps the largest empty space in all of the artist's works—is given a refined treatment that produces unprecedented effects of transparency.

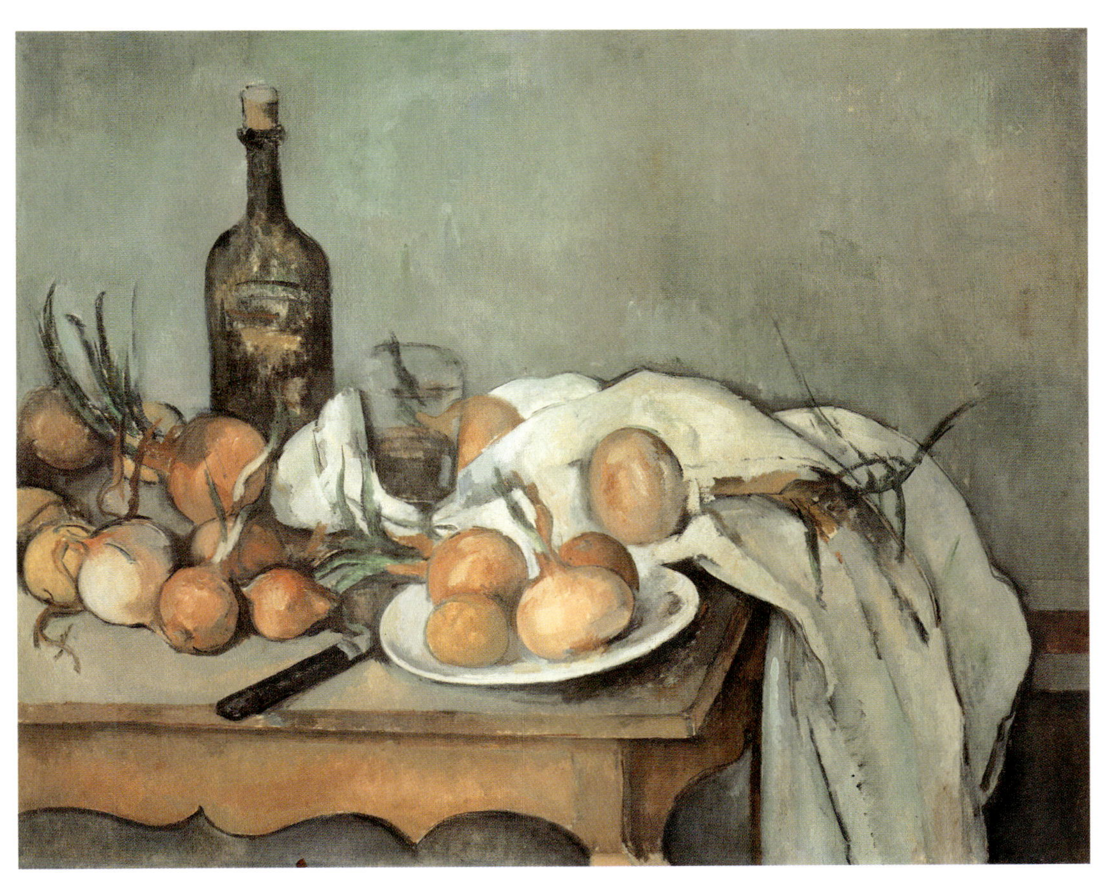

Turning Road at Montgeroult

1898
Oil on canvas, 81.2 × 66 cm
New York, The Museum of Modern Art
Digital image © 2003 Florence, The Museum of Modern Art, New York/Scala

The painting was executed in a village in the north of France, not far from Pontoise where Cézanne stayed in the summer of 1898. Montgeroult must have struck the artist for its potential to offer him the chance to study the spatial relationships between natural forms with no imposed order and the rigid constructions made by man.

The contrast between the mobility of the trees and bushes and the uniform shapes of the houses is the dominant motif in this view. The painting opens with the thick shrubs in the foreground through which the road to the village passes. The street curves steeply up the hill but gives no sense of depth to the painting, instead it brings out the strong angular thrust of the buildings over their natural surroundings. The houses at the top of the hill stand in the sun. They are created by the artist in the form of highly linear parallelepipeds whose explicit angularity is emphasized by heavy black outlines. Though we sense a keen desire for order and an impelling need to impose formal clarity on the natural environment, there remains the contrast between the rigorously geometrical elements made by the hand of man and their pulsating, organic, and formless counterparts that dominate in nature. This unresolved problem is accentuated by the distribution of the light which falls clear and strong on the houses but remains shady and dense on the vegetation which he rendered in cold, dark greens.

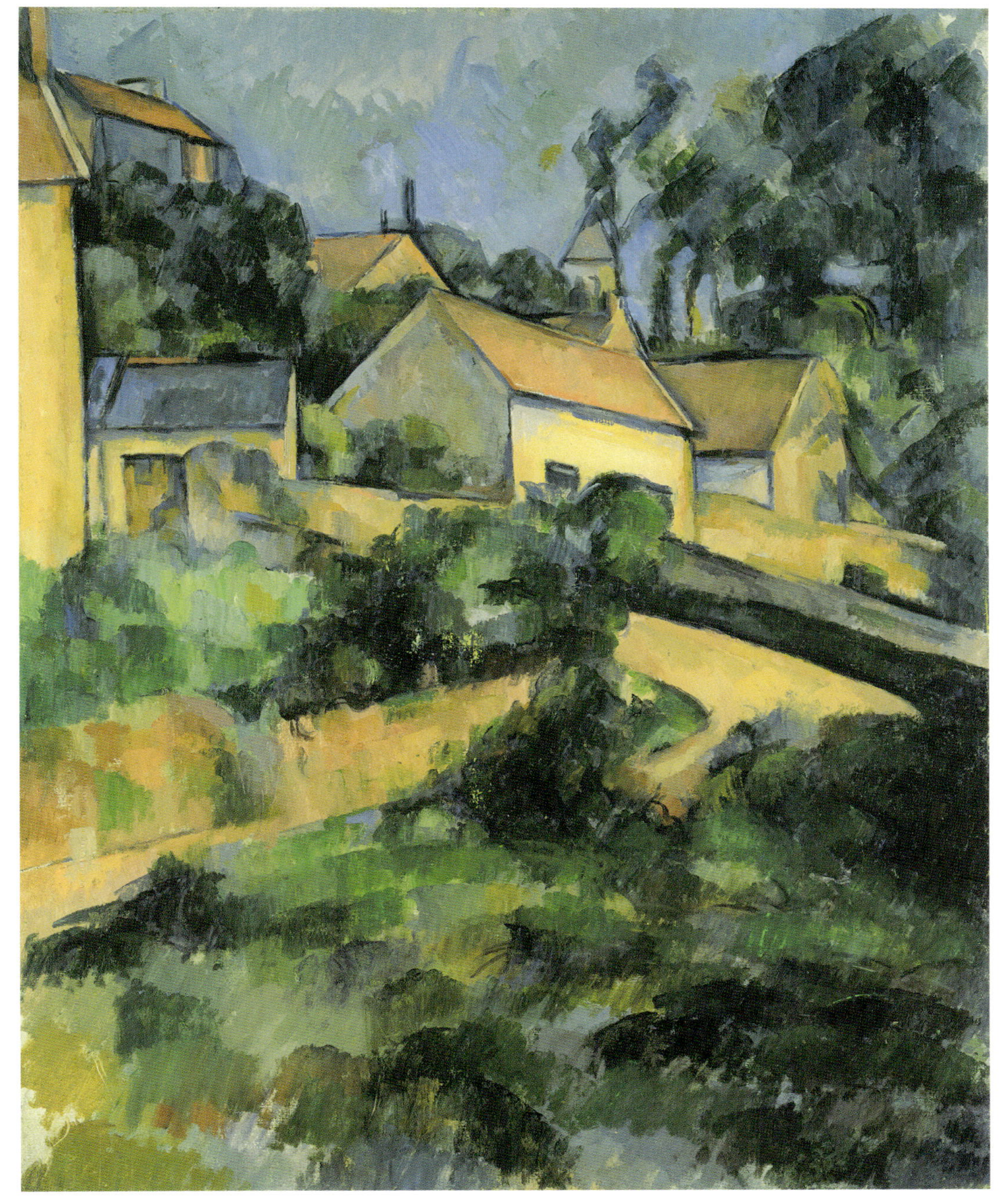

Still Life with Apples and Oranges

1899

Oil on canvas, 74 × 93 cm
Paris, Musée d'Orsay

Meyer Schapiro underlined the almost regal magnificence of this still life of apples and oranges that seems to radiate all the painter's joy in the abundance and profusion of colored objects. The space is markedly invaded by the oriental cloth with geometrical patterns over which the usual white tablecloth has been laid. With its oblique and faceted rucks and creases, the tablecloth almost seems as if it wants to absorb the splendid colors of the objects that have been placed upon it. The apples and oranges have been positioned on the table, plate and fruit bowl so that they can be viewed from different angles in order to reveal more clearly their volumes and precise pictorial function.

The painting has been constructed following the diagonal movement that runs from bottom left to right. The fruit, too, is arranged in a pyramidal shape to accentuate the dynamic ascensional effect of the composition. All contrast between depth and surface is duly masked and the objects project forward to vaunt their pure, essential forms and the manner in which they interact with space. The effect achieved is dense, almost jam-packed: the painting seems to have been orchestrated with geometric precision and it radiates the intense chromatism of the fruit in a symphony of yellows, oranges, and reds, which are reflected in the floral motif on the jug.

This is what the young artist Louis Le Bail had to say, who was present when Cézanne set out the composition: "The tablecloth was arranged on the table with great delicacy and innate taste. Cézanne then arranged the fruit so that their tonalities contrasted with one another, the complementary colors vibrated, the greens with the reds, the yellows with the blues, leaning, rolling and balancing the fruits until he found the position that he wanted, using a couple of coins for the purpose. He carried out this task with the utmost care and great caution; it was clear that to him it was a visual pleasure."

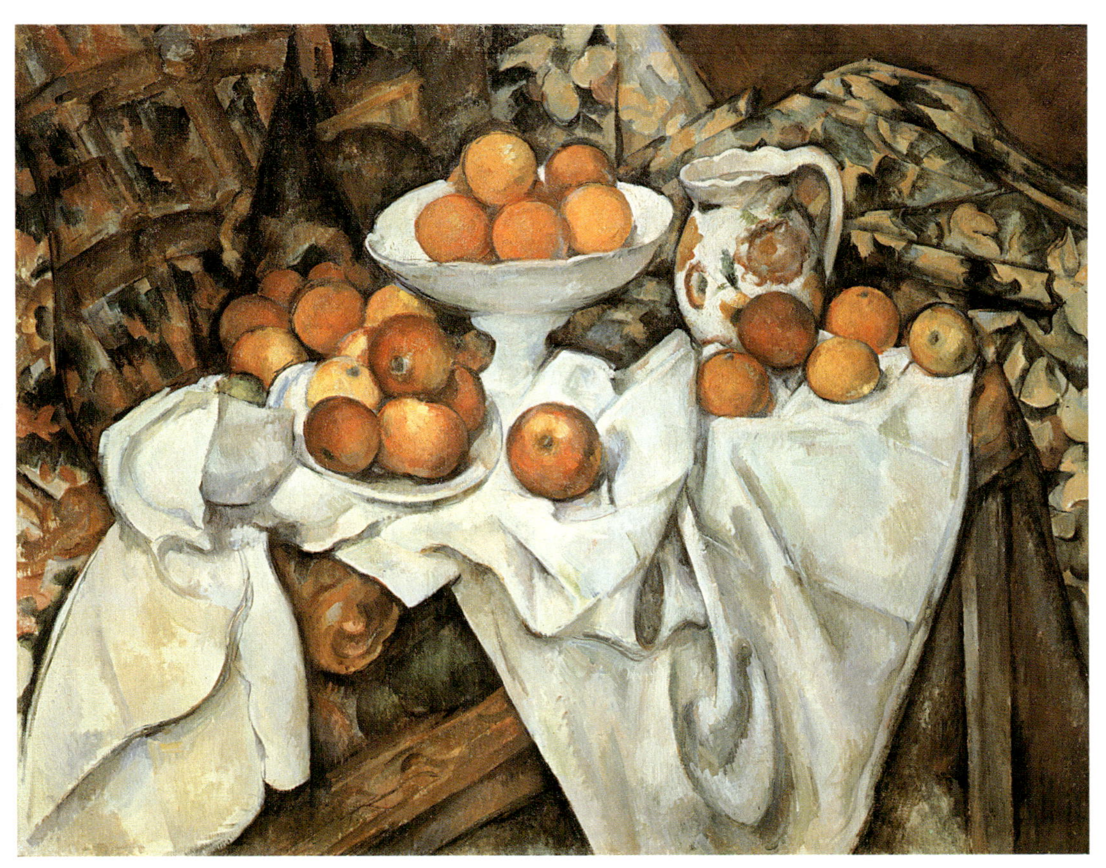

Bathers

1899–1900
Oil on canvas, 22 × 33 cm
Paris, Musée d'Orsay

There is a clear continuity between this small painting in the Musée d'Orsay and another in the same museum, which Cézanne painted in the early 1880s. This canvas appears to be a possible development of the previous composition, a sort of imaginary continuation of the scene Cézanne had already analyzed, though the number of figures has been reduced from nine to four. Like docile puppets in the skillful hands of the painter, the young bathers lay, stretch, bend, walk, and exhibit their "plastic substance." The man on the left beneath the tree, who before was shown leaning forward, is now immortalized with his right arm raised, while the monumental man with the cloth, chosen by Cézanne as the imposing protagonist in the other painting, now holds the blue cloth in his left hand and seems to be heading toward the water. The space reserved for the setting is open and wide though it is almost invaded by the thick vegetation sketched in summarily by the artist with rapid brushwork and a broad range of greens, ochers, and blues.

Fertile and dynamic, nature appears to be in complete harmony with the anatomies and tensed muscles of the young bathers who, arranged in a semicircle, create the space and are encircled by the natural world around them. A sense of limpid harmony dominates the scene: the landscape and figures are treated by Cézanne with the same close attention and rapid, darting touches of the brush that suggest we are looking at a sketch due to the freshness and immediacy of the pictorial *ductus*.

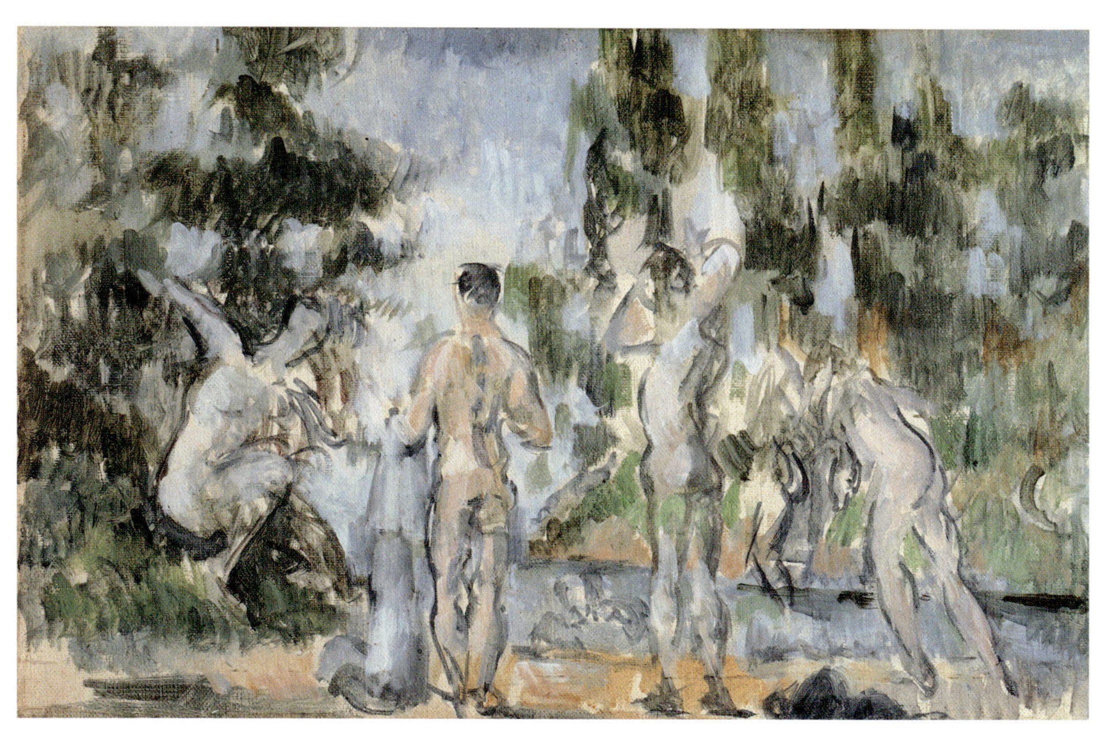

Bouquet of Flowers

1902–1904
Oil on canvas, 77 × 64 cm
Moscow, The Pushkin State Museum of Fine Arts

At the sale of the paintings that belonged to Cézanne's dear friend, Victor Chocquet, which was organized in 1899 after the death of Chocquet's widow, Ambroise Vollard purchased a watercolor by Delacroix titled *Bouquet of Flowers* for 1,325 francs. It was a watercolor that Cézanne was extremely fond of and which he considered one of the best works in Chocquet's exceptional collection. Vollard knew it and, perhaps in 1902, decided to give it to the master who wrote an affectionate letter of thanks in return. When Émile Bernard went to see Cézanne in Aix in 1904, he soon noticed the painting hung on the wall of the artist's bedroom but facing inward to protect it from the light and dust.

Cézanne adored Delacroix. In Paris he had spent a long time meditating on his predecessor's works—of his pictorial genius he appreciated above all the extraordinary chromatic power and unprecedented freedom of brushwork. Bernard wrote that Cézanne was thinking of painting an *Apotheosis of Delacroix* and had already made a sketch of it: "the Romantic master, dead, was carried by the angels; one had his brushes, the other his palette. Beneath there opened a landscape in which Pissarro, standing before his easel, was on the motif. To the right, Claude Monet, and in the foreground Cézanne, seen from behind, a pike in his hand and a game-bag at his side, wearing a vast Barbizon hat that covered his head; to the left Chocquet applauded the angels and in a corner a dog barking [a symbol of envy according to Cézanne] represented the art critics." The painting was never executed but the painter's regard for Delacroix was so high that he still felt the need to compare himself to him, and produced this enchanting and highly colorful *Bouquet of Flowers*. It is one of the rare paintings of flowers painted by Cézanne at the end of his career. Unlike the impressionists, he did not like painting them and he confessed to Joachim Gasquet on one occasion, "I have given up on flowers. They soon wither."

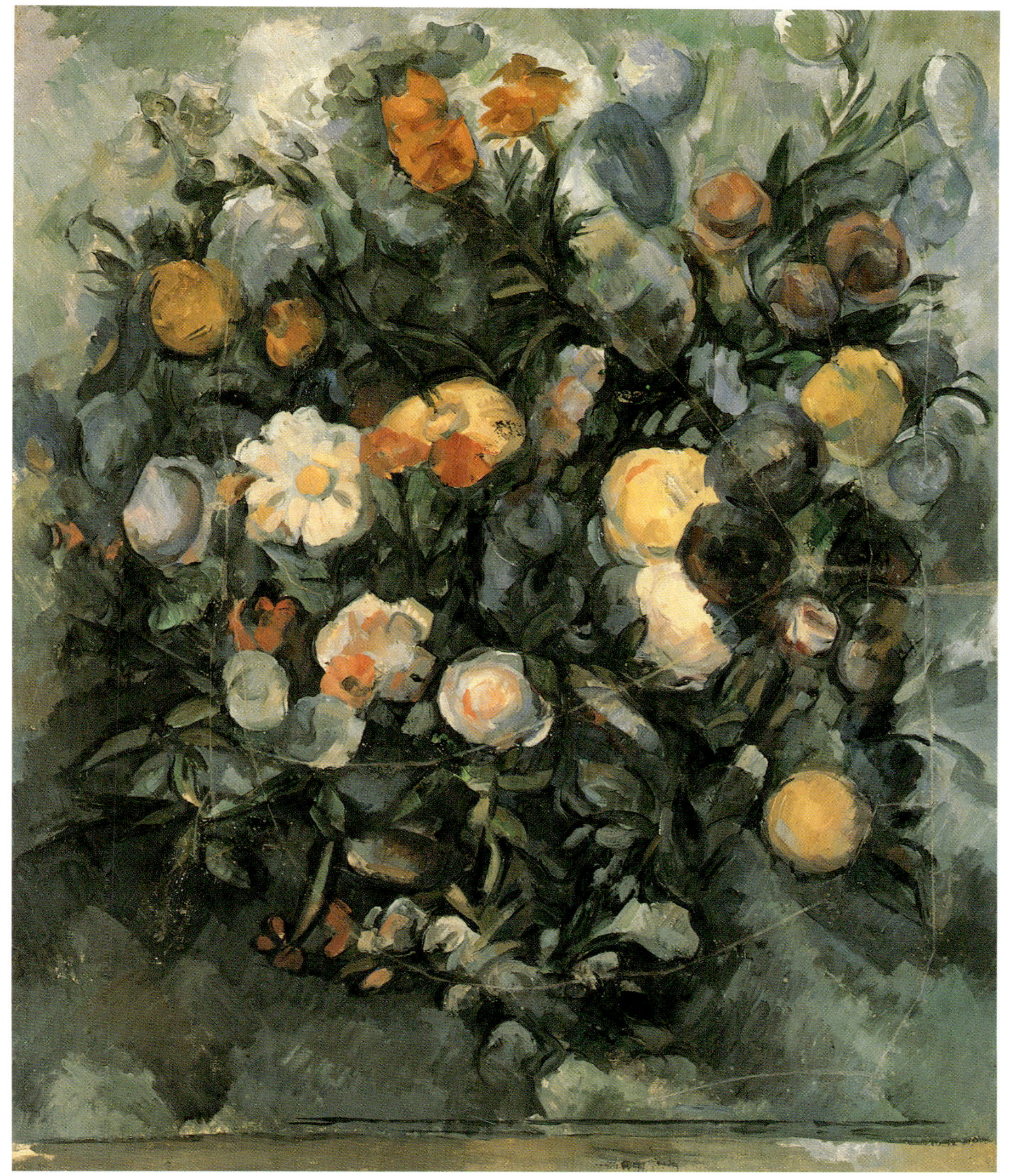

Woman in Blue

c. 1904
Oil on canvas, 88.5 × 72 cm
St. Petersburg, The State Hermitage Museum

A woman in blue sitting tiredly on a seat, her left hand resting on a table, with an absorbed expression filled with a wistful melancholy. This was one of the last female portraits painted by Cézanne, who was by this time at the end of his career. Executed perhaps in his studio in Lauves, the woman who posed for him was not Hortense, his wife and favorite model; the features are different but she is similar to a woman in another painting, *Woman with a Book*, today in Washington. According to Cachin, it might be Madame Brémond, the artist's housekeeper who lived with him in Rue Boulegon in Aix and was an excellent cook. Émile Bernard met her when he visited Cézanne in Provence in 1904 and soon noticed the woman's sincere attachment to the painter, whose bizarre behavior she tolerated with patience, for example, his requirement "to always pass by him without touching him, even with her skirt."

Cézanne's portrait of her is imbued with a great power of expression. Her figure is almost monumental and his refined use of color has allowed the chromatic modulations to define the volumes by themselves. Blue on blue, tone on tone: using masterly touches of pink, Cézanne highlights those parts of her figure that are most prominent and, with the use of a black outline, he gives her a greater degree of three-dimensionality. The colors he uses are bright and luminous: from pink he passes to pale yellow, then emerald green and finally the "local tone" of the cobalt blue with which he defines part of the background. The figure of the woman stands out vigorously against an abstract and unreal wall, partly as a result of the complex perspective that frames her and which pushes her forward toward the foreground. The corner of the table is characterized by a strong diagonal that seems to project beyond the narrow limits of the canvas toward the space occupied by the observer.

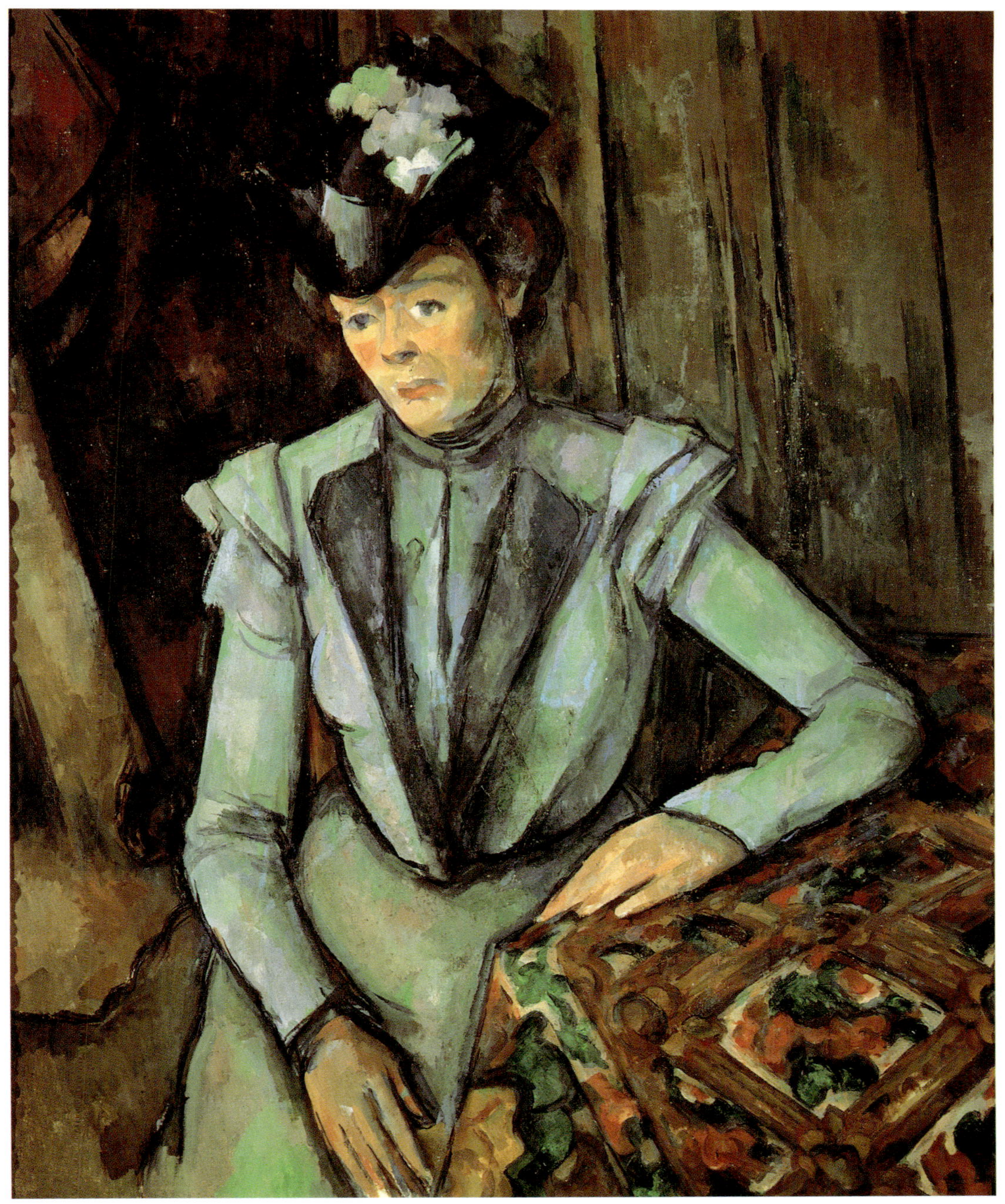

Mont Sainte-Victoire Seen from Les Lauves

1905
Oil on canvas, 60 × 72 cm
Basel, Kunstmuseum

The limestone massif of Mont Sainte-Victoire, with its characteristic peak right of center, dominates the valley near Aix-en-Provence. Its mysterious beauty attracted Cézanne and he worked tirelessly on this theme for over twenty years, producing a large number of drawings, watercolors, and oil paintings. The mountain appeared for the first time in his painting in the 1870s when it provided the backdrop to *The Railway Cutting*. He painted it from different angles continuously in the years that followed, concentrating on its profile, its massive monumentality, and the desire to impose order and control on nature.

When in 1901 Cézanne purchased the property of Les Lauves to the north of Aix and set up his studio there, it was Mont Sainte-Victoire that he saw from his terrace; with his customary doggedness he continued to paint its forms of the mountain and its valley. Between 1902 and 1906 it was a constant presence in his works, almost an obsession. He observed it for long periods and painted it with enthusiasm, trying to render, in its forms and subtleties of color, the mountain's profound sense of nature and the permanence of its structure.

The painting in the Kunstmuseum Basel represents one of the highest points Cézanne achieved in the depiction of the relation between form and color. He breaks nature down into a mosaic of colors so that the painting only exists through tonal modulations and relationships. His vision and the forms he wished to represent emerge from the pattern of colored tiles: the foliage in the valley blurs with the sky as do the houses and the trees. Only the profile of the mountain on the horizon remains recognizable, composed of dark and lighter blues and whites to emphasize its monumental presence.

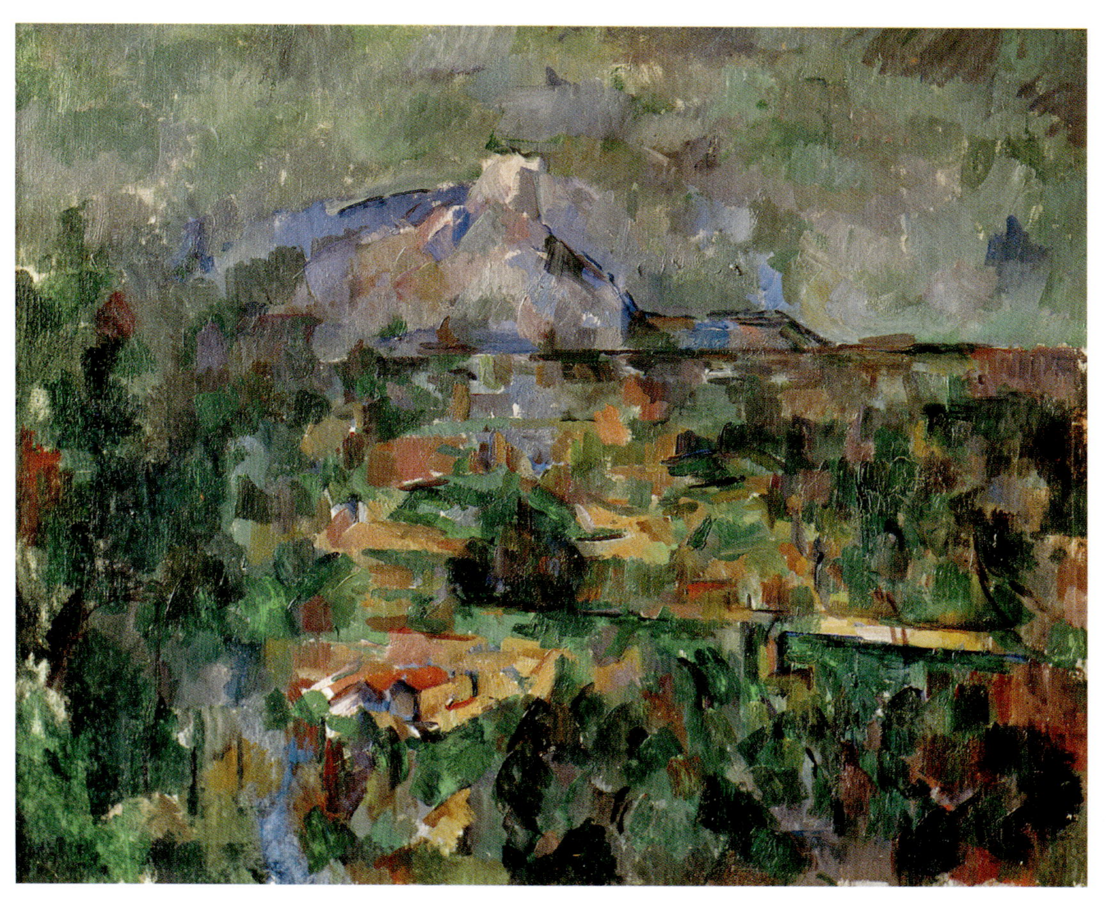

Mont Sainte-Victoire

1905

Oil on canvas, 63.5 × 83 cm
Zurich, Kunsthaus

Meyer Schapiro observed how Cézanne's painting in the last years of his career had become extraordinarily free. The intensity of expression he infused into the "romantic works of his youth" reappeared in a new form, as a "rhapsody of colors" that included the earth and mountain in a single hymn. It was color that he used to reconstruct his vision of nature on the canvas, a technique that took him to within a step of abstraction. In the vibrant interplay of the mosaics of color he produced, Cézanne discovered how to grasp not just the essence of things but also their spiritual dimension. Émile Bernard wrote to his mother on February 5, 1904, "He sees in small tones. His canvases are made up of tiny sections. Everywhere he leaves whites [...] proceeding from the details and completing some parts before taking the whole forward together."

This process *à la Ingres* is clearly followed in this painting in which the "whites" (the unpainted sections of the canvas) mentioned by Bernard can be seen, whereas the rest of the surface is covered with myriad vertical brushstrokes that play on chromatic contrasts to suggest forms and depth. Every element is represented by the daring chromatic mosaic which he rendered using just a few earthy and greenish tones applied with the painter's usual meticulous care. Nature for Cézanne was exclusively expressed "through patches of color that follow one another according to a law of harmony." No line or modeling exists, "just the contrasts" that strike the artist's perception as *chromatic sensation*. "The smell of the pines, which is harsh in the sun," he said, "must be matched with the green smell of the grass, the smell of the stones, and the smell of the distant marble of Mont Sainte-Victoire. It is this that must be rendered: and only using colors, without literature."

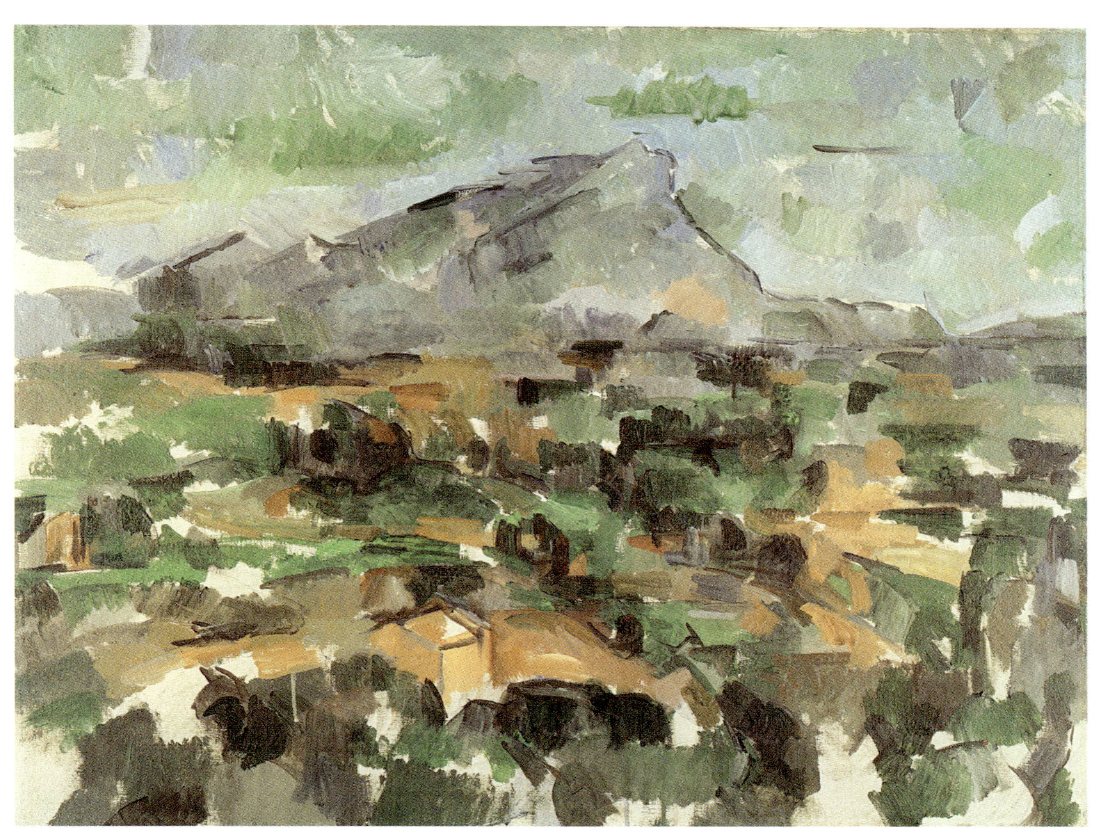

The Bathers

1906
Oil on canvas, 208 × 251 cm
Philadelphia, Philadelphia Museum of Art

Painted after long study, this is the largest canvas Cézanne produced in his series of bathers. During the last period of his career he returned to the theme with new determination, achieving effects of extraordinary monumentality and expressive power. The topics of form and the spatial relationships between figures and their setting reached surprising levels in this painting, resulting in one of the artist's most fascinating contributions to the avant-garde art of the early twentieth century.

In an open landscape bathed by a fluctuating, cerulean light, Cézanne carefully arranged his figures to give them the maximum expressiveness. He represented the dehumanized female body in the form of pure volumes to construct the space; he makes it twist, hunch up, and conform to the movement of the trees in order to display its material quality. These women are not provocative, no longer the languid temptresses of his paintings of the 1870s, but "herds of monstrous walruses interested in nothing but display, of opening to our perception their heavy flesh" (Renato Barilli). They are easygoing puppets that the artist arranges on his canvas to demonstrate spatial relationships.

Yet the painting—composed of patches of color employed by Cézanne to construct forms and reflect light—is permeated by an atmosphere of atavistic purity. A body of water lies beyond the two trees that act as a curtain to the scene and which embrace the figures gathered on the bank. From there our gaze runs to the other bank and the horizon, where, like Cézanne, we can imagine a timeless world consisting of silence, contemplation and the harmonious and subtle relationships between things.

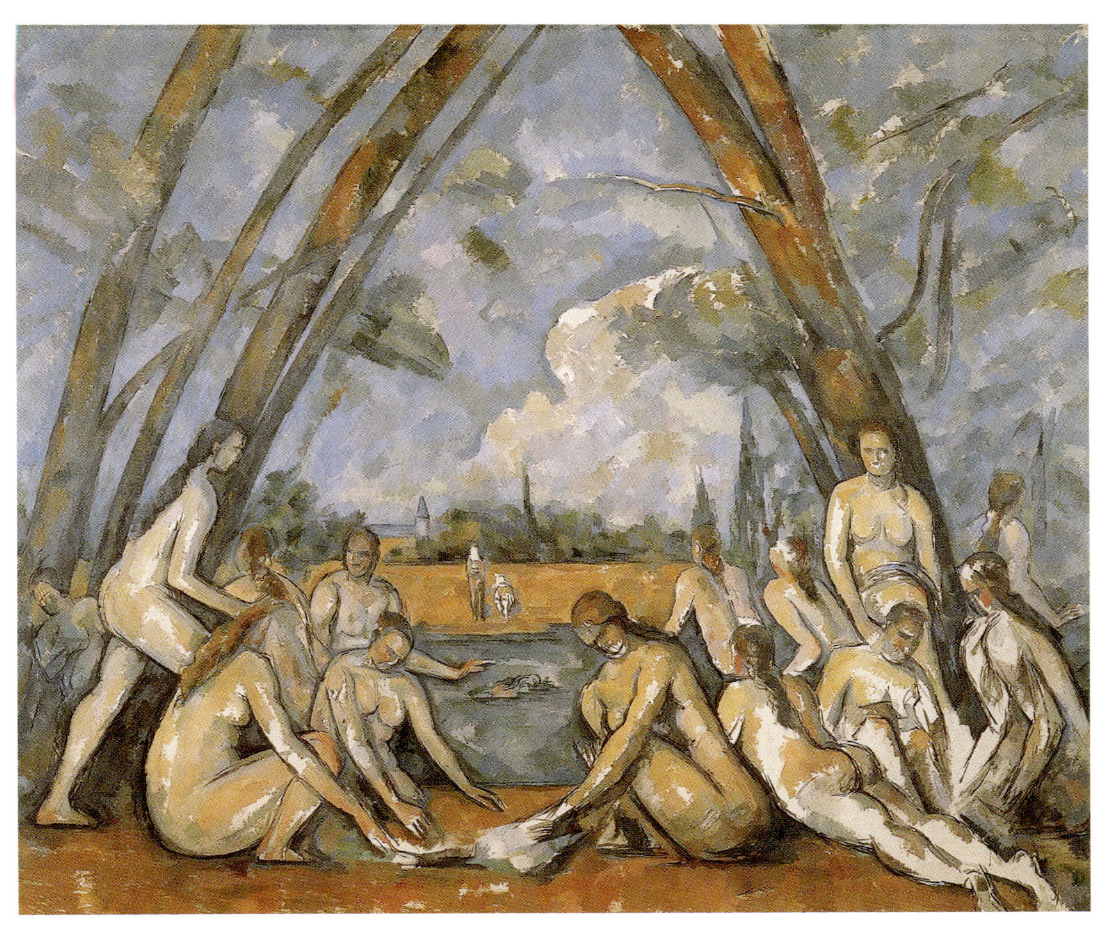

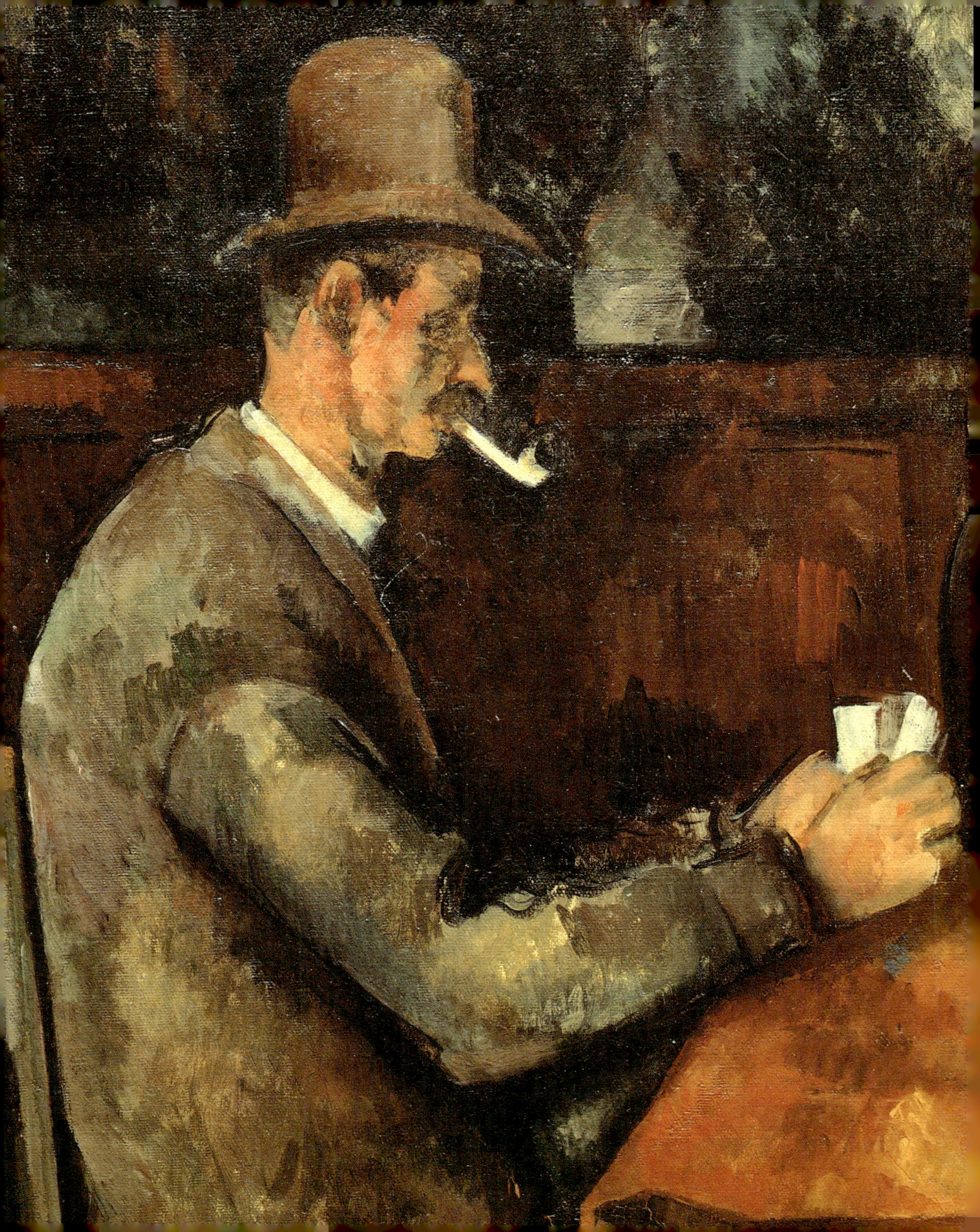

Appendix

Card Players
(detail), 1893–1896
Paris, Musée d'Orsay

Chronological Table

	Life of Cézanne	Historical and Artistic Events
1839	Paul Cézanne is born on 19 January in Aix-en-Provence.	Alfred Sisley is born in Paris.
1848		Louis Philippe forced to abdicate and presidential republic proclaimed in France.
1852	Attends Collège Bourbon. Begins his long friendship with Zola.	Louis Bonaparte becomes emperor under the title of Napoleon III.
1859	Studies law at the University of Aix. His father buys the house and farm of Jas de Bouffan on the outskirts of the city.	Work begins on the Suez Canal. Georges Seurat is born in Paris.
1861	In Paris, at the Académie Suisse, meets Pissarro.	
1863	Exhibits at the Salon des Refusés.	Manet exhibits his *Déjeuner sur l'herbe* at the Salon des Refusés.
1864	Spends the summer in Aix-en-Provence. Rejected by the Salon.	A retrospective of Daumier's work opens in Paris.
1865	Becomes a friend of Antony Valabrègue.	Manet exhibits *Olympia* at the Salon.
1869	Meets the model Hortense Fiquet.	Opening of the Suez Canal.
1871	Birth of his son Paul. Moves to Auvers-sur-Oise, where he lives near Dr. Gachet.	Proclamation of the Paris Commune.
1873	Meets the paint merchant Père Tanguy in Paris.	Foundation of the Société anonyme des artistes, peintres, sculpteurs, graveurs etc.
1874	Participates in the first exhibition of the Impressionists with *A Modern Olympia.*	First Impressionist exhibition in the studio of the photographer Nadar in Paris.
1877	Exhibits for the last time with the Impressionists.	Third Impressionist exhibition. Renoir exhibits the *Moulin de la Galette.*
1878	Spends the year in Provence with Hortense and his son and Paul.	
1880	Meets Huysmans in Médan, at Zola's house.	Fifth Impressionist exhibition; the young Gauguin participates. Flaubert dies.

	Life of Cézanne	Historical and Artistic Events
1881	Meets Gauguin in Pontoise, at Pissarro's house.	Sixth Impressionist exhibition. Manet receives the Legion of Honor.
1882	Winter in L'Estaque, where Renoir visits him.	Seventh Impressionist exhibition.
1884	Gauguin and Signac buy some of his paintings.	Retrospective of Manet's work at the École des Beaux-Arts in Paris.
1886	Marries Hortense Fiquet. Zola publishes *L'Oeuvre*.	Eighth and last Impressionist exhibition. Seurat and Signac take part for the first time.
1889	The *House of the Hanged Man* shown at the Paris World's Fair of 1889.	Monet organizes a subscription to buy Manet's *Olympia* for presentation to the Louvre.
1895	Exhibition of Cézanne's works organized by Vollard, who becomes his dealer.	The Dreyfus Affair explodes in France.
1897	Death of his mother. Paints Mont Sainte-Victoire.	Émile Zola writes his *J'accuse*.
1900	Some of his paintings shown in Berlin in the exhibition organized by Paul Cassirer.	
1903	Exhibits a number of works at the Vienna and Berlin Secessions.	
1904	The Salon d'Automne devotes a room to him with thirty paintings and two drawings.	
1905		Birth of the Fauves group in Paris.
1906	In October, caught in a storm while painting in the open air, falls sick, dying on 22 of the same month.	The French supreme court of appeals rehabilitates Dreyfus.
1907	Vast commemorative exhibition at the Salon d'Automne.	Pablo Picasso paints *Les demoiselles d'Avignon*.

Geographical Locations of the Paintings

Italy

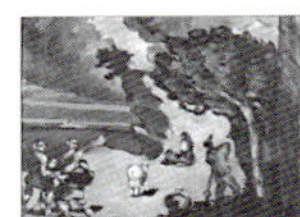

The Robbers and the Donkey
Oil on canvas, 41 x 55 cm
Milan, Civica Galleria d'Arte Moderna
1870

Brazil

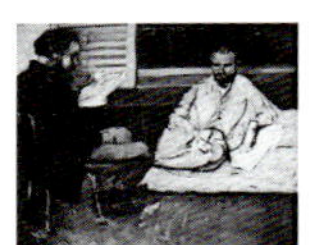

Paul Alexis Reading to Émile Zola
Oil on canvas, 130 x 160 cm
São Paulo, Museu de Arte
1869–1870

France

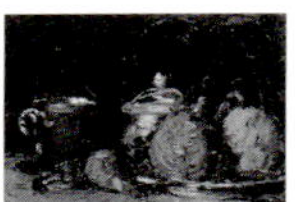

Still-life (sugar bowl, pears and blue cup)
Oil on canvas, 30 x 41 cm
Paris, Musée d'Orsay (on deposit at the Musée Granet, Aix-en-Provence)
*c.*1866

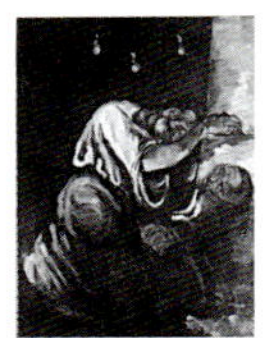

Sorrow – or The Magdalen
Oil on canvas, 165 x 124 cm
Paris, Musée d'Orsay
1865–1868

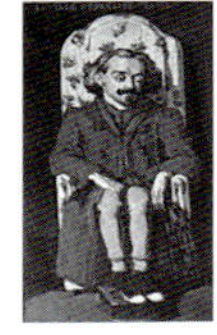

Portrait of Achille Emperaire
Oil on canvas, 200 x 122 cm
Paris, Musée d'Orsay
1867–1868

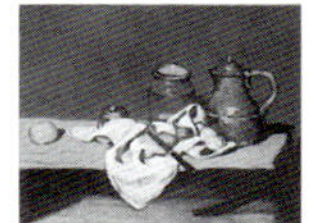

Still-life with Green Pot and Pewter Jug
Oil on canvas, 64 x 81 cm
Paris, Musée d'Orsay

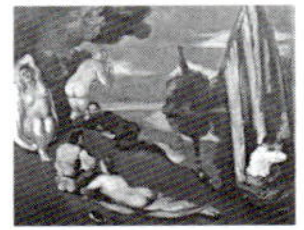

Pastoral
Oil on canvas, 65 x 81 cm
Paris, Musée d'Orsay
1870

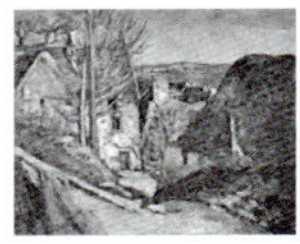

The House of the Hanged Man
Oil on canvas, 55 x 66 cm
Paris, Musée d'Orsay
1872–1873

France

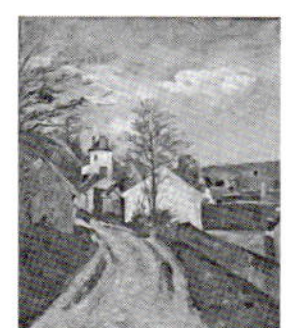

The House of Dr Gachet
Oil on canvas, 46 x 38 cm
Paris, Musée d'Orsay
1872–1873

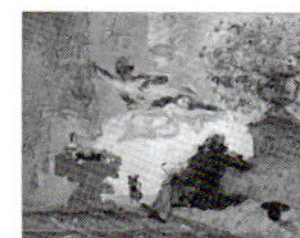

A Modern Olympia
Oil on canvas, 46 x 55 cm
Paris, Musée d'Orsay
1873–1874

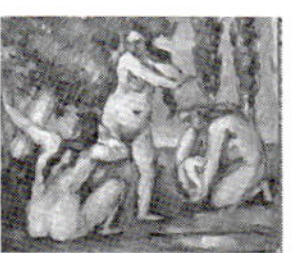

Three Bathers
Oil on canvas, 19 x 22 cm
Paris, Musée d'Orsay
1874–1875

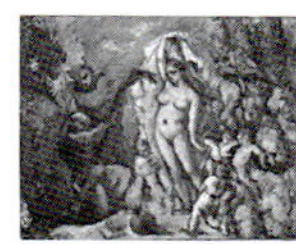

The Temptation of Saint Anthony
Oil on canvas, 47 x 56 cm
Paris, Musée d'Orsay
1875–1877

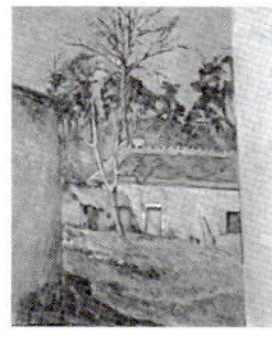

Farmyard in Auvers
Oil on canvas, 65 x 54 cm
Paris, Musée d'Orsay
*c.*1879

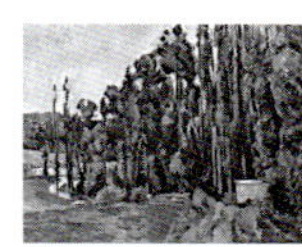

Poplars
Oil on canvas, 65 x 80 cm
Paris, Musée d'Orsay
1879–1880

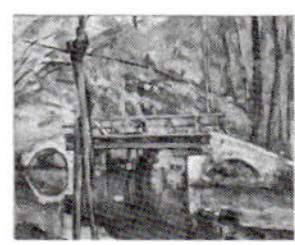

The Bridge at Maincy
Oil on canvas, 60 x 73 cm
Paris, Musée d'Orsay
1879–1880

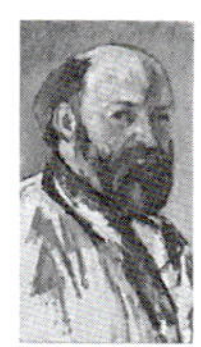

Self-portrait
Oil on canvas, 26 x 15 cm
Paris, Musée d'Orsay
1880

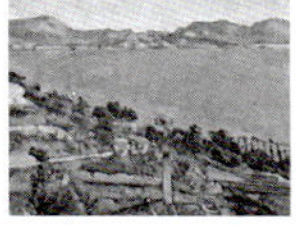

L'Estaque
Oil on canvas, 65 x 54 cm
Paris, Musée d'Orsay
1882–1885

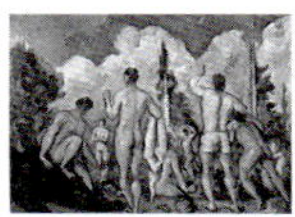

Bathers
Oil on canvas, 60 x 81 cm
Paris, Musée d'Orsay
*c.*1890

France

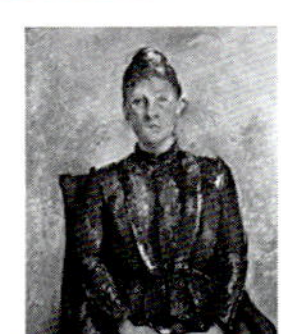

Portrait of Madame Cézanne
Oil on canvas, 81 x 65 cm
Paris, Musée de l'Orangerie
*c.*1890

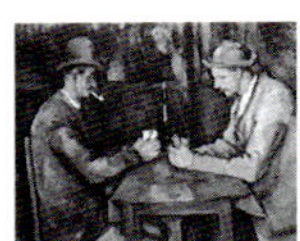

Card Players
Oil on canvas, 47 x 56 cm
Paris, Musée d'Orsay
1893–1896

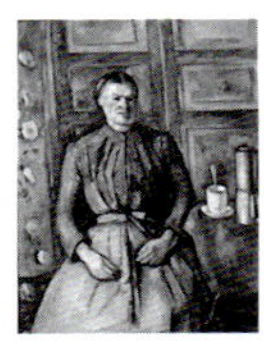

Woman with a Coffee Pot
Oil on canvas, 130 x 97 cm
Paris, Musée d'Orsay
*c.*1895

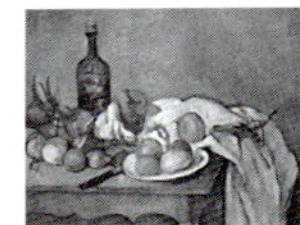

Still-life with Red Onions
Oil on canvas, 66 x 82 cm
Paris, Musée d'Orsay
1896–1898

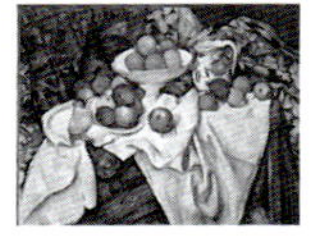

Still-life with Apples and Oranges
Oil on canvas, 74 x 93 cm
Paris, Musée d'Orsay
1899

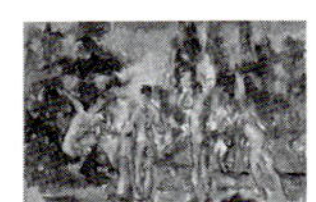

Bathers
Oil on canvas, 22 x 33 cm
Paris, Musée d'Orsay
1899–1900

Germany

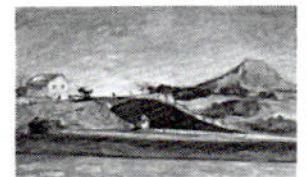

The Railway Cutting
Oil on canvas, 80 x 129 cm
Munich, Neue Pinakothek
1870

Russia

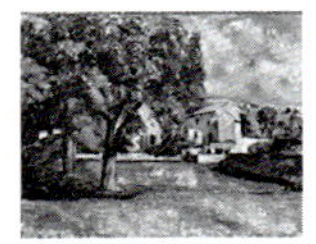

Chestnut Trees and Farm at Jas-De-Bouffan
Oil on canvas, 72 x 91 cm
Moscow, Pushkin Museum
*c.*1886

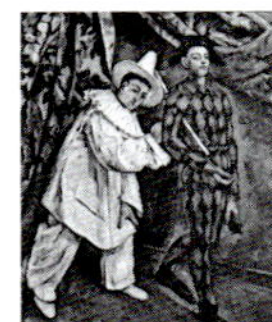

Pierrot and Harlequin (Mardi Gras)
Oil on canvas, 102 x 81 cm
Moscow, Pushkin Museum
1888

Russia

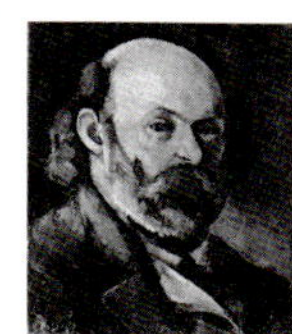

Self-portrait
Oil on canvas, 46 x 38 cm
Moscow, Pushkin Museum
*c.*1882

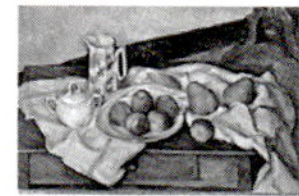

Sugar Bowl, Jug and Plate of Fruit
Oil on canvas, 61 x 90 cm
Moscow, Pushkin Museum
*c.*1890

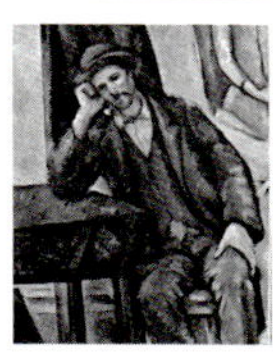

Man with Pipe Resting on a Table
Oil on canvas, 91 x 72 cm
Moscow, Pushkin Museum
1893–1896

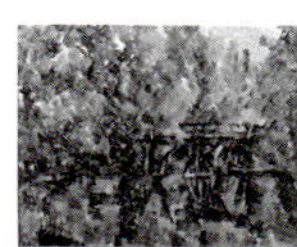

Bridge Over the Pond
Oil on wood, 64 x 79 cm
Moscow, Pushkin Museum
1895–1898

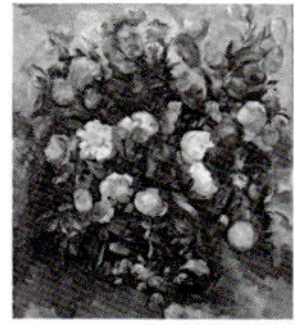

Bouquet of Flowers
Oil on canvas, 77 x 64 cm
Moscow, Pushkin Museum
1902–1904

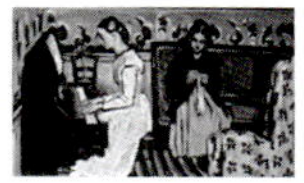

Young Girl at the Piano – Overture to Tannhauser
Oil on canvas, 57 x 92 cm
St Petersburg, The State Hermitage Museum
*c.*1869

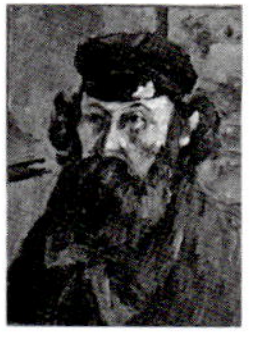

Self-portrait in a Casquette
Oil on canvas, 53 x 38 cm
St Petersburg, The State Hermitage Museum
*c.*1875

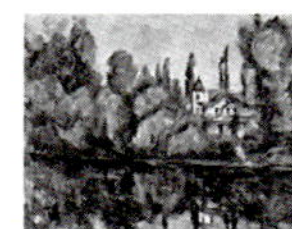

The Banks of the Marne
Oil on canvas, 65 x 81 cm
St Petersburg, The State Hermitage Museum
1888–1890

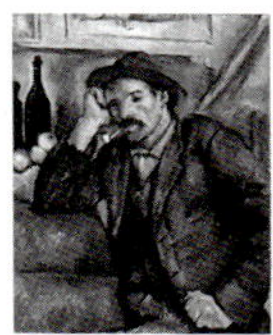

The Smoker
Oil on canvas, 91 x 72 cm
St Petersburg, The State Hermitage Museum
*c.*1891

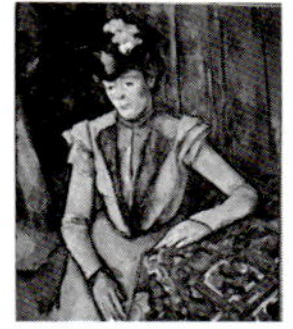

Woman in Blue
Oil on canvas, 88.5 x 72 cm
St Petersburg, The State Hermitage Museum
*c.*1904

Switzerland

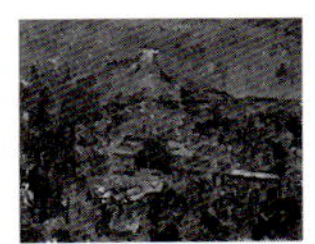

Mont Sainte-Victoire Seen From Les Lauves
Oil on canvas, 60 x 72 cm
Basel, Kunstmuseum
1905

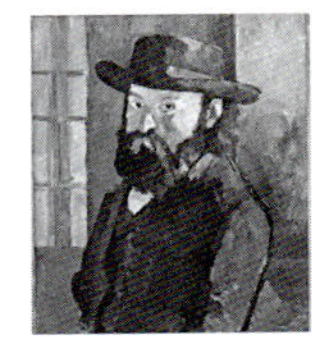

Self-portrait with Hat
Oil on canvas, 65 x 51 cm
Bern, Kunstmuseum
1879–1880

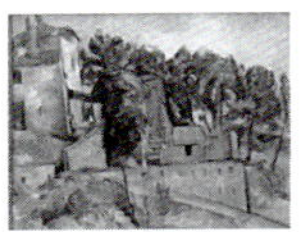

The House at Bellevue
Oil on canvas, 60 x 73 cm
Geneva, Musée d'Art et d'Histoire
1890

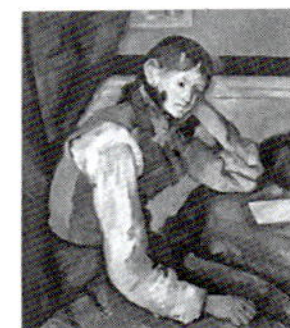

Boy in a Red Vest
Oil on canvas, 79.5 x 64 cm
Zurich, Bührle Foundation
1888–1890

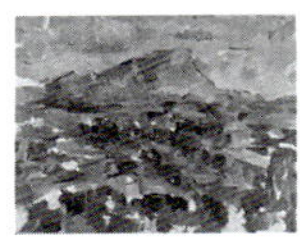

Mont Sainte-Victoire
Oil on canvas, 63.5 x 83 cm
Zurich, Kunsthaus
1905

United States

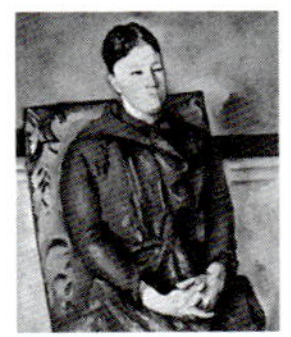

Madame Cézanne in a Yellow Chair
Oil on canvas, 81 x 65 cm
Chicago, The Art Institute
1888–1890

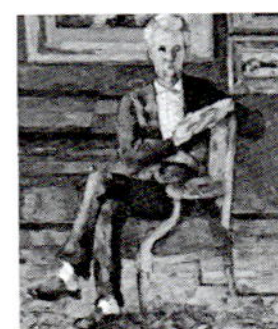

Portrait of Victor Chocquet
Oil on canvas, 46 x 38 cm
Columbus (Ohio), Columbus Museum of Art
1877

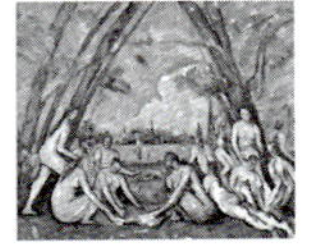

Large Bathers
Oil on canvas, 208 x 251 cm
Philadelphia (Pennsylvania), Philadelphia Museum of Art
1906

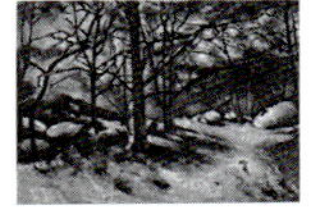

Melting Snow, Fontainebleau
Oil on canvas, 76.6 x 100.6 cm
New York, The Museum of Modern Art Digital image © 2003 Florence, The Museum of Modern Art, New York/Scala
1879–1880

United States

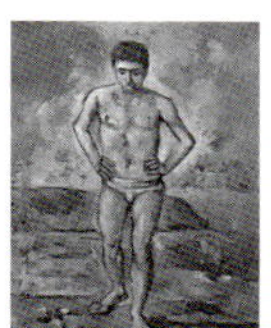

Bather
Oil on canvas, 127 x 96.8 cm
New York, The Museum of Modern Art Digital image © 2003 Florence, The Museum of Modern Art, New York/Scala
*c.*1885

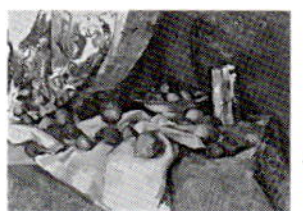

Still-life with Apples
Oil on canvas, 68.5 x 92.7 cm
New York, The Museum of Modern Art Digital image © 2003 Florence, The Museum of Modern Art, New York/Scala
1895–1898

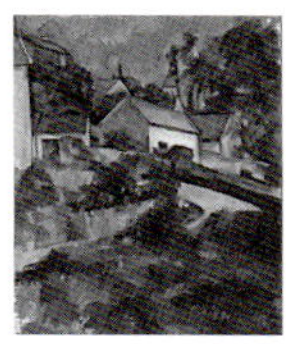

Turning Road at Montgeroult
Oil on canvas, 81.2 x 66 cm
New York, The Museum of Modern Art Digital image © 2003 Florence, The Museum of Modern Art, New York/Scala
1898

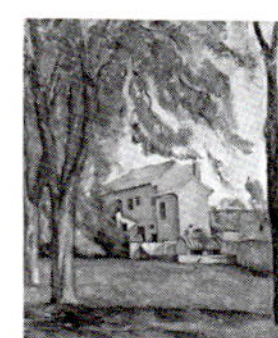

Farmhouse and Chestnut Trees at Jas-De-Bouffan
Oil on canvas, 92 x 73.7 cm
Pasadena (California), Norton Simon Museum
*c.*1884

Writings

Letter to Pissarro, July 1876

It's like a playing card. Red roofs over the blue sea [...]. The sun here is so tremendous that it seems to me as if the objects were silhouetted not only in black and white, but in blue, red, brown and violet. I may be mistaken, but this seems to me to be the opposite of modelling.

Letter to Emile Zola, May 1883

I have rented a little house and garden at L'Estaque just above the station and at the foot of the hill where behind me rise the rocks and the pines.

I am still busy painting—I have here some beautiful views but they do not make motifs—. Nevertheless, climbing the hills as the sun goes down one has a glorious view of Marseilles in the background and the islands, all enveloped towards evening to very decorative effect.

Letter to Louis Autenche, January 1904

In your letter you speak of my realization in art. I believe that I attain it more every day, although a bit laboriously. Because, if the strong feeling for nature—and certainly I have that vividly—is the necessary basis for all artistic conception on which rests the grandeur and beauty of all future work, the knowledge of the means of expressing our emotion is no less essential, and is only to be acquired through very long experience.

Letter to Emile Bernard, December 1904

This is true without any possible doubt—I am quite positive—an optical sensation is produced in our visual organs which allows us to classify the planes represented by colour sensations as light, half tone or quarter tone. Light, therefore, does not exist for the painter. As long as we are forced to proceed from black to white, with the first of these abstractions providing something like a point of support for the eye as much as for the brain, we flounder, we do not succeed in becoming masters of ourselves.

During this period (I am necessarily repeating myself a little) we turn towards the admirable works that have been handed down to us through the ages, where we find comfort, support, such as a plank provides for the bather. Everything you tell me in your letter is very true. [...] My wife and son are in Paris at the moment. We shall be together again soon I hope [...].

Letter to Emile Bernard, October 1905
Now, being old, nearly seventy, the sensations of colour, which give the light, are for me the reason for the abstractions which do not allow me to cover my canvas entirely nor to pursue the delimitation of the objects where their points of contact are fine and delicate; from which it results that my image or picture is incomplete. On the other hand the planes fall one on top of the other, from whence neo-impressionism emerged, which circumscribes the contours with a black line, a fault which must be fought at all costs. But nature, if consulted, gives us the means of attaining this end.

Letter to the artist's son, Paul Cézanne, September 1906
Today (it is nearly eleven o'clock) a startling return of heat. The air is overheated, not a breath of air. This temperature can be good for nothing but the expansion of metals, it must help the sale of drinks and bring joy to the beer merchants, a industry which seems to be assuming a fair size in Aix, and it expands the pretensions of the intellectuals in my country, a pack of ignoramuses, cretins and rascals.

The exceptions, there may be some, do not make themselves known. Modesty is always unaware of itself.

Finally I must tell you that as a painter I am becoming more clear-sighted before nature, but that with me the realization of my sensations is always painful. I cannot attain the intensity that is unfolded before my senses. I have not the magnificent riches of colouring that animates nature. Here on the banks of the river the *motifs* multiply, the same subject seen from a different angle offers subject for study of the most powerful interest and so varied that I think I could occupy myself for months without changing place, by turning now more to the right, now more to the left.

Cited in Joachim Gasquet, Cézanne, *1926*
An art which isn't based on feeling isn't an art at all [...]. Feeling is the principle, the beginning and end; craft, objective, technique—all these are in the middle [...]. Between you and me, Henri, between what makes up your particular character and mine there is the world, the sun [...] that which is transient [...] that which we both see [...].

Our dress, our flesh, reflections [...] That's what I have to concentrate on. That's where the slightest error with the brush can send everything off course [...]. If I am moved by emotion alone, then your eye goes askew [...]. If I weave around your expression, the infinite network of little blues and browns which are there, which marry together, I will make you look out from my canvas as you do in life [...].

One stroke after another, one after another [...]. And if I am just cold, as I draw or paint as they do in the schools [...] then I will cease to see anything. A conventional mouth and nose is always the same; no soul, no mystery, no passion [...].

And painting [...]. It's so fine and yet so terrible to stand in front of a blank canvas. Take that one—months of work have gone into it. Tears, laughter, gnashing of teeth. We were talking about portraits. People think that a sugar basin has no face, no soul. But even that changes day by day. You have to know how to catch and cajole these fellows [...]. These glasses and plates talk among themselves. Endless confidences [...]. As for flowers, I've given them up. They wither away so quickly.

Cited in Joachim Gasquet, Cézanne, *1926*
Fruits are more faithful. They like having their portrait painted. They seem to sit there and ask your forgiveness for fading. Their thought is given

off with their perfumes. They come with all their scents, they speak of the fields they have left, the rain which has nourished them, the daybreaks they have seen.

Cited in Emile Bernard, Some of Cézanne's Opinions

To read nature is to see it, as if through a veil, in terms of an interpretation in patches of colour following one another according to a law of harmony. These major hues are thus analyzed through modulations. Painting is classifying one's sensations of colour.

Cited in Joachim Gasquet, Cézanne, *1926*

You say that because two large pine trees are waving their branches in the foreground. But that's a visual sensation [...]. Moreover, the strong blue scent of the pines, which is sharp in the sunlight, must combine with the green scent of the meadows which, every morning, freshens the fragrance of the stones and of the marble of the distant Ste-Victoire. I haven't conveyed that. It must be conveyed. And through colours, without literary means.

Cited in Léo Larguier, Le Dimanche avec Cézanne, *1925*

Pure drawing is an abstraction. Drawing and colour are not distinct, everything in nature is coloured. Insofar as one paints, one draws. Accuracy of tone establishes both light and modelling for an object at the same time. The greater the harmony of colour, the greater the precision of the drawing.

Cited in Emile Bernard,
A Conversation with Cézanne

As you know, I have often done studies of bathers, both male and female, which I would have liked to make into a full-scale work done from nature; the lack of models forced me to limit myself to these sketches. Various obstacles stood in my way, such as finding the right place to use as the setting, a place which would not be very different from the one which I had fixed upon in my mind, or assembling a lot of people together, or finding men and women who would be willing to undress and remain still in the poses I had decided upon. And then I also came up against the problem of transporting a canvas of that size, and the endless difficulties raised by suitable or unsuitable weather, where I should position myself, and the equipment needed for the execution of a large-scale work. So I found myself obliged to postpone my plan for a Poussin done again entirely from nature and not constructed from notes, drawings and fragments of studies. At last a real Poussin, done in the open air, made of colour and light, rather than one of those works thought out in the studio, where everything has that brown hue resulting from a lack of daylight and the absence of reflections of sky and sun.

When I had met Monet and Pissarro, who had rid themselves of all these encumbrances, I realized that all one should ask of the past is that it provide an education in painting. Like me, they were full of enthusiasm for the great romantics; but instead of allowing themselves to be overawed by their vast paintings, they looked only at their innovations in colouring, which led to a new development of the palette. Pissarro represented nature like no one before him, and as for Monet, I have never met anyone with such compositional sense, such a prodigious facility for seizing upon what is true [...]. Imagination is a very beautiful thing; but one must also have a firm base.

As for myself, when I came into contact with the Impressionists, I realized that I had to become a student of the world again, to make myself a student once more. I no more imitated Pissarro and Monet than I did the masters in the Louvre. I tried to produce work which was my own, work which was sincere, naïve, in accordance with my abilities and my vision.

Sonnet by Cézanne, cited in Joachim Gasquet, Cézanne, *1926*

In an enchanting site of thick green branches
Closed on all sides against importunate glances,
Pure limpid water there of a clear spring
Slid slowly with a gentle murmuring.
[And there my child surprised the other day]
Willow and poplar above the watery way
Lift with their flexible boughs and softly sway
[And so my amorous son]
One day my dear son, seeking solitude.
To study at ease and pleasantly to brood,
A favourite book held near his arms with care,
By merest chance went wandering to his lair,
Sudden he halts, and, checking the least noise;
Enjoys a sight which his sole presence there,
Suspected in that place, would have disturbed [...].
That place unknown, forming like [...].

Here's the young woman with plump bottom, see,
In meadow-midst she stretches pleasantly
Her supple body, splendidly expanded.
Such sinuous curves in adders you'd not meet.
The sun obligingly beams down and sends
Some golden rays upon this lovely meat.

An excerpt from Paul Cézanne: His Life and Art *by Ambroise Vollard*

CÉZANNE PAINTS MY PORTRAIT (1896–1899)

My relations with Cézanne were not confined to the visit I made to Aix. I saw him again on each of his trips to Paris, and his good-will was such that one day I ventured to ask him to paint my portrait. He consented at once, and arranged a sitting at his studio in Rue Hégésippe-Moreau for the following day.

Upon arriving, I saw a chair in the middle of the studio, arranged on a packing case, which was in turn supported by four rickety legs. I surveyed this platform with misgiving. Cézanne divined my apprehension. "I prepared the model stand with my own hands. Oh, you won't run the least risk of falling, Monsieur Vollard, if you just keep your balance. Anyway, you mustn't budge an inch when you pose!"

Seated at last—and with such care!—I watched myself carefully in order not to make a single false move; in fact I sat absolutely motionless; but my very immobility brought on in the end a drowsiness against which I successfully struggled a long time. At last, however, my head dropped over on my shoulder, the balance was destroyed, and the chair, the packing case, and I all crushed to the floor together! Cézanne pounced upon me. "You wretch! You've spoiled the pose. Do I have to tell you again you must sit like an apple? Does an apple move?" From that day on, I adopted the plan of drinking a cup of black coffee before going for a sitting; as an added precaution, Cézanne would watch me attentively, and, if he thought he saw signs of fatigue or symptoms of sleep, he had a way of looking at me so significantly that I returned immediately to the pose like an angel—I mean like an apple. An apple never moves!

The sittings began at eight o'clock in the morning and lasted until half past eleven. Upon my arrival, Cézanne would lay aside *Le Pelerin* or *La Croix,* his favorite journals. "They're sensible papers," he would say. "They lean on Rome." It was the time of the war between the English and the Boers; and as Cézanne was always in favor of justice, he usually added: "Do you think the Boers will win?"

The studio in Rue Hégésippe-Moreau was even more simply decorated than the one at Aix. A few copies of Forain's drawings, clipped from the newspapers, formed the basis of the master's Paris collection. Cézanne had left what he called his Veroneses, his Rubens, his Lucas Signorellis, his Delacroix—that is to say the penny reproductions of which I have already spoken—at Aix. One day I told the painter that he could get very fine reproductions at Braun's. His answer was: "Braun sells to the museums." He looked upon a purchase from a purveyor to the museums as regal extravagance.

I can never forgive myself for having insisted on Cézanne's putting some of his own work on the walls of his studio. He pinned up about ten water-colors; but one day when the work was going badly, and after he had fretted and fumed and consigned both himself and the Almighty to the devil, he suddenly opened the stove, and tearing the water-colors from the walls, flung them into the fire. I saw a flicker of flame. The painter took up his palette again, his anger appeased.

When a sitting began, he would look at me his eyes intent and a little hard, his brush poised in the air. Sometimes he seemed restless. Once I heard him mutter fiercely between his teeth, "That fellow Dominique[1] is damnably good;" then, putting down a stroke, and leaning back to judge the effect; "but he gives me a pain!"

Every afternoon Cézanne would be off to copy in the Louvre or the Trocadéro. Not infrequently he would stop in to see me around five o'clock, his face radiant, and would say, "Monsieur Vollard, I have good news for you. I'm pretty well satisfied with my work so far; if the weather is 'clear gray' tomorrow, I think the sitting will be a good one!" That was his principal concern when the day was done: what kind of weather would we have tomorrow? Inasmuch as he was in the habit of going to bed very early, he usually woke up in the middle of the night. Haunted by his obsession, he would open the window. When he was satisfied about the weather, he would go and look over the work he had done, candle in hand, before getting back into bed. If he were pleased with her examination, he would wake up his wife so that she might share his satisfaction. And to make amends for disturbing her, he would invite her to play a game of checkers.

But for the sitting to be a real success, it was not enough for Cézanne to be satisfied with his study at the Louvre and for the weather to be "clear gray"; there were other conditions necessary, above all that silence should reign in the "pile driver factory." That was the nickname Cézanne had given to an elevator in the neighborhood. I took care not to tell him that when the noise stopped, it probably meant that the elevator was undergoing repairs; I left him to his hope that the owners would fail in business some day. In fact the noise stopped very often, and he reflected hopefully that the pile drivers stopped when business was not good.

Another noise that he could not endure was the barking of dogs. There was a dog in the neighborhood which made itself known occasionally—not very loud to be sure. But Cézanne had developed an extremely sharp ear for sounds which were disagreeable to him. One morning when I arrived he greeted me all smiles: "Lépine[2] is a good fellow! He has given an order for all dogs to be put in the pound; it's in *La Croix*." Thanks to this we had several good sittings: the weather continued to be "clear gray," and by a piece of good fortune, the dog and the pile driver factory never made a sound. But one day, when Cézanne had remarked to me for the thousandth time, "Lépine is a good fellow!" a faint "bow-ow-ow" came to our ears. With a start he let his palette fall and cried in a discouraged voice, "The wretch has got loose again!"

Very few people ever had the opportunity to see Cézanne at work, because he could not endure being watched while at his easel. For one who has not seen him paint, it is difficult to imagine how slow and painful his progress was on certain days. In my portrait there are two little spots of canvas on the hand which are not covered. I called Cézanne's attention to them. "If the copy I'm making at the Louvre turns out well," he replied, "perhaps I will be able tomorrow to find the exact tone to cover up those spots. Don't you see, Monsieur Vollard, that if I put something there by guesswork, I might have to paint the whole canvas over starting from that point?" The prospect made me tremble.

During the period that Cézanne was working

on my portrait, he was also occupied with a large composition of nudes, begun about 1895, on which he labored almost to the end of his life.

For his groups of nudes, the painter made use of sketches from life that he had made some years before in the Atelier Suisse; beyond that, he resorted to his memories of the museums.

His ambition was to pose nude models out of doors; but that was not feasible for many reasons, the most important being that women, even when clothed, frightened him. The only exception to this rule was an old servant whom he used to employ at the Jas de Bouffan, an odd creature with a craggy countenance about which he used to say admirably to Zola: "Look, isn't it handsome? You might also say it was a man!"

Imagine my surprise, then when one day he announced that he wanted to pose a nude female model. I could not help exclaiming, "What, Monsieur Cézanne, a nude model?"

"Oh, Monsieur Vollard, don't worry, I'll get some old crow!"

He found just the one he wanted, and after doing a study of the nude, he painted two portraits of the same model clothed; they remind one of the poor relations that people Balzac's stories.[3]

Cézanne assured me that he found this "camel" much less satisfactory as a model than me. "It is becoming very difficult to work from a female model," he explained. "And besides, I have to pay very high; the price has gone up to four francs, twenty sous more than before the war. Oh! if I can only realize your portrait!" The goal of his ambition was always the Salon of Bouguereau, until the Louvre should be open to him. He considered the Louvre the only sanctuary worthy of his art.

Cézanne used very pliable brushes made of sable or pole-cat hair; after each touch he washed them in a medium-cup filled with turpentine. No matter how many brushes he began with, he used them all during a sitting, and he daubed himself up to such a degree that once, at Aix, when he was coming back from his *motif,* the gendarmes asked him for his identification papers. Cézanne swore that he was a native; they insisted that they had never seen him before. "Well, I'm sorry," the painter said, with such an accent that the police could not have been left with the shadow of a doubt: a man with an accent like that must have been from Aix!

The solidarity of Cézanne's painting is readily explained when one knows his method of working. Inasmuch as he did not paint with a thick impasto, but put one layer of paint as thin as water-color over another, the paint dried instantly; he never had to fear the internal conflict of the colors which produces cracks when the upper and the lower layers dry at different times.

I have already said that Cézanne did not like to be watched when painting. Renoir, who used to accompany Cézanne on painting trips during his visit to the Jas de Bouffan, told me just how acute the painter's susceptibilities were. An old woman was in the process of installing herself with her knitting a few paces from where they used to paint. He proximity always threw Cézanne into a state of extreme exasperation. One day he could stand it no longer. Seeing her approach, with his keen and piercing eyes, from a great distance, he cried: "Here comes the old cow!" and in spite of all Renoir's efforts to stay him, he packed up his traps and marched off in a rage.

It is easy to imagine his anger if he were surprised with brush in hand. One day when he was working in the field with a young painter named Le Bail, whom he had put in front of him so that the younger man could not watch him work, a passer-by who had approached unheard said in a loud voice, "I like the young man's picture better." Cézanne quit at once, furious that anyone should have spied on him while he was painting, and very much annoyed at the lout's reflection on his work. Nevertheless he steadfastly believed that the public really knew whether a picture was "well realized" or not. Small wonder that by dint of hearing Cézanne complain of not being able to "realize," that same irreverent public should have found in the end a certain lack of assurance in his work. When some one propounded the idea that this peculiarity was due to a certain irregularity in the painter's visual field, Cézanne seized upon the notion as a fresh excuse for bewailing his inability to realize. Even Huysmans, in his estimate of the painter, gave credence to this myth about a malformation of the eyesight: "An artist with diseased retinae, who, exasperated by faulty vision, has discovered the prodromes of a new art."[4]

Though Cézanne did not permit me to utter a single word during the sittings, he would talk willingly enough while I was getting ready, and also during the all too short rests that he allowed me. Upon entering one morning I found him grinning from ear to ear. He had discovered in *Le Pelerin* that some shares in the Sosnowice (which he had pronounced *Sauce novice*) were being offered to the public. "They'll go bankrupt," he said. The public isn't fool enough to buy anything with a name like that." Some days later I found him sobered; the stock had gone up. "Too bad, Monsieur Vollard," he said, "they've found some easy marks. Life's frightful, isn't it!" Then, with the sort of self-satisfaction that we feel when others are being made sport of while we ourselves are out of harm's way, he added: "I'm not used to the ways of the world, so I lean on my sister, she leans on her confessor, a Jesuit (they're mighty wise, those people), and he leans on Rome."

Superficial observers, hearing the great painter complain of such childish things, and seeing him take everything for granted without the slightest examination, could not resist the temptation to turn such naïveté to their profit; but when Cézanne was pulling himself together--and he was forever pulling himself together—he went at them hammer and tongs, and, once well rid of an intruder, he would pronounce his favorite phrase: "The wretch, he tried to get his hooks on me!" Cézanne did not adopt the laissez-faire attitude with any idea of hoodwinking the public. Did he not say of himself: "After an event has occurred or an idea has been propounded, it takes me a long time to perceive clearly its character and import."

I had been told that Cézanne had made a slave of his models. I proved it to my own satisfaction from sad experience. From the moment that he put down the first brush stroke until the end of the sitting, he treated the model like a simple still-life. He loved to paint portraits. "The goal of all art," he would say, "is the human face." If he did not paint it more often, the reason lay in the difficulty of procuring models who were as tractable as I. Consequently, after painting himself and his wife many times, and also a few obliging friends (at the time that Zola still had faith in Cézanne, the future novelist consented to pose for the nude), he resorted to painting apples, and even more frequently flowers—flowers did not decay: he used paper ones. But "even they, confound 'em! faded in the long run." Therefore, in certain moments of exasperation against the "contrariness" of things, Cézanne would even fall back upon the plates in the *Magasin Pittoresque,* of which he possessed some bound volumes, or, as a last resort, upon his sister's fashion magazines! Beyond that there was left but to hope for a clear gray sky, and to dread the barking of dogs, the noise of the pile driver factory, and a few inconveniences of a like nature.

Cézanne had found in me, or so I like to think, his ideal model; hence he made no haste to finish my portrait. "It makes a good study," he would say, setting to work again on some part that was fairly well realized. And he would add, expecting me to be overwhelmed with joy, "You are beginning to learn how to pose."

One day when his bad humor had manifested itself several times during the sitting, and when I had departed after arranging to meet on the morrow, Cézanne suddenly said to his son, "The sky is turning clear gray. When Monsieur Vollard has had time to get a bite to eat, run over to his place and fetch him back."

"But aren't you afraid that Monsieur Vollard will get all tired out?"

"What difference does that make, as long as the weather is good?"

"But if you exhaust him today, perhaps he won't be able to pose tomorrow."

"You're right, son. We must spare the model! You've got the practical view of life."

While pretending to deplore his utterly impractical outlook on life, Cézanne really prided himself on it privately. One very cold winter, I remember, happening to stop in the middle of a bridge to look at the Seine heavy with ice, I espied someone washing brushes on the bank of the river. It was Cézanne. "The water is frozen at the studio," he shouted. "I hope that doesn't happen here!" and he shot an anxious glance at the ice blocks drifting closer and closer together.

While posing for my portrait, I feared above all the entrance on the scene of the terrible palette-knife. With what care did I guard my merest words! You may be sure I never spoke of painting, nor of literature, nor savants, nor teachers; in fact I usually held my peace, lest Cézanne, who thought of nothing but his work, might misconstrue whatever I said into a desire to contradict, and my portrait might momentarily run the risk of destruction. I thought it most prudent to wait until he spoke to me—but even that had its hidden dangers, as we shall see.

Cézanne had said, "You must go to see the Delacroix in the Choquet collection; they are up for auction." He mentioned in particular a very important water-color of flowers bought by Monsieur Choquet at the Piron sale. Piron had acquired it at the sale which followed the death of Delacroix, whose executor he was. Cézanne informed me that Delacroix, by his last wish, had given his heirs the right to choose any picture from among his works with the exception of this water-color, which was to figure at the sale of his effects. Wishing to show Cézanne the interest I had taken in his narrative, I looked up Delacroix's will; he actually does mention a large water-color representing flowers placed, as it were, 'at random against a gray background.'"

"You idiot," he shouted, taking a couple of steps in my direction and brandishing his fists in my face, "don't you dare say that Delacroix painted anything at random!"

I explained the misunderstanding; he calmed down. "I love Delacroix," he said by way of apology. Meanwhile I promised myself to redouble my precautions in the future. Another time, all omens presaged a favorable sitting; the sky was "clear gray," no dogs, silence in the pile-driver factory, a good copy the day before at the Louvre; and last but not least *La Croix* had announced a victory for the Boers that day. While I was rejoicing over these auspicious portents, I heard of a sudden resounding oath, and turning around, I saw Cézanne wild-eyed, his palette-knife raised over my portrait. I was petrified with fear for what might happen; at last, after moments which seemed like hours, Cézanne turned his fury against another canvas, which was instantly reduced to shreds. The reason for this wrath, it seems, was this: in a corner of the studio opposite to where I was posing, there had always been an old faded carpet. On that particular day, unfortunately, the mind had taken it away with the laudable intention of beating it. Cézanne explained that it was intolerable not to have that carpet in its accustomed place; it would be impossible for him to continue my portrait; he would never touch a brush again as long as he lived. Happily he did not keep his word, but the fact remains that he could not paint another stroke that day.

After a hundred and fifteen sittings, Cézanne abandoned my portrait to return to Aix. "The front of the shirt is not bad"—such were his last words on parting. He made me leave the clothes in which I posed at the studio, expecting, when he returned to Paris, to paint in the two white spots on the hands, and then, of course, to work over certain parts. "I hope to have made some progress by that time. You understand, Monsieur

Vollard, the contour keeps slipping away from me!" But he had not counted on the moths, "the little wretches!" which devoured my clothes in short order.

When Cézanne laid a canvas aside, it was almost always with the intention of taking it up again, in the hope of bringing it to the point of perfection. We can readily understand, then, those landscapes, already "classified" and taken up again the following year—sometimes even two or three years in succession. This procedure did not bother him in the least, since for him, "to paint from nature was not a question of copying the subject, but solely of realizing his sensations." It is easy to see how, from this unheard-of conscientiousness, this perpetual repainting of his work, the legend gained credence that he was powerless to realize his visions. Cézanne himself did all he could to spread this belief; he would solemnly and with the utmost conviction tell you, "I don't seem to posses the power to realize." That epitomizes "Cézanne the provincial," darting furtive glances about him, and imagining himself hedged in by enemies whose sole purpose in life was to obstruct his admission to the Salon of Bouguereau. It was those imaginary enemies whom he tried to disarm with a humble, timid mien. What a contrast to "Cézanne the master," who, when someone bumped into him by accident one day at work, shouted furiously: "Don't you know that I'm Cézanne?"

His friends bantered him a great deal about his obstinate determination to get into the great Salons; but we must not forget his conviction that, if ever he could slip into the Salon of Bouguereau with a "well-realized canvas," the scales would fall from the eyes of the public, and they would desert Bouguereau to follow the great artist that he felt himself capable of becoming.

It is only fair to add that every trace of this conceit vanished the moment he sat down to his easel. Picture him with all his faculties concentrated on the "exactness of the form," searching out the line, with the same conscientiousness that the guild apprentices might have lavished on the *chef d'oeuvre* which was to bring them their mastership. If he were satisfied with a sitting, a very unusual occurrence, he shouted like a schoolboy who has just received a good mark. Therefore it is not hard to understand how great must have been his irritation if he were suddenly awakened from his dreams and brusquely brought back to earth again. One day when someone had disturbed him at his work, and he had slashed up one of his pictures, he said to me, "Excuse me, Monsieur Vollard, but when I am studying, I must have absolute quiet."

From *Paul Cézanne: His Life and Art* by Ambroise Vollard. Translated by Harold L. Van Doren. Published by Nicholas L. Brown, New York, 1923.

[1] Dominique Ingres

[2] The prefect of police at the time.

[3] Among the women who posed for Cézanne, a certain old woman who had formerly been a nun's attendant, and who had suffered many misfortunes, might be mentioned. It was she who posed for the *Woman with a Rosary.*

[4] J. K. Huysmans. *Certains.*

Concise Bibliography

Armstrong, Carol, Deborah Gribbon, and Paul Cézanne. *Cézanne in the Studio: Still Life in Watercolors.* Los Angeles: J. Paul Getty Trust Publications, 2004.

Athanassoglous-Kallmyer, Nina Maria. *Cézanne and Provence: The Painter in His Culture.* Chicago: University of Chicago Press, 2003.

Cachin, Françoise. *Cézanne.* New York: Harry N. Abrams, 1996.

Doran, Michael, Julie Lawrence Cochran, and Paul Cézanne. *Conversations with Cézanne.* Berkeley: University of California Press, 2001.

Geist, Sydney. *Interpreting Cézanne.* Cambridge: Harvard University Press, 1988.

Machotka, Paul. *Cézanne: Landscape into Art.* New Haven: Yale University Press, 1996.

McPherson, Heather. *The Modern Portrait in Nineteenth-Century France.* London: Cambridge University Press, 2001.

Rewald, John. *The Paintings of Paul Cézanne: A Catalogue Raisonné.* New York: Harry N. Abrams, 1996.

Rilke, Rainer-Maria, Clara Rilke, and Joel Agee. *Letters on Cézanne.* New York: Fromm International, 1985.

Shiff, Richard. *Cézanne and the End of Impressionism: A Study of the Theory, Technique, and Critical Evaluation of Modern Art.* Chicago: University of Chicago Press, 1984.

Vollard, Ambroise. *Paul Cézanne: His Life and Art.* Trans. Harold L. Van Doren. New York: Nicholas L. Brown, 1923.